The Coming of Keynesianism to America

To Julie Johnson Kidd and in memory of Ewing T. Boles

The Coming of Keynesianism to America

Conversations with the founders of
Keynesian Economics

Edited by

David C. Colander
Middlebury College, US

and

Harry Landreth
Centre College, US

Edward Elgar
Cheltenham, UK • Brookfield, US

HB
99.7
.C635
1996

Published by
Edward Elgar Publishing Limited
8 Lansdown Place
Cheltenham
Glos GL50 2HU
UK

Edward Elgar Publishing Company
Old Post Road
Brookfield
Vermont 05036
US

British Library Cataloguing in Publication Data
Coming of Keynesianism to America:
Conversations with the Founders of
Keynesian Economics
I. Colander, David C. II. Landreth, Harry
330.1560973

Library of Congress Cataloguing in Publication Data
The coming of Keynesianism to America : conversations with the
founders of Keynesian economics / edited by David C. Colander and
Harry Landreth.
Includes index.
1. Keynesian economics—History. 2. Economics—United States–
–History. 3. Economists—United States—History. I. Colander,
David C. II. Landreth, Harry.
HB99.7.C635   1996
330.15'6'0973–dc20   95–19493
                                                                                        CIP

ISBN 1 85898 087 9

Typeset by Manton Typesetters, 5–7 Eastfield Road, Louth, Lincs LN11 7AJ, UK
Printed and bound in Great Britain by
Biddles Limited, Guildford and King's Lynn

Contents

v

Preface

This book has had a long gestation period. The initial idea for it came from a conversation between Abba Lerner and Dave Colander. They were sitting around one day discussing economics, as they generally did when they were together, and Abba started to talk about how the Keynesian revolution progressed. Dave found it fascinating. The conversation was, unfortunately, unfinished; they had pressing deadlines to meet.

During these talks Abba told Dave of a taped interview with Alvin Hansen and himself on the Keynesian revolution, conducted at Boston University in the 1970s. Dave had the tape transcribed and he put it in the files. He and Abba were going to use it as the basis for a formal interview on the subject. They did discuss the issues informally, but they never got around to discuss them formally before Abba had a stroke which impaired his language ability, and made further discussion impossible.

Colander was kicking himself for never carrying through on the idea, and he vowed to do better. He set out to interview participants of the Keynesian revolution and to put the interviews together in a book. Over the next decade he interviewed a number of Keynesians when the opportunity presented itself, including Lorie Tarshis, Walter Salant, John Kenneth Galbraith, Paul Samuelson, Evsey Domar, Richard Musgrave and Tibor Scitovsky. He also interviewed Leon Keyserling both because he was a friend and because Leon's strong views added some context from which to consider the policy aspects of the Keynesian revolution.

In 1988 Dave organized a Christian A. Johnson Symposium at Middlebury College on the Keynesianization of America. At that symposium Bob Bryce, Lorie Tarshis and Paul Sweezy discussed their role in the Keynesian revolution. Harry Landreth, who was then a visiting professor at Middlebury College, attended the symposium and found it fascinating. At that point the basis for a book was there, but somehow, as often happens with projects, the raw material never coalesced into a book. There was always some book or paper project that had more urgency.

In the early 1990s Dave told Edward Elgar of the unfinished project. Edward said he was very interested, and encouraged Dave to finish it. To encourage him more, Edward sent Dave a contract for a book. Still, other projects kept getting in the way. One of those other projects was Dave's collaboration with Harry Landreth on the third edition of their history of economic thought book. The collaboration was great fun, and satisfying for both of them. The pleasure of working with Harry on the history of thought book gave Dave a bright idea. He brought up in a casual conversation with Harry how interesting the Middlebury conference was, and how he had been thinking about the book, but how he just wasn't finding the time to do the job right. He suggested that, if Harry would work with him on it, it would be a lot more fun, and it might even get done. Harry agreed to join the project and, from then on, the project progressed nicely.

We decided from the beginning that the interviews were to be the backbone of the book and that we would supplement them with a short essay which put the interviews in context, gather biographical information and work up a selective bibliography.

The Interviews

The first point we should make about the interviews is that they were friendly, not investigative. Our purpose was to facilitate the interviewees in telling the story they remember, not to determine how good their memories were. Second, we should emphasize that the tapes were edited not for content but for clarity of expression and organization. Where possible we checked the general arguments made and found them correct, but for the most part we have not tried to determine if specific memories fit the events exactly.

Readers who check specifics will find that memories of events differ even among the interviewees in this book. For example, one will find differences in the reminiscences of Keynes's visits to the United States and of the exchanges between Lerner and Keynes that led Keynes to feel, if not say, that he was not a Keynesian. The same is true of Leon Keyserling's memory of the events leading to various legislative actions related to the New Deal. While other accounts of that era tell a somewhat different story, the general point Keyserling makes, that much of the New Deal legislation had little to do with Keynes and Keynesian economists and that the legislation would have proceeded even in the absence of the Keynesian revolution, is expressed forcefully and is, we believe, correct.

After we had edited the interviews, when possible we returned them to the interviewees and asked them to review and correct their interview in any way that they saw fit. All who could did so, and did a superb job. (Lorie Tarshis and Leon Keyserling died before this could be done, and Robert Bryce's illness prevented his responding.) In short, the interviews are not formal historical documents, but are, instead, informal stories as the participants remember them. That, we believe, gives them much of their charm.

The Background Essay

To make the book complete we felt that we needed an introduction that would provide context for the interviews. To write that we had to catch up with the literature coming out on the Keynesian revolution. That proved an enormous task since that literature has been expanding exponentially. Although both of us had followed the literature before, we uncovered much more to read and reread than we had imagined, discovering facts and insights that provided new perspectives to the interviews.

After reading that literature we decided that we had some differences from the story that we thought this literature was telling, and we decided to make the initial essay focus on those differences. An early draft of the introduction began in the usual style of a journal article, that is, with lots of documentation and detail, and concern not to push tentative conclusions too far.

Rereading it, we felt the reference to other literature was becoming oppressive, and was eliminating the informal charm that we thought characterized the interviews. To avoid that oppression we decided to give up the formal journal style as too constraining, and to tell our interpretation of what happened in the Keynesian revolution in the same fashion that we asked our interviewees to tell their story – informally. In doing so we believe we have made the book relevant to a much broader audience, and we hope that we have not too much offended historians of thought.

We have significantly condensed and placed in an appendix to our essay two topics which will be of more interest to specialists: 'The Keynesian Revolution and the Methodology of Science' is in Appendix A and 'The Second Coming of Keynes' in Appendix B.

Acknowledgements

The book has benefited from much competent and energetic help. Our biggest thanks go to the Keynesian revolutionaries. We appreciate their giving of their valuable time, first to submitting to an interview and then to checking their account in its written form. We also want to thank Helen Reiff who transcribed the interviews and, as usual, was helpful at every stage. Next on the list come our wives; Patrice Colander put up with Dave, and Donna Gardt Landreth not only put up with Harry, but also improved the prose with her usual efficiency. We would also like to thank Perry Mehrling, Robert Dimand, and Paul Wonnacott for helpful comments on an early draft of the introduction; Craufurd Goodwin for helpful comments on the design of the project; Don Moggridge and Susan Howson for help in getting letters and permissions to publish these letters; Christopher Johnson for permission to publish the Lionel Robbins letter; and King's College, Cambridge, for permission to publish the Keynes letters.

A number of people helped with specific research work. Billy Gooch helped gather the biographical material, and Nicole Shown and Robert Alford helped greatly in finding and checking references and in the editing process. Mary Beth Garriott, Connie Klimke and Judy Nystrom demonstrated, as always, the necessity for and benefits of librarians who contribute their time and expertise so generously to our projects. We want to thank them all.

In carrying out the project we each benefited from our associations with our respective colleges. Harry received financial assistance with funds from his Boles Professor of Economics Chair at Centre College and David Colander received financial assistance from his Christian A. Johnson Distinguished Chair in Economics at Middlebury College. We thank the donors of our chairs. Individuals, such as these, who have made significant contributions to colleges by endowing chairs make work such as this possible. We are pleased to dedicate this book to the donors of our chairs.

Once the manuscript went to Edward Elgar a number of people were exceptionally helpful. These include the project editor and A.J. Waterman, the copyeditor. And last, but not least, we want to thank Edward Elgar who, with his friendly encouragement, got us to finish the project.

1. Introduction

The Keynesian revolution continues to fascinate and delight both economists and the lay public. It does so because it was the triumph, at least temporarily, of an idea, in all the strange and wonderful ways that ideas triumph. This book is about the Keynesian revolution in the United States – about what that revolution was, why it occurred and how it occurred. It considers the period from the early 1930s, when the early seeds of the Keynesian revolution were first sown, to the early 1950s, when Keynesian economics, while still controversial, had become king of the academic mountain and the mainstream paradigm used in macroeconomics.

The core of the book is a set of interviews with what might be called the Keynesian revolutionaries – the economists who were at the center of the U.S. Keynesian revolution.[1] In these interviews the Keynesian revolutionaries describe their perceptions of what was happening in the revolution. Their story is fascinating. They give the reader a sense of what the Keynesian revolution was and how it spread, but they do more than that. They also tell of the political persecution Keynesians found themselves facing, and point out the similarities among their views as well as differences. The interviews show how ideas challenge vested interests and how, consequently, they are not easily adopted.

The Continuing Interest In The Keynesian Revolution

More than fifty years have passed since the revolution placed Keynesian economics on the map. The passage of time, however, has heightened, rather than diminished, interest in it. There have been numerous articles and books on Keynes, on what he "really" meant, "should have" meant and "must have" meant. In this literature it is generally accepted that there are two intertwined aspects of the Keynesian revolution and the Keynesianization of America: (1) a theoretical revolution marked by the development of a new set of theoretical tools coupled with a significant widening of the scope of economics, and (2) a policy revolution marked by a new view about the proper role for government in stabilizing the aggregate economy through fiscal and monetary policies. Although related, these two aspects of the revolution progressed at different rates and were often unconnected.

Why so many books? So much interest? One of the reasons is that the Keynesian revolution is an almost unique case history in which there was a major shift in the thinking of a social science. It created a new field of economics – macroeconomics. Moreover, it was accompanied by both a major shift in economic policy and a major shift in economists' thinking about economic policy. One might think that separating these two is unnecessary, but, as will become clear in the interviews, the two events, while parallel, are quite unconnected. In terms of paradigmatic shifts, the Keynesian revolution was felt by some to be as important to economics as the Copernican revolution was to physics. Yet by the 1960s, the theoretical portion of the Keynesian revolution had essentially been relegated to a minor role in economic theory, and by the early 1970s, with the development of the new classical revolution, the theoretical portion was seen as having nearly ended. Then the tables turned again, and in the early 1990s, new Keynesian economics developed and reopened discussion about the Keynesian theoretical revolution.

Ironically, the policy revolution course followed that of the theoretical revolution – but in reverse: Keynesian policy was king in the 1960s, and in the 1990s, as *theoretical* Keynesianism was making a comeback, Keynesian *policy* (or at least what had become known as Keynesian policy) was dead. This swinging pendulum of both theory and policy provides a second reason for the continuing interest in the Keynesian revolution, which might be elucidated by the story of the violinist who was performing a new concerto. Although he felt his performance was lacking, the cries of "Encore!" encouraged him to continue. After he played his encore, the cries continued, only louder. Two more encores led to even louder cries, and finally he announced to the audience: "Thank you for your kindness, but I really must stop." Then he heard someone scream, "No way! You're going to keep playing until you get it right!"

Another reason for the continuing interest in the Keynesian revolution involves methodological and philosophical implications of the Keynesian revolution. The Keynesian revolution's uniqueness has continually elicited the intense interest of philosophers of science and, with the appearance of each new approach to a philosophy of knowledge, there has followed a renewed interest in Keynesianism.

The Keynesianization of America is interesting not just to historians of economic thought but also to other economists who want to know something of the development of their discipline and to interested lay people and historians who follow the spread of ideas. Despite its general familiarity to Keynesian specialists, we think the story told by the interviews will be absorbing to them as well as to the general public, even though much of it will be a familiar one. The reason is twofold. First, the participants' telling provides otherwise inaccessible insights, and second, our reading of the story as told by these interviews differs slightly from the story derived from other sources by previous writers. Specifically, we find a *three-part* rather than a *two-part* revolution. The third part of the Keynesian revolution is a pedagogical revolution, a revolution in the tools and models used to teach macroeconomics.

Pedagogy has not received much attention in other examinations of the Keynesian revolution, but we believe pedagogy and pedagogical tools played an important role in it. Textbooks and textbook models not only reflected the theoretical and policy developments, but also played a significant role in determining the course of the other revolutions. This interwoven three-part story helps explain the ebbs and flows of Keynesian economics. Other discussions of the Keynesian revolution often have not made clear what revolution they were talking about.

Before we consider these broader issues, let us begin with a brief recounting of the events that set the stage. It all starts in the early 1930s with a number of our future revolutionaries sitting in undergraduate introductory economics classrooms listening to lectures in economic theory and hearing nothing about the depression going on around them. They were learning microeconomics, and it had little or nothing to say about the problems the economy was experiencing. Some went to Cambridge, England, to find out a bit more about it. The story then moves to Cambridge, Massachusetts, and then into the journals, textbooks and classrooms of academia. Two seminars featured in the development and transmission of Keynes's ideas: the Cambridge Circus at Cambridge, England, and the fiscal-policy seminar at Harvard in Cambridge, Massachusetts.

Cambridge, England

Let us start at Cambridge University, England, in 1930.[2] Maynard Keynes was in his late forties, and in October his two-volume *A Treatise on Money* was published. He would spend Tuesday to Friday in London and Friday evening to Tuesday morning at Cambridge. There were thirteen members of the graduate staff of the faculty in Economics and Politics, and Keynes did not have a position on the faculty. Since macroeconomics had not yet been born, much of the intellectual ferment concerned microeconomics: a re-examination of Marshall's value theory which led to Joan Robinson's *The Economics of Imperfect Competition* (1933).

Students were important in bringing Keynes to America. One important way ideas are spread is through the influence of teachers on students – the syllabus, books read, the force of the personality of the professor. Ideas spread in chain-letter fashion, with a professor influencing one hundred perspiring Ph.D. candidates during a lifetime. Some of these students become professors who mold hundreds more Ph.Ds, while others go on to teach thousands of undergraduates. Over time a network is established, and an idea becomes entrenched. It is such a casual network that is the mortar of mainstream orthodoxy, which makes one marvel at, and appreciate, the uniqueness of grand paradigmatic shifts such as the Keynesian.

The strength and force of the personality of the messiah is a crucial factor in this spread of new ideas, and the recruitment of prophets in this case began even before the vision was seen. A.F.W. Plumptre was a student at Cambridge for two years beginning in the fall of 1928. His essay on Keynes as a teacher reveals his lifelong admiration of him. In a letter written home in October, 1928, he says: "Keynes is far beyond my hopes and expectations – cleverer, wittier, and more genial ... In any pedantic sense Keynes was not my best teacher, but in terms of impact and influence he was incomparable."[3] Plumptre was Tarshis's teacher at Toronto and also taught Robert Bryce's sister. He significantly influenced Tarshis, who under Plumptre became an ardent disciple of Keynes's *Treatise on Money*. And it was Plumptre, in networking fashion, who funneled Tarshis and, through Tarshis, Bryce to Cambridge. Plumptre later became part of the spread of Keynesian ideas in the Canadian government.[4]

Keynes regarded his *Treatise* as his *magnum opus*,[5] but it was criticized by Ralph Hawtrey, Dennis Robertson and Friedrich von Hayek. Upon its publication, however, a group of Cambridge economists, all under thirty-five, began a seminar to examine the *Treatise*. This so-called "Circus" consisted of Richard Kahn, James Meade, Piero Sraffa, Joan Robinson and Austin Robinson. Keynes did not attend these seminars but was informed of their discussions by Kahn who also brought back communications from Keynes.

When Keynes was at Cambridge he did find time to spend each Monday evening with students and some faculty in what came to be called the "Keynes Club". Not all students were invited to join the Political Economy Club, or Keynes Club, but those who were had an opportunity to give and discuss papers. The Canadians Robert Bryce and Lorie Tarshis attended both Keynes's lectures and the Keynes Club, while Walter S. Salant attended only the lectures in 1933. It was these colleagues and students of Keynes at Cambridge who became the first phalanx of academics to carry his message to the world, although the influence of many of them, multifaceted and talented as they were, eventually extended beyond their role in advancing the Keynesian paradigm.

Richard Kahn has great interest for historians of thought in that he played a significant role in the writing of *The General Theory*. In its preface Keynes notes that he "depended on the constant advice and constructive criticisms of Mr. R.F. Kahn. There is a great deal in this book which would not have taken the shape it has except at his suggestion."[6] James Meade went on to publish extensively in international trade and was awarded the Nobel Prize in Economics in 1977. He was one of the first to use Keynesian theory in a textbook, *An Introduction to Economic Analysis and Policy* (1936, 2nd ed. 1938). Joan Robinson popularized Keynes among the academic community in the years immediately after the publication of *The General Theory* with her *Introduction to the Theory of Employment*. She later went in several directions, one of which led to the seminal foundation of the modern school of Post-Keynesian economics. Piero Sraffa and Austin Robinson mostly plowed non-Keynesian fields.

Maynard Keynes was a towering figure at Cambridge. Austin Robinson, who was an undergraduate at Cambridge, aptly describes the impact of Keynes: "As undergraduates those of us who attended his Club were, almost to a man, Keynesians in whatever were the issues of the moment, but Keynesians because we had made ourselves Keynesians."[7] Harry Johnson, however, described Keynes as arrogant, and an editor in an obituary asserts, "his capacity for rudeness was unequalled". Yet all who observed Keynes commented on a difference in his treatment of his peers and his students, which may account for these inconsistencies.[8] He was always kind in criticism of student efforts and never sharp or rude, and his good relations with them were rewarded by their devotion to the transmission of his ideas. The same apparently cannot be said of his treatment of academic equals.

The Canadians Tarshis and Bryce became particularly important in the spread of Keynes's ideas in America. Their notes, taken in lectures given by Keynes in 1932 through 1935 and combined with the notes of others, became part of a composite set of notes of a "representative student" constructed by Thomas Rymes and published as *Keynes's Lectures 1932–35*.[9] Although

Tarshis and Bryce later became enthusiastic retailers of Keynesian ideas, their first year at Cambridge in 1932–3, when they were attending Keynes's lectures, found them wanting to drop economics. Bryce spent three years at Cambridge. In the interviews he recalls that it was "in the second year of my study there, I saw the light ... I was hooked by then."[10] He began to do what he called missionary work with the heathen, going to the London School of Economics to attend a seminar offered by Hayek, a leading exponent of non-Keynesian theories about business cycles. Bryce wrote a paper summarizing his views of the essence of Keynes's new theory and presented it to Hayek's seminar: "Hayek was very kind to me and let me have four consecutive weeks of his seminar to explain these ideas to them." Bryce then went to Harvard as a Commonwealth Fund Fellow. Kahn had advised him to concentrate on his thesis, but Bryce ignored this advice: "This was nothing to tell a missionary. I was polite about it, but went to Harvard and followed my own agenda." During Bryce's two years at Harvard he spread the gospel "first on the basis of this piece of paper I had brought over and then on the basis of Keynes's book."

The role that Bryce played at Harvard undoubtedly accounts for Schumpeter's referring to Keynes as Allah and Bryce as the prophet.[11] What an unusual situation for the senior faculty members at Harvard in 1935, to have a graduate student trying to capture the minds of fellow students with heterodox ideas still not in print. Bryce left Harvard in two years, without taking a degree, to spend the remainder of his professional life first in business, then as a Canadian public servant, and finally with the International Monetary Fund. Lorie Tarshis attended Cambridge as a student for four years, and of the nine extant sets of students' notes of Keynes's lectures, Tarshis's is the only set covering the four years of lectures from 1932 through 1935.[12] Plumptre had advised Tarshis to start over at Cambridge as an undergraduate, which he did, and in two years he had his B.A. While Tarshis could not remember all of his courses and teachers, he recalls that he "always went to Keynes".[13] He was also a member of the Keynes Club, believing that "Plumptre arranged it." Like Bryce,

Tarshis speaks of the intensity of his attachment to Keynes and his ideas: "I was impressed with Keynes's lectures ... The end of the second year I was excited beyond belief ... There were a couple of points that he made in the second year that stuck with me. I can still feel the funny prickling-in-the-back-of-your-neck feeling when he mentioned them ... God! You have to listen to this as hard as you can. This is the most important thing you'll ever hear."

Keynes Comes to America

On to Cambridge, Massachusetts, where the Canadian Bob Bryce, after three years at Cambridge, England, had returned to North America to study at Harvard. Keynes's *General Theory* was not yet published, but Bryce began to spread the new economics in discussion groups by reading the paper he wrote in England setting down the essence of *The General Theory*. Some Harvard graduate students showed interest in the new Keynesian ideas conveyed by Bryce, but few older faculty. Earlier in the fall of 1933, once each month a group of seven economists teaching at Harvard had gathered for dinner and discussion. Called the "shop club" by O.H. Taylor, it consisted of J.A. Schumpeter as its senior member and six "younger scholars 'sitting at his feet'".[14] Their reaction to some of the policies of the early New Deal led to the book, *The Economics of the Recovery Program*, published in 1934.[15] Five of the authors had analyzed and criticized various New Deal programs, Schumpeter had written about the depression in the context of business-cycle theory, and Taylor had written a concluding, broader essay examining economic, political and ethical questions and the New Deal. Of the seven, only Seymour Harris moved into the Keynesian camp.

A different, Keynesian interpretation of the depression appeared four years later in a book written by younger Cambridge, Massachusetts, economists, entitled *An Economic Program for American Democracy*. The book was authored by R.V. Gilbert, G.H. Hildebrand Jr., A.W. Stuart, Maxine Yaple Sweezy, Paul M. Sweezy, Lorie Tarshis and J.D. Wilson.[16] It influenced Roosevelt somewhat, showing up on his nightstand as George Gilder's book later appeared on Reagan's.

In 1937 the newly appointed Littauer Professor of Economics, Alvin Hansen, joined in, making Keynesian economics the central focus of a seminar he ran with John Williams. Together they challenged the students to new heights. Thus the revolutionary seeds were sown deeply in high quality students who spread Keynesian ideas through publication, teaching and positions in government. The fiscal policy seminar initiated a Harvard–Washington policy nexus and the mixing of the Keynesian seeds with institutionalist New Deal seeds produced a beautiful garden – or a weed field – beauty being in the eyes of the beholder. By the early 1950s the economics journals were filled with Keynesian models, the Committee for Economic Development (C.E.D.) had signed on, Samuelson's textbook was published and would become the model for future texts, and the three-part revolution was essentially complete.

A Revolution of the Young

One interesting aspect of the spread of ideas relates to the stature in the intellectual community of those spreading the new gospel. In regard to the ideas of Keynes it was, with few exceptions, the young untenured professors who converted and the established senior professors who fought a rearguard action. The most notable exceptions would be Alvin Hansen and Milton Friedman. The relationship between Keynes and the young revolutionaries has few precedents in the history of economic thought. Few of the great innovators in economics have been able to build such a phalanx of believers – not Smith, Ricardo, J.S. Mill, Marshall or Veblen, although the latter two came closer than the others. Schumpeter, perhaps reflecting his own feelings towards Keynes, captures the fervor and allegiance of the revolutionaries as manifested in the interviews:

> A Keynesian school formed itself, not a school in that loose sense in which some historians of economics speak of a French, German,

Italian school, but a genuine one which is a sociological entity, namely, a group that professes allegiance to One Master and One Doctrine, and has its inner circle, its propagandists, its watchwords, its esoteric and its popular doctrine. Nor is this all. Beyond the pale of orthodox Keynesianism there is a broad fringe of sympathizers and beyond this again are the many who have absorbed, in one form or another, readily or grudgingly, some of the spirit or some individual items of Keynesian analysis. There are but two analogous cases in the whole of history of economics – the Physiocrats and the Marxists.[17]

The Intellectual Ferment in the 1930s

Analysis of the spread of Keynes's ideas is complex because much more than just changes in macroeconomic theory was occurring during the 1930s. There was a massive movement of intellectual capital from Europe and Britain to the United States. Lerner had been born in Russia and studied at the London School of Economics; Robert Bryce was a Canadian who studied under Keynes at Cambridge, England, and brought his ideas to Harvard and Cambridge, Massachusetts; Lorie Tarshis was a Canadian who studied at the University of Toronto and Cambridge, England, and brought Keynes to the United States as a teacher at Tufts in 1936 and later advanced his cause in his introductory textbook in 1947; Richard Musgrave was born in Germany, earned an undergraduate degree at Heidelberg, and came to study at Harvard in 1933; Tibor Scitovsky was born and received his undergraduate education in Hungary, studied law in England in the early 1930s, went back to Hungary, returned to study at the London School of Economics, served with the British forces in World War II, and came to the United States in 1946; Evsey Domar was born in what is now Poland, educated at UCLA, and later completed his Ph.D. at Harvard in 1947. The spread of Keynes's ideas in America must be set in this broader context of a movement of graduate education in economics and other disciplines from Germany and England to the United States and its acquisition of intellectual capital as a consequence of the policies of Hitler, Mussolini and Stalin.

The growth and spread of Keynesian ideas must also be viewed in the context of the increased mathematization and quantification of economics which had begun long before publication of *The General Theory*. The form of Keynes's work in both his *Treatise* and *General Theory*, with its concepts of aggregate demand; consumption, investment and liquidity preference functions; multipliers and accelerators; and implicit national income accounts, invited formalization, specification and empirical testing. This was centrally important to the spread of the Keynesian policy and theoretical revolutions, but ultimately contributed to its demise. That empirical implementation of Keynes's theory gave it an aura of scientific objectivity and definitiveness which made it much easier for advocates of policies flowing from the model. Thus there appeared a large United Nations project, with Ragnar Frisch as project leader, designed to model the macroeconomy by means of models that could be "solved" and so that policy could be used to find "better" solutions for the problems the economies were experiencing. It also provided a large number of dissertation topics for students. Likewise, with national income accounting, the process of creating new definitions and terminology relating the aggregate economy to Keynesian economics meant that Keynesian ideas structured the debates and almost guaranteed success for Keynesian economics. If you talk in Keynesian terms, it is difficult not to come up with Keynesian results. Ironically, Keynes was not especially supportive of econometrics; he saw the limitations of the formal models and the empirical specification of those relationships, but he played little role in the later developments, since his time, which was limited by ill health, was spent on policy issues such as setting up the post-war international monetary system.

The Political Resistance to Keynesianism

The Keynesianization of America must also be viewed in the larger context of the political ferment in America in the 1930s, 1940s and early 1950s. Economy and society appeared in deep trouble for which many explanations were offered. Marx had written about the collapse of capitalism, and intellectuals studied Marx and other socialist writers to find answers. Some of the Keynesian revolutionaries studied Marx and found little of value, other than a broad vision of the instability of capitalism and the crucial role of investment spending in economic fluctuations. Some of the revolutionaries turned to Marx and became convinced that Marx's analysis was more fruitful than all others. Many non-academics who rejected both Marxism and Keynesianism had difficulties in distinguishing between the two and actively tried to remove adherents of either view from government and the academy. Others simply wanted to remove Keynesian ideas from Washington and the colleges. Hence Keynesian ideas encountered stiff political winds.

The three revolutions, theoretical, policy and textbook, all met with political resistance. The trouble began in 1938, when a number of graduate students at Harvard, a professor at Tufts and "others" published *An Economic Program for American Democracy* presenting an analysis of the depression and suggestions for a Keynesian policy response.[18] The main reason "others" did not want to be identified was that they were employed by government. The book cost Tufts some alumni support[19] because one of its authors was Lorie Tarshis, on the staff at Tufts. Thus it became apparent early on that advocacy of Keynesian ideas could result in political problems for the advocator. Tarshis's principles of economics book published in 1947 met an even stronger political response. An organized attack against the book led to a piece critical of it being sent to university trustees throughout the United States.[20] Galbraith in his interview relates that his Keynesianism held up his Harvard appointment for a year.[21] James Conant, the President of Harvard at the time, has written about outsiders' concern over the make-up of the economics department. Conant relates that "Keynes's name had taken on a symbolic value. Among economists, his book was controversial. To a certain type of businessman, it was the proverbial red rag. In the eyes of many economically illiterate but deeply patriotic (and well-to-do) citizens, to accuse a professor of being a Keynesian was almost equivalent to branding him a subversive agent."[22]

Overcoming the ideological resistance to Keynesianism was not easy. William F. Buckley's *God and Man at Yale* (1951) had recounted the "evil ideas" being purveyed at Yale. Keynesianism was given a great deal of attention. This ideological reaction to Keynes reached its zenith (or nadir?) with the publication, *Keynes at Harvard*, in 1960, an anonymously written book sponsored by the Veritas Foundation that found Fabian socialists, Marxists, Keynesians and others of such ilk under every academic rock.[23] These political issues influenced each of the three revolutions, and they can only be understood within this context.

Let us now consider the three revolutions separately.

The Keynesian Theoretical Revolution

The Keynesian theoretical revolution began mainly among the young. As Paul Samuelson wrote:

> To have been born as an economist before 1936 was a boon – yes. But not to have been born too long before!
> *Bliss was it in that dawn to be alive,*
> *But to be young was very heaven!*
> The *General Theory* caught most economists under the age of thirty-five with the unexpected virulence of a disease first attacking and decimating an isolated tribe of South Sea Islanders. Economists beyond fifty turned out to be quite immune to the ailment.[24]

In examining this "youth" aspect of the Keynesian revolution, it is useful to separate out a deep structure of theory and what might be called a surface structure. The deep structure is the formal complex core of theory. The surface structure is the simple model or vision conveyed of that complex core to those who do not fully understand the complex theoretical core itself. Keynes's revolution was a surface revolution with an undeveloped complex core. Classical economics had a much more developed complex core, but a simple surface structure. A number of classical economists fully recognized that the simple surface structure of classical economics was misleading, but their efforts concentrated on modifying the complex core. Their reaction to Keynes's work is best seen in this light. It was a surface revolution that left many issues of the core untouched. Young economists had yet to be imbued with the complex core of classical economics; they were more interested in surface issues, and to them the Keynesian revolution was a true revolution.

This dual aspect of the theory helps explain the ascendancy of Keynesian ideas even though in many ways they were far less sophisticated than those of some of his contemporaries. For example, Dennis Robertson's work in England on sequential equilibria was an attempt to get at some of the same issues, but in such a complicated way that it was lost on most of his contemporaries. Similarly, as Perry Mehrling has pointed out, Allyn Young's work in monetary theory was starting to deal with similar issues and his student Lauchlin Currie was developing a classical monetary disequilibrium theory, and hence was open to Keynes's ideas.[25] The interviews with Walter Salant and Richard Musgrave indicate that, in the view of a number of students, Currie was a forerunner and possibly an even more sophisticated theorist than Keynes. Why then is the revolution known as the "Keynesian" revolution rather than the Robertson or Young revolution? Partly because of the *simplicity* of the Keynesian model. In many aspects Robertson's, Young's and Hayek's reasoning accorded with and surpassed Keynes's but was too complex to be fully understood and appreciated without a deep understanding of classical monetary thought. It was only for leading-edge theorists. Keynes's work invited simplification because it created a whole new terminology and was couched in a totally different framework. Younger students, who had not been steeped in classical reasoning, were presented with a different operating system that was easy to comprehend. That simplicity made Keynesian economics infectious to the young and made it seem too simple to the old. Thus it is not surprising that an undergraduate engineering student, who had previously studied little economics, was a key Keynesian prophet.

There were many ways in which the Keynesian revolution could have developed. It could have extended to core theory and connected to Robertson's and Hayek's work, but it did not, in large part because of the interest of the Keynesian revolutionaries in policy. Complex core theory has little to say about policy; surface theory has much to say. Thus much of the early work in Keynesian economics involved the development of policy-related surface theory. A key place for this development was the Harvard seminar centered around Alvin Hansen, who had come from the University of Minnesota as the first Littauer Professor and who became the one tenured Harvard faculty member accepting Keynesian ideas. With Hansen the young Keynesians had a powerful faculty ally who, like them, was primarily interested in policy, not complex theory. Thus, like a river, the Keynesian revolution followed the path of least resistance, and it was this area of theoretical policy that constituted that path.

Keynes had created an illusion in his Procrustean portrayal of contemporary economists as "classical" and rigidly monolithic in their acceptance of mainstream theory *and* policy, but that was clearly not the case for theoretical policy.[26] The Keynesian theoretical revolution was the beginning of a revolution, but one which skirted the main issues at debate: the multiplicity of aggregate equilibria and whether dynamic forces were strong enough to return the economy to a unique, desirable equilibrium. Instead of focusing on these abstract issues, the Keynesian revolution focused on a different branch of theory – what might be called theoretical policy. It developed underlying theory only far enough to justify its policy prescriptions and would accept any basic theory which would lead to that policy conclusion. This theoretical policy revolution was quite different from the pure theoretical revolution, which never occurred, and the practical policy revolution, which guided what policies were actually accepted. Theoretical policy connects the abstract theoretical models with specific policy conclusions. In the case of Keynesian macroeconomics, models led to an advocacy of fiscal policy and monetary policy.

For example, it was easy to get academic economists to accept as a practical policy "pump priming" in the form of fiscal deficits. Indeed, many of them, such as Knight and Pigou, had supported deficits before the *General Theory* was published, as had Keynes himself.[27] Yet as the interview with Evsey Domar shows, getting economists to accept deficits as a theoretical policy, a theory of functional finance, was quite another matter. The reason was that it forced economists to deal with the question of multiple equilibria, and the failure of economic forces to lead the economy automatically to the "best" position. In functional finance, the depression was not simply a friction which was preventing the aggregate dynamic equilibrating processes from working; it was instead endemic to the system: *the economy was not self-regulating and needed to be controlled.* That view attacked the core of classical theory. But the new Keynesian theory had many rough edges which were left, for the most part, unexamined. It was these rough edges that would later lay the groundwork for the classical counter-revolution.

Instead of being a core revolution, the Keynesian revolution was primarily a textbook or pedagogical revolution. The pedagogical revolution was built upon a simple model, Samuelson's aggregate expenditure/aggregate product model at the introductory level, IS/LM at the intermediate level, and a metaphor to accompany it. The Keynesian metaphor is probably best seen in Abba Lerner's conception of the economic steering wheel. The government should steer the economy with fiscal and monetary policy practicing functional finance, in contrast to pre-Keynesian macroeconomic laissez-faire policy with its sound finance. Functional finance's three central rules were:

1. The government shall maintain a reasonable level of demand at all times. If there is not enough spending so that there is excessive unemployment, the government shall reduce taxes or increase its own spending. If there is too much spending the government shall prevent inflation by reducing its own expenditures or by increasing taxes.
2. By borrowing money when it wishes to raise the rate of interest and by lending money or repaying debt when it wishes to lower the rate of interest, the government shall maintain that rate of interest which induces the optimum amount of investment.
3. If either of the first two rules conflicts with the principles of

"sound finance" or of balancing the budget or of limiting the national debt, so much the worse for these principles. The government press shall print any money that may be needed in carrying out these rules.[28]

Even though functional finance was the natural policy which followed from the Keynesian model as it was then conceived, most economists found it difficult to accept the implications of functional finance: that the level of the deficit or debt did not matter or that government fiscal policy should be judged by its consequences, not by any precepts about the policy.

It is hard to assess whether the reluctance for public endorsement by economists of functional finance was a strategy – economists agreed with Lerner but felt the public was not ready for such a radical conclusion – or if economists did not accept Lerner's conclusion. We suspect it was primarily the latter; economists talked a macroeconomic theory, but if one scrapes the surface for what they truly believed one finds a macroeconomist whose complex core ideas remained classical microeconomic. It was in large part for this reason that the theoretical Keynesian revolution was short-lived – why it succumbed to the microfoundations attack.

Our view is that the Keynesian revolution initially involved a major theoretical revolution – a significant change in vision of the workings of the macro economy – but that theoretical revolution was progressively lost in the focus on theoretical policy issues which obscured the underlying pure theoretical issues and later the "development" of the microfoundations of Keynesian economics. The Keynesian theoretical revolution is only now being regained with the development of multiple-equilibria macroeconomic models in a game-theoretic context. In this new work the essence of the theoretical Keynesian revolution is that the disequilibrium dynamic path can affect the final equilibrium of an economy and it harkens back to the work of Robertson and Young as much as it does to Keynes.[29] It involves microeconomic foundations but it is microfoundations in dynamics, not statics, and one in which there are important macro feedbacks which make it possible to analyze microeconomics only in its macro-economics context.

The Keynesian Policy Revolution

As was the case with the Keynesian theoretical revolution, the Keynesian policy revolution in the United States did not need to be tied to *The General Theory*. It could have occurred without *The General Theory*, and much of it – specifically the emphasis given to monetary and fiscal policy – was as much a C.E.D. revolution as it was a Keynesian revolution.[30] Our interviews support this view, and it explains an interesting event recounted in a story about a seminar at which Keynes repudiated what was then thought to be Keynesian economics.[31] This Keynesian policy revolution could be garnered from the *Treatise* as easily as from *The General Theory*, and indeed was.[32]

Ironically, this policy revolution, while in many ways the least revolutionary aspect of the Keynesian revolution, was the most contentious at the time. People care about policy in ways they do not care about theories or textbooks. That it took place in the 1930s made this policy revolution all the more contentious. The period under study was not just one of severe depression in the industrialized world, but one of the development and growth of fascism in Germany and Italy and of so-called communism in the Soviet Union.

Harvard and its fiscal policy seminar run by Alvin Hansen and John H. Williams were important in the policy revolution. Here policy makers from Washington, D.C. exchanged ideas with aca-demics. The use of academics in helping to formulate solutions to social and economic problems had first been done on a large scale by LaFollette in Wisconsin. The economics department at Wisconsin under the leadership of John R. Commons had helped to draft, pass and administer legislation regulating public utili-ties, industrial safety, workmen's compensation, child labor, mini-mum wages for women and unemployment compensation. Alvin Hansen was a student of Commons and it is not surprising that the idea of a cooperative relationship between academia and government was institutionalized at Harvard in 1936 in the Littauer School of Public Administration. Alvin Hansen immediately became involved with the federal government as member of the Advisory Council on Social Security. Hansen's interests became primarily focused on explaining and extending Keynes's ideas as they related to policy, and he played a key role in the Keynesianization of America and its policy focus.

There is an aspect of the Keynesian policy revolution, the call for greater government intervention in the society, that has led some observers to find parallels between Keynesianism and mercantilism. We would suggest that there exists another similarity between Keynesianism and mercantilism which is a precondition for the more government interventionist mode of these two systems of thought. Let us term this commonality "certainty of knowledge". As mercantilistic ideas developed, mercantilists became more and more certain that they understood how the economy operated. Given this certainty of knowledge, they recommended specific governmental policies aimed at advancing the wealth of the nation. Often the mercantilist used the metaphor of a doctor prescribing for a patient.

Had Keynesian economics focused on the complex core theory, with its multiplicity of equilibria, rather than surface theory, this certainty of knowledge would not have existed: neoclassical economics' laissez-faire theory would have been challenged, but no alternative Keynesian prescription would have been forthcoming from theory. The core is complex and it is difficult to draw any unambiguous policy conclusion from it. One of Adam Smith's differences with the mercantilists was his uncertainty of knowledge. He was much more humble and tentative, and this attitude is part of his opting for laissez-faire rather than government action. As classical economics developed, and itself was formalized, that tentativeness and humility started to disappear. Laissez-faire became a policy that followed from a theory of the economy, not from our lack of understanding of the working of the economy. Once that had happened, if a macroeconomics policy revolution was to occur, it had to counter that certainty with its own counter-certainty.

It is not surprising that the Keynesian revolutionaries and many of those who later were merely teachers of introductory and intermediate economics also *believed* they understood the economy and could not only specify the appropriate government policy to bring about full employment but could also, because of knowledge of multipliers, accelerators and their interactions, prescribe the amount of the needed stimulus. The younger members of the economics profession went from a period of utter bewilderment in the early 1930s[33] to an arrogant certainty that Keynes had the answers. As Lorie Tarshis aptly put it, Keynes supplied hope and "The opportunity for all us to be part of a great adventure. ... In those years many of us felt that by following Keynes ... each one of us could become a doctor to the whole world."[34]

This Keynesian arrogance on policy matters, while it may have been necessary to counter the classical arrogance, was one of the ingrained weaknesses that led to its ultimate demise. Even if the aggregate economy has multiple equilibria – the idea that we believe to be the core of the Keynesian theoretical revolution – there is no presumption that government policy can, in general, lead it to a preferable equilibrium. Given the strategic nature of the decision making that leads to the multiple equilibria, there is a necessarily strategic, and hence uncertain, nature to policy. In the Keynesian policy revolution, that uncertain nature of policy was lost. Keynesian theory as applied to policy was as noncontextual as was neoclassical: it was naive beyond belief in its view of the way governmental budgets are determined and public choices are made. The same can be said of the C.E.D. and the many business executives who signed on to the use of government as a compensatory agent to fluctuating demand.

Perhaps it had to be. Had Keynesians admitted the flimsy theoretical basis for their policy conclusions, they might never have been adopted.

The Pedagogical (Textbook) Revolution

The final Keynesian revolution has been least commented on, but in many ways is the most important, in that it ties together the other two Keynesian revolutions and creates the vision within which the Keynesian contribution is viewed. It is sometimes said that an army travels on its stomach, and understanding supply routes is crucial to comprehending successful military campaigns. Academic economists travel on their textbook models, and understanding the role of those textbook models is part of the key to discerning the spread of economic ideas and successful theoretical and policy revolutions. The simple textbook models students learn serve as an operating system for their minds. These models limit students' imagination and consideration of alternatives as they focus their vision within the model they learn. Thus part of the key to the other two Keynesian revolutions lies in the textbook models which were used to teach Keynesian ideas.

From Keynes's lectures before the publication of *The General Theory*, Robert Bryce had perceived that, although Keynes's new ideas were intellectually formidable, they could be simplified and effectively presented.[35] Lerner and Robinson also wrote simplified translations of Keynes's ideas in the 1930s, of which Keynes also approved.[36] Others, most notably Tarshis, Samuelson, Dillard and Hansen, had also recognized the possibilities of presenting Keynes's ideas in a simpler, more understandable framework that gave up some theoretical intricacies to achieve more clear-cut policy implications.[37] It was these publications, particularly Samuelson at the introductory textbook level, Hansen at the intermediate textbook level, and Lerner at the non-specialist economist level, which brought about the pedagogical revolution and directed the focus of the Keynesian revolution.

The revolution would focus on a simple policy model which explicated the precise role of monetary and fiscal policy. It would not deal with the more radical policy issues or the more revolutionary theoretical issues that could also have been culled from *The General Theory*. It was an accommodating revolution that would fit in with the liberal business view as exemplified by the C.E.D. Thus we find Paul Sweezy in the interviews explaining how the Keynesian revolution failed to come to grips with the difficult political–economic issues that he saw coming out of Keynes's work.

In many ways, given the institutional structure of economics which focuses mainly on teaching economic policy ideas, this was the only way the Keynesian revolution could have proceeded. The institutional reality is that a social science revolution implicitly prescribes a role for the state and policy in a way fundamentally different from many natural scientific theories. It does not make much difference for government policy whether or not the world started with a big bang or a series of little bangs.[38] It does make a big difference for policy whether the economy gravitates towards a "natural" equilibrium or whether there are multiple equilibria towards which it could gravitate, and whether the government policy can change the economic dynamic trajectory. The multiple equilibria view gives a much stronger sense that government policy makes a difference. Thus the political aspect of the revolution shaped the revolution. We see this in the tales of the textbooks told by our interviewees.

Lorie Tarshis gave Keynes's ideas their first significant American exposure in an introductory economics textbook in 1947. The book's popularity was immediately confronted by efforts to educate trustees and donors of adopting colleges on the heresy of Keynesian theory and policy.[39] These reactions to Tarshis's introductory textbook crushed the adoptions of what had appeared to be an innovative and successful new text. The pedagogical revolution could have come to a halt or been seriously delayed if the apparently successful ideological reaction to the Tarshis textbook had been carried over to other texts.

The pedagogical revolution was saved by Samuelson, whose book gave Keynesian economics an aura of scientific legitimacy. To fight against his text was not only to fight against a policy prescription, it was to fight against scientific models. Because Keynesian economics could be reduced to a simple mathematical model, it was not questionable on political grounds. It was simply "positive economics". Samuelson's textbook was crucial because it influenced a generation of students who became influential in economic and political affairs. It did this not in just the number of readers – over three million copies printed and, with a used-book multiplier of 2.5, over eight million readers – but in the way introductory texts were organized and how Keynes's theory came to be understood.[40] Thus the Keynesianization of America was importantly assisted by Paul Samuelson. He played a major role in the theoretical, policy and pedagogical revolutions. Great theoreticians, and Samuelson ranks with the greats, seldom *directly* influence popular opinion. An interesting aspect of Samuelson's non-theoretical impact is that it was the result of a conscious decision on his part to influence events. He said, "I don't care who writes a nation's laws – or crafts its advanced treaties – if I can write its economics textbooks."[41] Samuelson wanted not just to influence the foundations of economics in the rarefied air of high theory, but to influence people and events. George Feiwel held that "the coin for which he [Samuelson] works is influencing the mind of a generation".[42] Although Samuelson had not read Tarshis's textbook when he wrote his *Principles*, he confesses that he "wrote carefully and lawyer-like".[43]

How does one account for the demise of the Tarshis book and the spectacular success of Samuelson? Kenneth Elzinga holds that "Samuelson out-Keynesianized Tarshis".[44] Samuelson's greater use of graphs and mathematics was helpful in avoiding the ideological reaction that undermined Tarshis's book. He also borrowed Frank Knight's wheel of wealth in introducing circular-flow diagrams and invented and introduced the Keynesian cross which gave macroeconomics its totem to correspond to microeconomics' supply and demand totem.[45] Samuelson's first edition not only offered students a new field, macroeconomics, and new policy considerations, the problems and ways of maintaining full employment, but its organization emphasized the new material by presenting it before microeconomics. The book was also important in the spread of Keynes's ideas throughout the world. It has been translated into 30 foreign languages.

The most successful American introductory economics text of all time, by Campbell R. McConnell, was first published in 1960, some twelve years after Samuelson's first edition, and it closely followed the Samuelson book in its emphasis and organization. Legions of students used these books and their clones and acquired a different set of ideas about the workings of capitalistic-market economies and the role of government than had their parents. The pedagogical revolution was essential to the policy revolution that followed. Samuelson's textbook presentation also helped set the tone for the structure of macroeconomic research in the future, that also helped sow the seeds of its demise.

What is important about this pedagogical revolution was that it separated microeconomics from macroeconomics and, in the microeconomics portion, presented a general-equilibrium vision of a single equilibrium toward which the economy gravitated. Thus while presenting the Keynesian model, in which the outcome of the economic forces was a multitude of equilibria, Samuelson and the economics profession accepted a microeconomics that allowed only one outcome. Keynesian economics was separate and tangential to that larger general-equilibrium vision. But all work on microeconomics began from that single equilibrium vision, and hence its conclusions were preordained. The Keynesian revolution would be a supernova. By accepting a unique equilibrium general equilibrium micromodel to which Keynesian economics had to conform, they made it inevitable that Keynesian economics would become an addendum to classical economics. That acceptance removed the "general" from Keynesian theory.

Conclusion

The interpretations and views expressed above are not the only ones that can be garnered from the interviews. We have developed them here to put the interviews in context for those readers who do not have an extensive background in the history of economics and economic theory. We remind such readers that our views are not solely the product of those interviews, nor are they the only views of this time period. Interpretations of the nature and significance of the Keynesian revolution are many and, if history is any guide, will be unending.

Notes

1. To add perspective, we also include an interview with Leon Keyserling, a very non-Keynesian advocate of many policies associated with Keynesians. He was a government employee who saw the spread of Keynesian ideas from the other side.
2. See Austin Robinson, 'Keynes and His Cambridge Colleagues', in Don Patinkin and J. Clark Leith (eds), *Keynes, Cambridge and The General Theory* (Toronto: University of Toronto Press, 1978) 25–38.
3. A.F.W. Plumptre, 'Maynard Keynes as a Teacher', in Milo Keynes (ed.), *Essays on John Maynard Keynes* (Cambridge: Cambridge University Press, 1975) 248, 252.
4. A.F.W. Plumptre, *Three Decades of Decision: Canada and the World Monetary System. 1944–75* (Toronto: McClelland and Stewart, 1977). Robert W. Dimand, in commenting on an early draft of this essay, directed us to the Plumptre connection and pointed out that Plumptre later brought Tarshis back from Stanford to chair the social science division at Scarborough.
5. Don Patinkin, 'The Process of Writing *The General Theory*: A Critical Survey', in Patinkin and Clark Leith, (eds), 4.
6. John Maynard Keynes, *The Collected Writings of John Maynard Keynes*, vol. VII, *The General Theory of Employment Interest and Money (1936)*, ed. Donald Moggridge (Cambridge: Cambridge University Press, 1973) xxiii. Also see Richard F. Kahn, *The Making of Keynes' General Theory* (Cambridge: Cambridge University Press, 1984).
7. Austin Robinson, 'A Personal View' in Milo Keynes (ed.), *Essays on John Maynard Keynes* 10–11.
8. Elizabeth S. Johnson and Harry G. Johnson, *In the Shadow of Keynes* (London: Basil Blackwell, 1978) 133.
9. Thomas K. Rymes (ed.), *Keynes's Lectures, 1932–35* (Ann Arbor: University of Michigan Press, 1989).
10. Material and quotations from this paragraph taken from the Bryce interview. His paper on Keynes was published for the first time in 1978: Robert B. Bryce, 'An Introduction to a Monetary Theory of Employment', in Patinkin and Clark Leith, (eds), 129–45. See also Keynes's 1935 letter to Bryce approving of this summary of his ideas (127–8). For other comments by Bryce on his Cambridge, England years, see Robert Bryce, 'Keynes as Seen by His Students in the 1930s', in Patinkin and Clark Leith (eds), 40–41.
11. Galbraith recalls this Schumpeter comment in his interview.
12. Rymes, ix.
13. Material and quotes in this paragraph taken from Tarshis interview. For other comments by Tarshis on his Cambridge, England experience, see Lorie Tarshis, 'Keynes as Seen by his Students in the 1930s', in Patinkin and Clark Leith (eds), 50–52.
14. O.H. Taylor, *Economics and Liberalism* (Cambridge, Mass.: Harvard University Press, 1955) 7.

15. Douglass Brown, E.H. Chamberlin, Seymour Harris, Wassily Leontief, Edward Mason, J.A. Schumpeter and O.H. Taylor, *The Economics of the Recovery Program* (New York: McGraw-Hill,1934).

16. R.V. Gilbert, *et al.*, *An Economic Program for American Democracy* (New York: Vanguard Press, 1938). There were several others who had a role in writing the book, but who chose not to be identified as authors. Alan Sweezy lists himself, Emile Despres and Walter Salant. See, Alan R. Sweezy, 'The Keynesians and Government Policy, 1933–1939', *American Economic Review*, May, 1972, 122. We have not edited the interviews to give a "correct" list of authors, but note the varying recollections of those interviewed of who were the unsigned authors.

17. Joseph A. Schumpeter, *Ten Great Economists From Marx to Keynes* (New York: Oxford University Press, 1951) 287–8.

18. R.V. Gilbert, *et al.*

19. See Tarshis interview. Also see G.C. Harcourt, 'Occasional Portraits of the Founding Post-Keynesians: Lorie Tarshis', *The Social Science Imperialists: Selected Essays by G. C. Harcourt*, ed. Prue Kerr (London: Routledge & Kegan Paul, 1982) 371.

20. See Tarshis interview. Also see G.C. Harcourt, 'Occasional Portraits of the Founding Post-Keynesians: Lorie Tarshis', 371–3.

21. Also see Peggy Lamson, *Speaking of Galbraith: A Personal Portrait* (New York: Ticknor & Fields, 1991) 92–5.

22. James B. Conant, *My Several Lives* (New York: Harper & Row, 1970) 440–41.

23. *Keynes at Harvard: Economic Deception as a Political Credo* (New York: Veritas Foundation, 1960). The author was later identified by the Foundation after his death in 1962 as Olin Glen Saxon, a Yale professor. The book is curious and amusing. Schumpeter is accorded the designation of one of the world's outstanding Marxists. Many economists, such as Alfred Marshall, were classified as Fabian socialists. The author did not comprehend the cruel tricks history plays on propagators of partisan views. For example, the London School of Economics, founded by the Fabian socialists, had on its staff Friedrich von Hayek and Lionel Robbins. There is a revised and enlarged edition by Zygmund Dobbs (1969) with new chapters by Dobbs.

24. Paul A. Samuelson, 'The General Theory' reprinted (1946) in Robert Leckachman (ed.), *Keynes's General Theory Reports of Three Decades* (New York: St Martin's Press, 1964), 315–16.

25. Perry Mehrling, 'The Monetary Thought of Allyn Abbott Young', *Working Paper Series*, 94–04, Barnard College, Columbia University: New York, February, 1994; 'Allyn Young and the Chicago Tradition', *Working Paper Series*, 94–06, Barnard College, Columbia University: New York, March, 1994.

26. Harry G. Johnson argues that Keynes's method of debate 'posits a nameless horde of faceless orthodox nincompoops, among whom a few recognizable faces can be discerned, and proceeds to ridicule a travesty of their published, presumed, or imputed views'. See Johnson's memoir, 'How Good was Keynes' Cambridge?' *Encounter*, August, 1976, 90.

27. See J. Ronnie Davis, *The New Economics and the Old Economists* (Ames, Iowa: Iowa State University Press, 1971); Herbert Stein, *The Fiscal Revolution in America* (Chicago: University of Chicago Press, 1969); T.W. Hutchison, *On Revolutions and Progress in Economic Knowledge* (Cambridge: Cambridge University Press, 1978); and Robert W. Dimand, 'The New Economics and American Economists in the 1930s Reconsidered', *Atlantic Economic Journal*, **XVIII** (4) 42–7.

28. Abba P. Lerner, 'The Economic Steering Wheel', *The University Review*, June 1941, 2–5.

29. Because of its relationship to classical ideas, this work is more properly called post-Walrasian rather than Keynesian. See David Colander (ed.), *Post Walrasian Macroeconomics: Beyond Microfoundations*, London: Cambridge University Press, forthcoming. See also Appendix B.

30. For the role of the Committee for Economic Development (CED) see Herbert Stein, *Presidential Economics*, 2nd edn (Washington: American Enterprise Institute, 1988) and Stein, *The Fiscal Revolution in America* (1969).

31. See the Lerner–Hansen interview.

32. Peter Clarke, *The Keynesian Revolution in the Making 1924–1936* (Oxford: Clarendon Press, 1988).

33. Paul A. Samuelson, 'Succumbing to Keynesianism', *Challenge*, Jan.–Feb. 1985, 4–11.

34. Robert Skidelsky, *John Maynard Keynes*, 2 vols (New York: Viking, 1983–92) II, 574.

35. Written in 1935 and published for the first time in 1978: Robert B. Bryce, 'An Introduction to a Monetary Theory of Employment', in Patinkin and Clark Leith (eds), 129–45. See Keynes's 1935 letter to Bryce approving of this summary of his ideas (127–8).

36. Abba P. Lerner, 'Mr. Keynes' "General Theory of Employment, Interest and Money"', *International Labour Review*, October 1936, 435–54; Joan Robinson, *Introduction to the Theory of Employment* (London: Macmillan, 1937).

37. Lorie Tarshis, *The Elements of Economics: An Introduction to the Theory of Price and Employment* (Boston: Houghton Mifflin, 1947); Paul A. Samuelson, *Economics, an Introductory Analysis* (New York: McGraw-Hill, 1948); Dudley Dillard, *The Economics of John Maynard Keynes* (New York: Prentice-Hall, 1948); Alvin Hansen, *A Guide to Keynes* (New York: McGraw-Hill, 1953).

38. The two are not totally distinct. Copernicus's theory that the earth traveled around the sun rather than vice versa challenged the view of the earth as the center of the universe, and thus was treated in much the same way as was the Keynesian revolution.

39. The young Buckley, writing about the use of the Tarshis book at Yale, held that, "When this book, generally classified as 'the most frankly Keynesian of all full-length elementary textbooks,' was published, it was immediately put to use as the basic textbook in Economics 10. It was withdrawn after a year due in large part, I am certain, to the ire its use

evoked in so many alumni" (William F. Buckley, Jr. *God and Man at Yale*, Chicago: Henry Regnery, 1951, 98).
40. Kenneth G. Elzinga, 'The Eleven Principles of Economics', *Southern Economic Journal*, **58**, (4), 861–79.
41. Paul A. Samuelson, 'Foreword,' in *The Principles of Economics Course*, ed. Philip Saunders and William B. Walstad (New York: McGraw-Hill, 1990) ix. In another place Samuelson makes the same remark: "Let those who will write the nation's laws if I can write its textbooks", (Paul A. Samuelson, 'Economics in My Time', in William Breit and Roger W. Spencer (eds), *Lives of the Laureates*, Cambridge: MIT Press, 1986, 68).
42. George R. Feiwel (ed.), *Samuelson and Neoclassical Economics* (Boston: Kluwer-Nijhoff, 1982) 19.
43. See Samuelson interview. Also see Feiwel (ed.), 19.
44. Elzinga, 863.
45. For the origins of the circular-flow diagram, see Don Patinkin, 'In Search of the "Wheel of Wealth": On the Origins of Frank Knight's Circular-Flow Diagram', *American Economic Review* (December, 1973); for the origins of the Keynesian cross, see Elzinga, 863, fn 5.

Bibliography

Adelman, Irma, 'Scitovsky, Tibor', *The New Palgrave: A Dictionary of Economics*, London: Macmillan, 1987.

Allen, William R., 'Economics, Economists, and Economic Policy: Modern American Experiences', *History of Political Economy*, **9**, (1), (1977), 48–88.

Arestis, Philip and Malcolm Sawyer (eds), *A Biographical Dictionary of Dissenting Economists*, Brookfield: Edward Elgar, 1992.

Bailey, Stephen Kemp, *Congress Makes a Law*, New York: Vintage, 1950.

Barber, William J., *From New Era to New Deal: Herbert Hoover, the Economists, and American Economic Policy*, Cambridge: Cambridge University Press, 1985.

——, 'The Career of Alvin H. Hansen in the 1920s and 1930s: A Study in Intellectual Transformation', *History of Political Economy*, **19**, (2), (1987), 191–205.

Bergson, Abram, 'Paul A. Samuelson: The Harvard Days', in George R. Feiwel (ed.), *Samuelson and Neoclassical Economics*, Boston: Kluwer-Nijhoff, 1982, 331–5.

Blaug, Mark, *Great Economists Since Keynes*, Totowa, New Jersey: Barnes and Noble, 1985.

——, 'Second Thoughts on the Keynesian Revolution', *Economic Theories, True or False?*, Brookfield: Edward Elgar, 1990, 88–106.

Brazelton, Robert W., 'Alvin Harvey Hansen', *American Journal of Economics and Sociology*, **48**, (4), (1989), 427–40.

Brown, E. Cary, 'Domar, Evsey David', *The New Palgrave: A Dictionary of Economics*, London: Macmillan, 1987.

Bryce, Robert B., 'Keynes as Seen by His Students in the 1930s' and 'An Introduction to a Monetary Theory of Employment', in Don Patinkin and J. Clark Leith (eds), *Keynes, Cambridge and The General Theory*, Toronto: University of Toronto Press, 1978.

Buckley, William F., Jr., *God and Man at Yale*, Chicago: Henry Regnery, 1951.

Clarke, Peter, *The Keynesian Revolution in the Making 1924–1936*, Oxford: Clarendon Press, 1988.

Clower, Robert W., 'The State of Economics: Hopeless But Not Serious?', in David C. Colander and A.W. Coats (eds), *The Spread of Economic Ideas*, Cambridge: Cambridge University Press, 1989. 23–9.

Colander, David (ed.), *Post Walrasian Macroeconomics: Beyond Microfoundations*, London: Cambridge University Press, forthcoming.

Collins, Robert M., *The Business Response to Keynes, 1929–1964*, New York: Columbia University Press, 1981.

Conant, James B., *My Several Lives*, New York: Harper & Row, 1970.

Council of Economic Advisers Oral History Interviews, 1964.

Currie, Lauchlin, 'Comments and Observations', *History of Political Economy*, **10**, (4), (1978), 541–8.

——, 'Causes of the Recession' (written 1 April 1938), *History of Political Economy*, **12**, (3), (1980), 316–35.

Currie, Lauchlin and Martin Krost, 'Federal Income-Increasing Expenditures, 1932–1935', (written circa November, 1935), *History of Political Economy*, **10**, (4), (1978), 534–40.

Davis, J. Ronnie, *The New Economics and the Old Economists*, Ames: Iowa State University Press, 1971.

Dillard, Dudley, *The Economics of John Maynard Keynes*, New York: Prentice-Hall, 1948.

Dimand, Robert W., *The Origins of the Keynesian Revolution*. Stanford: Stanford University Press, 1988.

——, 'The New Economics and American Economists in the 1930s Reconsidered', *Atlantic Economic Journal*, **XVIII**, (4), (1990), 42–7.

Ekelund, Robert B., 'Hansen, Alvin', *The New Palgrave: A Dictionary of Economics*, London: Macmillan, 1987.

Elzinga, Kenneth G., 'The Eleven Principles of Economics', *Southern Economic Journal*, **58**, (4), (1992), 861–79.

Feiwel, George R. (ed.), 'Samuelson and the Age After Keynes', *Samuelson and Neoclassical Economics*, Boston: Kluwer-Nijhoff, 1982, 202–43.

Fischer, Stanley, 'Samuelson, Paul Anthony', *The New Palgrave: A Dictionary of Economics*, London: Macmillan, 1987.

Fletcher, Gordon A., *The Keynesian Revolution and its Critics*, New York: St Martin's Press, 1987.

Foster, John Bellamy, 'Sweezy, Paul Malor', *The New Palgrave: A Dictionary of Economics*, London: Macmillan, 1987.

Galbraith, John Kenneth, 'How the Keynesian Revolution Came to the United States', *Economics, Peace, and Laughter*, Boston: Houghton Mifflin Company, 1971.

——, *A Life In Our Times*, Boston: Houghton Mifflin Company, 1981.

Gilbert, R.V. *et al.*, *An Economic Program for American Democracy*, New York: Vanguard Press, 1938.

Hall, Peter A. (ed.), *The Political Power of Economic Ideas*, Princeton: Princeton University Press, 1989.

Hansen, Alvin, 'Mr. Keynes on Underemployment Equilibrium', *Journal of Political Economy* (Oct. 1936), 686.

——, *A Guide to Keynes*, New York: McGraw-Hill, 1953.

Harcourt, G.C. 'Occasional Portraits of the Founding Post-Keynesians: Lorie Tarshis', *The Social Science Imperialists: Selected Essays by G.C. Harcourt*, ed. Prue Kerr, London: Routledge & Kegan Paul, 1982. A shorter version appeared as 'An Early Post-Keynesian: Lorie Tarshis', *Journal of Post Keynesian Economics*, **IV**, (Summer, 1982), 609–19.

Harris, Seymour (ed.), *The New Economics*, New York: Alfred A. Knoff, 1952.

Harrod, R.F., *The Life of John Maynard Keynes*, 2 vols, New York: Harcourt, Brace and Company, 1951.

Himmelberg, Robert, *The Origins of the National Recovery Administration*, New York: Fordham University Press, 1976.

Hirschman, Albert O., 'How the Keynesian Revolution Was Exported from the United States, and Other Comments', *The Political Power of Economic Ideas: Keynesianism Across Nations*, in Peter A. Hall (ed.), Princeton: Princeton University Press, 1989, 347–59.

Hutchison, T.W., *On Revolutions and Progress in Economic Knowledge*, Cambridge: Cambridge University Press, 1978.

Johnson, Elizabeth S., 'Keynes as a Literary Craftsman', in Don Patinkin and J. Clark Leith (eds), *Keynes, Cambridge and The General Theory*, Toronto: University of Toronto Press, 1978.

Johnson, Elizabeth S. and Harry G. Johnson, *In the Shadow of Keynes*, London: Basil Blackwell, 1978.

Johnson, Harry G. 'How Good was Keynes' Cambridge?' *Encounter* (August, 1976), 90.

Jones, Byrd L. 'The Role of Keynesians in Wartime Policy and Postwar

Planning, 1940–1946', *American Economic Review* (May, 1972), 125–33.

——, 'Lauchlin Currie, Pump Priming, and New Deal Fiscal Policy, 1934–1936', *History of Political Economy*, **10**, (4), (1978), 509–24.

——, 'Lauchlin Currie and the Causes of the 1937 Recession', *History of Political Economy*, **12**, (3), (1980), 303–15.

Keynes, John Maynard, *The Collected Writings of John Maynard Keynes*, vol. VII, *The General Theory of Employment Interest and Money (1936)*, ed. Donald Moggridge, Cambridge: Cambridge University Press, 1973.

Keynes, Milo (ed.), *Essays on John Maynard Keynes*, Cambridge: Cambridge University Press, 1975.

Klein, Lawrence R., *The Keynesian Revolution*, New York: Macmillan, 1961.

Kuhn, Thomas, *The Structure of Scientific Revolutions*, Chicago: University of Chicago Press, 1962.

Lamson, Peggy, *Speaking of Galbraith: A Personal Portrait*, New York: Ticknor & Fields, 1991.

Lebowitz, Michael A., 'Paul M. Sweezy', in Maxine Berg (ed.), *Political Economy in the Twentieth Century*, Savage, Md.: Barnes & Noble, 1990, 131–61.

Leckachman, Robert (ed.), *Keynes's General Theory Reports of Three Decades*, New York: St Martin's Press, 1964.

Lerner, Abba P., 'Mr. Keynes' "General Theory of Employment, Interest and Money"', *International Labour Review* (October 1936), 435–54.

——, 'The Economic Steering Wheel', *The University Review* (June 1941), 2–5.

Mehrling, Perry, 'The Monetary Thought of Allyn Abbott Young', *Working Paper Series*, 94-04, Barnard College, Columbia University: New York, February, 1994.

——, 'Allyn Young and the Chicago Tradition', *Working Paper Series*, 94–06, Barnard College, Columbia University: New York, March, 1994.

Mehta, Ghanshyam, *The Structure of the Keynesian Revolution*, New York: St Martin's Press, 1978.

Mieszkowski, Peter, 'Musgrave, Richard Abel', *The New Palgrave: A Dictionary of Economics*, London: Macmillan, 1987.

Moggridge, D.E. *John Maynard Keynes*, New York: Penguin, 1976.

——, 'Tarshis, Lorie', *The New Palgrave: A Dictionary of Economics*, London: Macmillan, 1987.

——, *Maynard Keynes*, New York: Routledge, 1992.

Musgrave, Richard A., 'Alvin Hansen: Caring for the Real Problems', *Quarterly Journal of Economics*, **XC**, (1), (1976), 1–7.

Patinkin, Don, 'Keynes and Econometrics: On the Interaction Between the Macroeconomic Revolutions of the Interwar Years', *Econometrica*, **44**, (1976), 1091–1123.

——, 'Monetary Economics', *Paul Samuelson and Modern Economic Theory*, in E. Cary Brown and Robert M. Solow (eds), New York: McGraw-Hill, 1983, 157–67.

Patinkin, Don and J. Clark Leith (eds), *Keynes, Cambridge and The General Theory*, Toronto: University of Toronto Press, 1978.

Portelli, Alissandro, 'What Makes Oral History Different', *The Death of Luigi Trastulli and Other Stories*, Albany: State University of New York Press, 1991.

Robinson, Austin, 'A Personal View', in Milo Keynes (ed.), *Essays on John Maynard Keynes*, Cambridge: Cambridge University Press, 1975.

——, 'Keynes and his Cambridge Colleagues', in Don Patinkin and J. Clark Leith (eds), *Keynes, Cambridge and The General Theory*, Toronto: University of Toronto Press, 1978.

Robinson, Joan, *Introduction to the Theory of Employment*, London: Macmillan, 1937.

Rymes, Thomas K. (ed.), *Keynes's Lectures, 1932–35*, Ann Arbor: University of Michigan Press, 1989.

Salant, Walter S., 'Alvin Hansen and the Fiscal Policy Seminar', *Quarterly Journal of Economics*, **XC**, (1), (1976), 14–23.

——, 'Keynes as Seen by his Students in the 1930s', in Don Patinkin and J. Clark Leith (eds), *Cambridge and The General Theory*, Toronto: University of Toronto Press, 1978.

——, 'The Spread of Keynesian Doctrines and Practices in the United States', in Peter A. Hall (ed.), *The Political Power of Economic Ideas*, Princeton: Princeton University Press, 1989, 27–51.

Samuelson, Paul A., 'The General Theory' reprinted (1946), in Robert Leckachman (ed.), *Keynes's General Theory Reports of Three Decades*, New York: St Martin's Press, 1964.

——, *Economics, an Introductory Analysis*, New York: McGraw-Hill, 1948.

——, 'Economics In A Golden Age: A Personal Memoir', in Gerald Holton (ed.), *The Twentieth Century Sciences: Studies in the Biography of Ideas*, New York: W. W. Norton, 1972.

——, 'The Balanced-Budget Multiplier: A Case Study in the Sociology and Psychology of Scientific Discovery', *History of Political Economy*, **7**, (1), (1975), 43–55.

——, 'Alvin Hansen as a Creative Economic Theorist', *Quarterly Journal of Economics*, **XC**, (1), (1976), 24–31.

——, 'My Life Philosophy', *The American Economist*, **27**, (1983), 5–12.

——, 'Succumbing to Keynesianism', *Challenge*, **27**, (6), 1985, 4–11.

——, 'Economics in My Time', in William Breit and Roger W. Spencer (eds), *Lives of the Laureates*, Cambridge: MIT Press, 1986, 59–76.

——, 'In the Beginning', *Challenge*, **31**, (4), (1988), 32–4.

Sandilands, Roger L. *The Life and Political Economy of Lauchlin Currie: New Dealer, Presidential Advisor, and Development Economist*, Durham: Duke University Press, 1990.

Scitovsky, Tibor, 'Lerner, Abba Ptachya', *The New Palgrave: A Dictionary of Economics*, London: Macmillan, 1987.

Shinn, Terry and Richard Whitley (eds), *Expository Science: Forms and Functions of Popularisation*, Dordrecht: D. Reidel, 1985.

Skidelsky, Robert (ed.), *The End of the Keynesian Era*, New York: Holmes & Meier, 1977.

——, *John Maynard Keynes*, 2 vols, New York: Viking, 1983–92.

Stein, Herbert, *The Fiscal Revolution in America*, Chicago: University of Chicago Press, 1969.

——, *Presidential Economics*, 2nd edn, Washington: American Enterprise Institute, 1988.

Sweezy, Alan R., 'The Keynesians and Government Policy, 1933–1939', *American Economic Review* (May 1972), 116–24.

Tarshis, Lorie, *The Elements of Economics: An Introduction to the Theory of Price and Employment*, Boston: Houghton Mifflin, 1947.

——, 'Keynes as Seen by his Students in the 1930s', in Don Patinkin and J. Clark Leith (eds), *Keynes, Cambridge and The General Theory*, Toronto: University of Toronto Press, 1978, 48–63.

Taylor, O.H., *Economics and Liberalism*, Cambridge, Mass: Harvard University Press, 1955.

Thurow, Lester C., 'Galbraith, John Kenneth', *The New Palgrave: A Dictionary of Economics*, London: Macmillan, 1987.

Tobin, James, 'Hansen and Public Policy', *Quarterly Journal of Economics*, **1**, (1976), 32–37.

——, 'Macroeconomics and Fiscal Policy', in E. Cary Brown and Robert M. Solow (eds), *Paul Samuelson and Modern Economic Theory*, New York: McGraw-Hill, 1983, 189–201.

Turgeon, Lynn, 'Keyserling, Leon Hirsch', *The New Palgrave: A Dictionary of Economics*, London: Macmillan, 1987.

Veritas Foundation, *Keynes at Harvard: Economic Deception as a Political Credo*, New York: Veritas Foundation, 1960.

Wattel, Harold L., *The Policy Consequences of John Maynard Keynes*, Armonk, New York: M.E. Sharpe, 1985.

Winch, Donald, *Economics and Policy A Historical Study*, New York: Walker and Company, 1969.

Appendix A: The Keynesian Revolution and the Methodology of Science

One of the reasons for interest in the Keynesian revolution is its relevance as an example for debate in the philosophy of science. While we find this period full of interesting issues relevant to the philosophy of science, we did not want to clutter up the story of the coming of Keynes to America with topics of less interest to most readers. Hence this appendix and the next. Let us begin with a brief summary of the evolution of views on the philosophy of science. In the early 1900s logical positivism was dominant—science was the truth. In the mid-1900s logical positivism was replaced by Popper's falsificationism which held that theories could not be proven true but could be shown to be false. In logical positivism and falsificationism the progression of science was viewed as a progression of thinking toward the "truth", or at least the "less false". Keynesian economics seemed to fit this optimistic view about the progression of science toward truth.

The view of science progressively moving toward truth which was inherent in logical positivism and falsificationism was challenged by Kuhnians and Lakatosians, who saw science as more of a contest among competing research programs in which the truth would not necessarily win out, but in which the truth would nonetheless have a good chance of winning. This view fit the Keynesian–classical debate of the 1960s in which the monetarist and Keynesian theories both had significant followers.

That modified view of the "sort-of progression" of science was modified still further in other work, including Feyerabend's nihilism, the rhetorical and sociological schools, and the post modernist approaches to the philosophy of science. These perspectives to the philosophy of science see science as biased anarchy in which the truth plays a minor role. The current chaotic state of macroeconomics appears to fit these views.

The more current sociologies of knowledge have made a study of the history of thought and the sociology of the profession more important. Under logical positivism and falsificationism, the invisible hand of truth would win out over competing theories independent of the events and institutions; so studying the events and institutions was primarily of intellectual and historical interest. In the Kuhnian and Lakatosian views, the nature of the profession and individuals could affect the timing of the paradigm shift. And finally, in the rhetorical and sociological views, the nature of the profession is everything: the theory that wins out is not necessarily true; its advocates are simply better at promoting it.

Given this increasing importance assigned to the nature of the profession, and to individuals' roles, it is easy to recognize the ever-heightening interest in the pulsating theoretical and policy Keynesian revolutions. If the new classical model does supplant the Keynesian model, it means that the Keynesian revolution was not a revolution; it was simply a fifty-year wrong turn leading to a dead-end. For a sociological or rhetorical methodologist the Keynesian revolution is a wonderful case study of the arbitrary nature of choice variables or paradigms–one can study the reasons why Keynesian economics won out in the 1930s and lost out in the 1970s and, through that study, better understand the theories. Was there anything more to the Keynesian revolution than slick salesmanship? Why was there a movement back to the classical school? And does the recent surge of theoretical interest in Keynesianism move us back to a Lakatosian or even falsificationist understanding of the progression of macroeconomic thought?

Our view of the Keynesian revolution's relevance for the philosophy of science is mixed. It is clear from our consideration of its theoretical, policy and pedagogical phases that personalities, sociological considerations and incentives for researchers played a large role in what "theories" were accepted. The strength of the Keynesian metaphors and their ability to provide conundrums for researchers to explain exerted a major role in the theory's growth and ascendancy. The Keynesian policy and theoretical revolutions contributed something to economics approved by nearly all economists: increased standing as a science that understood its subject matter, could predict outcomes, and that could formulate policies that would bring about a new era of prosperity. The dismal science became a euphoric science. Building the Keynesian revolution into the textbooks made it easier for the society to accept deficit spending, as millions of students were trained to think in a Keynesian mode. But we do not quite move to the methodological nihilism of post modernism. We find that the ascendancy was confined by both logical and empirical, albeit, informal, tentative verifications of Keynesian and classical theory. Thus modified positivism in which there is some hope for a general movement forward retains some credibility. It is not total chaos that determines our theories, it is a limited chaos.

Neither classicals nor Keynesians worked towards definitive empirical tests, and both had a pot-pourri of ad hoc explanations of why outcomes may not come out as expected. When empirical tests are non-definitive, other issues take charge, specifically the underlying vision held by the researchers that influenced their interpretation of events. It was the Keynesian revolution's failure to change the underlying unique equilibrium microeconomic vision of economists, and to develop a pedagogical model which changed that vision, that doomed it and set in motion the revolt against it. It is only now in the 1990s, as work in game theory and strategic complementarities is beginning to change the unique equilibrium vision, that a Keynesian theoretical revolution is taking place.

Appendix B: The Second Coming of Keynes

A key element of the simple Keynesian model was the multiplicity of equilibria: aggregate income was not uniquely determined by the system. Classical economists could accept that in the short run, but in the back of their mind they had a vision of economic forces pushing the economy toward a unique equilibrium. The debate about the multiplicity of aggregate equilibria was initially hidden as debate focused on other issues, such as the role of monetary policy relative to fiscal policy and the nature of the consumption function. IS/LM analysis, which was the intermediate model in which Keynes's ideas were presented, was essentially a multiple equilibria model. It was only in the late 1960s, after the period we are considering, that the classical vision was reintroduced in the form of the natural rate of unemployment and the vertical long-run Phillips Curve.

If there were a variety of macroeconomic equilibria towards which the economy could gravitate, there would also be a variety of microeconomic equilibria—each associated with a macroeconomic result. If the aggregate economy gravitated toward a less than optimal equilibrium, then the sum of all the individual markets that make up the aggregate would also have to gravitate toward less than optimal equilibria. The textbooks explicitly did not make this step and instead relied upon a competitive model in which the market led to a unique optimal equilibrium. But this presented a contradiction. If each individual market was led to a desirable equilibrium, how could the aggregate of those individual markets be an undesirable equilibrium? It was this tension that ultimately led to the new classical revolution and the theoretical demise of the theoretical Keynesian revolution. Microeconomics and macroeconomics had to be compatible, and the new classical revolution made them compatible on microeconomics' unique equilibria terms.

It is interesting that it was only a small specification difference that set the theoretical Keynesian revolution on its unique equilibrium route. Samuelson and other Keynesians implicitly accepted the classical aggregate production function which had a unique equilibrium. Given a set amount of capital and labor, only one aggregate output was possible. Since this model only relates capital (K) and labor (L) to output (X), the only way it allows output to fall is to have labor or capital not being used. In competitive markets that can only happen if some wages or prices are rigid. If an alternative textbook specification of aggregate production had been used which allowed for coordination failures, Keynesian economics could have been interpreted as an equilibrium phenomenon in which, for example, because individuals expect low output, they produce little, create little demand, and confirm their negative expectations. Notice that in this coordination interpretation the Keynesian problem is not a fixed-wage or fixed-price problem, it is a problem of self-fulfilling expectations and multiplicity of equilibria. Put in more technical, modern terms, the dynamic disequilibrium adjustment process affects the new equilibrium of the economy so that the equilibrium cannot be studied independently of the dynamics.

This coordination failure interpretation of the Keynesian revolution answers the question of whether one needs fixed wages and prices to arrive at an under-full equilibrium. The answer is no. Coordination failures can cause a less than desirable equilibrium independent of wage and price flexibility. Only some variant of this coordination specification would have been consistent with Keynes's theory being a general theory and classical theory being a special case. It is to these issues that a modern new Keynesian debate is returning. Thus we foresee a second coming of the Keynesian revolution, this one with a different mix of policy, theory and pedagogy. Because the second coming will be far less concerned with policy and more concerned with core theory, its supporting pedagogy can provide a firmer foundation for the theoretical revolution.

2. Robert Bryce (b. 1910)

Birthplace: Toronto, Canada

Education:

1931:   B.S. in Engineering, University of Toronto
1934:   B.A. Cambridge
1935–6:   Studied at Harvard

Significant publications:

'An Introduction to a Monetary Theory of Employment', in Don
    Patinkin and J. Clark Leith (eds), *Keynes, Cambridge and The
    General Theory*, Toronto: University of Toronto Press, 1978.
*Maturing in Hard Times: Canada's Department of Finance
    Through the Great Depression*, Kingston: McGill-Queens Uni-
    versity Press, 1986.

Significant honors:

Commonwealth Fund Fellowship

Experience:

1937:   Business
1938:   Joined Canadian Department of Finance
1954:   Appointed Clerk of the Privy Council
        Secretary to the Cabinet
1963:   Deputy Minister of Finance
1971:   Canadian Executive Director to International Monetary
        Fund
        Chair–Royal Commission on Corporate Concentration

This interview with Bob Bryce was conducted on 24 September 1987 in Burlington, Vermont, following a symposium on Keynesian economics at Middlebury College.

How did you get into economics?

As an undergraduate I initially studied engineering. I never studied economics until the depths of the Depression. However, when I graduated in engineering in 1932, there were no jobs for engineers in either Canada or in the United States so I had to follow a different path.

In my last year or two at the University of Toronto doing engineering, I had become interested in debating and history. Those interests led me into an interest in current affairs, and that meant that I should learn something about the Depression and why it occurred. Thus my interest in economics.

I was very puzzled as to why there was a Depression. I asked my friend Lorie Tarshis where I could go to find out. He told me the best place to go to learn about that was Cambridge, which is where he was going. So I went over there with him. I was able to go because my father happened to be in the gold-mining business, which was the only prosperous business during the Depression.

I went over to Cambridge with Lorie in the worst stateroom of the oldest ship that still went across the Atlantic. Anyway, we got there. After arriving I was very lucky in being invited, along with Lorie and some other Canadians that year, to join Keynes's "Club", as he called it, which met in his rooms on Monday nights during the term. It was really there and at the pubs that we had the conversations.

My coming into economics late gave me a distinct advantage over other students. I had never learned the pre-Keynesian economics which was founded on the belief that you didn't have any unemployment. In that pre-Keynesian view if you had unemployment, it was only a temporary condition that occurred because of business cycles. They had elaborate statistics and elaborate explanations showing what these cycles were. Most students had had the view that there could be no long-term unemployment drilled into them throughout their undergraduate studies. I hadn't, which made it easier for me to pick up Keynes's alternative arguments.

Actually, it isn't quite true that I went over there having studied no economics. In preparation for my studies in England I took books that I was supposed to read in this coming year with me and spent three months at Rocky Island in Lake Huron studying economics. I rented a cottage, and read and studied on my own. I remember reading Marshall's *Principles* and Keynes's *A Treatise on Money*, which I thought was terrific. But I didn't have to worry too much about it since when I got to Cambridge I quickly discovered that there was a real ferment going on, that all the really serious books that Keynes had written prior to the 1930s were based on past theory, which he had discarded. I might add that he had, however, written a number of popular pamphlets that departed from past theory into common sense prior to the 1930s. These, however, did not provide the intellectual background to stand up against the analysis not only of the academics of the time but also of the British Treasury.

How did you find your first year?

What was going on in the period from 1931–2 until 1935 was the evolution of Keynes's ideas. He was trying to switch over, broadly speaking, from a kind of economic analysis that dealt with price levels and things that related to them, to a macroeconomic analysis that dealt with levels of output and employment. This switchover led to much confusion, which bothered me.

While it was absorbing, because I was learning something quite new, I found it frustrating because it was so imprecise a subject, and I felt, at that stage, that it didn't give me the answer I had been looking for on how the Depression came about. This was in part because in that particular year Keynes's ideas were changing; they hadn't been crystallized yet in his lectures or on paper. The other subjects I was taking were better developed, but they were not the main thing in my interest.

I, fresh from studying engineering, which is done with some precision, came to the conclusion that economics was a fuzzy subject. I concluded that economists didn't know what they were talking about, and that there was little reason that I should care about economics. I was sufficiently disenchanted that I made one move to go back into science. I had an expensive exchange of cables with my father and mother, who were financing me, and said that I wanted to go back and do science again, where at least people seemed to know what they were talking about. They had enough sense to tell me, "Carry on for another year and get your degree," as I could at that stage, "and then we'll talk."

So you took another undergraduate degree at Cambridge?

Yes. I took a B.A. In the second year of my study there, I saw the light. I got what it was that was on Keynes's mind. He was trying to work out a system where the amount of output, production and employment, and such things, were variables and were not re-garded as given as they were in the classical analysis. In Keynes's new view it was the variation in output and the components of it that was what was really important. He hadn't got the inter-relationship worked out by that time, but he was moving toward it. So, I was hooked by then.

Having devoted a couple of years to understanding Keynes's ideas, I decided I'd stay on a third year as a research student and really get the feel of what was happening. During the third year I made expeditions down to the London School of Economics. I was determined to be a missionary for Keynesian ideas. They had sent a missionary up from London to Cambridge to spy on us, by the name of Lerner. I went down and spent half of each week at the London School of Economics. In order to indicate to them what was going on, I had to write Keynes's ideas up with-out having seen his book – he hadn't finished his book yet. So I had a clandestine publication that I had mimeographed in non-copyright form, and nonpublishable because it was Keynes's ideas. But, anyway, I circulated them.

Hayek at the London School was very kind to me and he let me have four consecutive weeks of his seminar to try to explain these ideas to them. The students were very interested.

Did you notice any acceptance of the ideas?

The students were very interested in the new ideas. They were baffled and annoyed by the definitions because Keynes's last major work in print had been *A Treatise on Money*. He had an arbitrary definition of savings which made it very hard for people to know what his new ideas were and how they related to what they had seen in his 1930 book. But anyway, that worked, and I made the acquaintance of some of the other people at LSE at that time, whose names I've forgotten now, I'm sorry to say.

Having had some success at LSE, I decided I should tackle something dramatic, and so I applied for a fellowship, the Commonwealth Fund Fellowship to go to the United States, and was fortunate to get it. So I went with the same idea to Harvard, where I spent two years. The Commonwealth Fund Fellowship was a very generous fellowship. It provided me with nice rooms in Dunster House and enough to pay my fees and some spending money to boot. It also gave me $600 for the summer for making a trip around the United States. I took Alec Cairncross who was then at Cambridge with me on this grand tour.

Technically, for my fellowship I had to have a research project, and before I left, Richard Kahn, who was Keynes's assistant in all sorts of matters, told me, "When you get to Harvard, there's a good library. They've got all the statistics. Don't bother with the lectures; don't bother with the seminars; spend your time in the library and write a good thesis for us." This was nothing to tell a missionary. I was polite about it, but I went over to Harvard and followed my own agenda.

I listened and talked and talked some more and listened again. I did this by going to lectures. My supervisor, which I had to have because of my fellowship, was Joseph Schumpeter, who was really a tremendous scholar of economics.

Who recommended that you study under Schumpeter? Where would you have gotten that idea?

Well, I wanted to be attached to it a pretty senior professor, and of course he was that. He had also written books on some of the related subjects, but most of Harvard was doing the kind of things that Keynes had been writing about; they were dealing with them as aspects of the trade cycle. Schumpeter either had written or was writing a book on the trade cycle. I found Schumpeter an interesting and very pleasant man to work with. He didn't endeavor to dispute Keynes's ideas with me. He was interested in my essay about them and interested in asking me various questions about them, but he didn't absorb them and acknowledge them, partly because he was intensely jealous of Keynes. He thought Joseph Schumpeter should be regarded as the leading living economist, not Maynard Keynes. One of the reasons for Schumpeter's jealousy was that he thought that Keynes was getting all the press. Keynes, of course, was a far more popular writer and speaker than "Schupie".

While at Harvard I got to know Schumpeter personally fairly well. Schumpeter opened my eyes to some of the pureness of economics, the scholarship of economics – but I regarded that as ornament. My sights were on what the good post-graduate students were thinking and what the members of the faculty there – those who were still open-minded – were thinking about things.

I spent most of my two years at Harvard engaged in controversy. My notes at the time indicate that Paul Sweezy and I organized an informal seminar on Keynes's economics. I am not sure whether Paul really, unbeknownst to me, hadn't organized some Marxist seminars, because I got into trouble many years later. But anyway we did have quite a group that met, disputed and discussed what Keynes was doing and thinking – first on the basis of this piece of paper I brought over and then on the basis of Keynes's book, *The General Theory*.

I might point out that *The General Theory* wasn't written to be easy to understand; it was written to try to carry a detailed argument through to a conclusion. Anyone who studies that book is going to get very confused. It was a very provocative book. It is written and addressed to other professional economists.

Who attended the informal seminars?

These were informal groups meeting usually in the evening. The people who attended them were other graduate students plus the younger members of the faculty, such as the Sweezy brothers and occasionally some of the people working on money, like Seymour Harris. Seymour Harris was the supervisor of studies at Dunster House, which was similar to a College at Cambridge, and I got to know him by living next to him. He worked in the field of money. He was prolix rather than pro-found, and he had to be: he had a very sick wife to look after, and he just had to write all he could. Ken Galbraith would occasionally come. I don't know whether Paul Samuelson came to those meetings or whether I saw him at other people's semi-nars, but Paul was at that time a post-graduate student with the title of, I believe, Junior Fellow. He was involved in our discus-sions one way or another. Then I was also drawn into what they called The Theory Subcommittee of the Committee on Business Cycle Research. The Committee on Business Cycle Research was a joint committee of the Business School and the Arts and Science faculty at Harvard. The Littauer School had not yet been established.

And they put students on this committee?

Well, whether I was on it officially or not I don't know, but I was at many of their meetings, because I've got notes of things I wrote for them. I was the only Keynesian around.

Did you feel you were the only Keynesian?

In the first year I was there I felt like the only expert on Keynes's work around. The book had not yet been published, and it wasn't published until the middle of that academic year – it was the end of January, 1936. It was published in England first and then a few weeks later in New York. But in most of the first academic year I was the only one who was familiar enough with it to be willing to argue in defense of it.

When the book came out, gradually more and more people became interested in reading the book. The book was a difficult, provocative book, not really a textbook but a book addressed to other economists, in order to persuade them to change their minds, and at times it was deliberately provocative to make his point. Anyway, that, I think, was why I got involved in groups like the Business Cycles Committee, because they were interested in whether the ideas of Keynes contributed something to it. They also had enormous amounts of statistical data from the National Bureau and I was doing some statistical work on Kuznets's figures of the national accounts. I discussed some of that work. Anyway, I attended their meetings, and I got to speak when I wanted to.

This is all before Hansen came to Harvard?

Yes. I had left when Hansen arrived. I knew something of Hansen's work.

When you left did you feel that most of the students at Harvard that mattered were Keynesians?

No. Many of the younger ones were making progress. Among the older ones, only Leontief – and he was really in-between in age – really understood it. You know, it wasn't in its nature too far away from his input–output analysis, and he was used to aggregating. Indeed, it was Leontief who suggested to me that I should try taking the Keynesian concepts and making some equations out of them and seeing whether there was enough data to solve the equations. He wrote an article on implicit theories which was one of the really sophisticated criticisms of Keynesian argument.

Did you leave Harvard because you thought you had completed your missionary work?

No. When my fellowship was over I was under an obligation to leave the United States and go back to some part of the British Commonwealth, so I went to Montreal. This was not a binding legal contract, but it was the understanding on which I accepted the commission.

Did you do your dissertation while at Harvard?

No. I did a little on it. I did intend eventually to write a thesis, but I never got beyond the methodological introduction, and I didn't much like that. The rest of my work on it at Harvard was prefatory. Specifically, I was working on developing the statistical knowledge to proceed.

I had done a fair amount of work developing Kuznets's series of macroeconomic statistics at that time. I went to see him down in New York, and I was familiar with his writings. My first year as a graduate student in Cambridge I had been attached to Colin Clark, who was originally a chemist and had become an economist by contact, I guess, with economists whom he knew in London and Cambridge, and then he was one of the most expert statisticians in the economic field. But he wasn't an advanced practitioner in statistics himself, as Cromwell at Harvard was.

The leading statistician in Cambridge at that time was Mueller, whose field was vital statistics, and he set the statistics paper for the Tripos examination that I wrote, and I made a mess of it. I didn't understand fully all the terms that he was using and what he wanted, and I was getting frustrated. I remember at the end I was down on the floor trying to pick up some of the paper I had discarded, because I was taking more time than I expected. But I took statistics at Harvard from Cromwell, and I wrote the examination. I wanted to make sure that I got my A+ eventually. But I never did finish my thesis.

Even after I left I tried to keep the thesis option open. After leaving Harvard, I continued studying economics, first in the investment department at the Sun Life, and finally in being an economist in the Department of Finance, where I was an assistant to the Deputy Minister. Then the war came along and there was little time to worry about economic theory. I would have been able to go back after the end of the war and re-open it, I think, but by that time I was too involved in my work as an economist.

3. Lorie Tarshis (1911–93)

Birthplace: Toronto, Canada

Education:

1931:   B.S. University of Toronto
1934:   B.A. Cambridge
1939:   Ph.D. Cambridge

Significant publications:

'Real Wages in the United States and Great Britain', *Canadian Journal of Economics and Political Science*, **4**, August 1938, 362–76.

'Changes in Money and Real Wages', *Economic Journal*, **49**, March 1939, 150–54.

The Elements of Economics: An Introduction to the Theory of Price and Employment, Boston: Houghton Mifflin, 1947.

'Price Ratios and International Trade: an Empirical and Analytical Survey', *The Allocation of Economic Resources: Essays in Honor of B.F. Haley*, Stanford: Stanford University Press, 1959.

'The Elasticity of the Marginal Efficiency Function', *American Economic Review*, **51**, (1961) 958–85.

'Retained Earnings and Investment', in K. Kurihara (ed.), *Post Keynesian Economics*, London: Allen & Unwin, 1962.

The United States Balance of Payments in 1968, edited with W.S. Salant, E. Despres and A. Rivlin, Washington: Brookings Institution, 1963.

Modern Economics, Boston: Houghton Mifflin, 1967.

'The Dollar Standard', in P.A. David and M.W. Reder (eds), *Nations and Households in Economic Growth*, New York: McGraw-Hill, 1974.

'The Aggregate Supply Function in Keynes's *General Theory*', in M. Boskin (ed.), *Economics and Human Welfare: Essays in Honor of Tibor Scitovsky*, New York: Academic Press, 1979.

World Economy in Crisis: Unemployment, Inflation and International Debt, Toronto: James Lorimer for Canadian Institute for Economic Policy, 1984.

Significant honors:

Massey Scholarship

Experience:

1936–9:	Tufts University
1942–6:	Tufts University
1946–71:	Stanford
1970–78:	University of Toronto
1978–88:	York University

The interview was conducted on 30 September 1986, at York University in Toronto.

How did you get into economics?

Up until the age of 16 or so I wanted to be a doctor. My father, who died when I was four, had been a doctor, but my mother's second husband was emphatically not a doctor. The summer before I went up to university, however, I was at a camp in Algonquin Park. The head of the camp knew I was going to university and asked me whether I would like to talk to a friend of his who was a counselor. He said, "I don't know what these people are, but I think they give advice to high school students as to their careers." Nobody had ever given me any advice, and I thought that would be fine. So we walked up the creek and sat down on a log and he started asking questions. "I hear you want to be a doctor?" and I said, "Yes." In those days there was no problem being admitted – you just went to a medical school on registration day and said, "I'd like to sign up."

He said being a doctor offered great opportunities to serve, and so forth, and I was impressed. He said, "How do you do in biology?" We had two sets of matriculation exams – one at the end of fourth year high school and one at the end of fifth year high school. I'd had As. Then he said, "How did you do in chemistry?" and in chemistry I'd had As. "Physics?" – "As." Finally he said, "How do you do in mathematics?" And like a fool – I should have just said I got As, but instead I said, 'Oh, I love it – I get As." He said, "You know, you'd be crazy to go into medicine. With a mathematical ability you ought to become an economist."

I didn't know what economics was. But he was wearing long pants and I was wearing short, so I said, "Yes sir." In effect. And I went down a month later to the University of Toronto and said, "I want to sign up for economics."

That's how I got into economics. The first year I didn't know what it was all about. We had economic geography, economic geology, and some other course which had economics in the title, but I can't remember what it was. It must have been unmemorable. But I still didn't know what economics was. The second year, in Principles of Economics, we had for our textbook Marshall's *Principles of Economics*, which gave me a dose of what economics was about. It was exciting.

In those days, once you got in, when you concentrated in the field you *concentrated*. All my courses – with one exception – were in economics. The exception was a half-year American history course. All others were economics and economics-related courses, such as Accounting, Actuarial Science, Calculus and a little bit of Algebra.

What did they be teach you about economic policy?

As I said earlier, it was only in my second year, when I started reading Marshall's *Principles of Economics*, that I started realizing what economics was all about. But there was very little policy involved in it; it was just straight Marshall. From time to time we talked about policy, but there was no day-to-day discussion of policy.

But that was the year of the Great Stock Market Crash?

Yes, I know. We had economic history, but as with everything in Canada in those days, it was British economic history. No American economic history and no Canadian economic history.

We had a British lecturer, C.R. Fay, a Cambridge man. He was a World War I veteran and somebody said he'd been shell-shocked; he was strange. He was a close friend of Keynes, I learned afterward. I think he was an Apostle. He had a speech problem, and from time to time he became very absent-minded, from all we could detect. The morning after the Great Crash he came in, and he waited till we all shut up, and said, "Gentlemen, you will remember yesterday for the rest of your lives." That's all he said. But it made a deep impression, because we were all gabbing about it, you see; we were all investing in the stock market but not with any real funds: I gave myself $5000, my friends $5000, and we ran pools to see who would come out ahead, so we were interested. But we didn't get much about the decline in the economy in class.

Next year we were very lucky. The third year included a course called Money and Banking. It was to be taught by a young man, A.F.W. Plumptre, who had preceded me by four years at Toronto, and then went to Cambridge for two, where he encountered Keynes. He came back to Toronto with, the story was, two trunks full of the just-published two-volume *Treatise on Money*. In any case, *A Treatise* was our textbook. I still have my copy on my bookshelf. That course was, to me, the key course of the third year. I became an ardent disciple of *A Treatise on Money*. I thought it was the greatest thing on earth, and I really thought I understood it.

So they taught more than simply theory?

Oh, yes. Policy was really being taught, but it was policy as applied to Britain. I was, however, becoming aware of what it was all about. I recall coming down on the train from summer camp the next year – that was in 1931 – to begin my fourth year, and seeing the headlines on a copy of a newspaper of September

21: BRITAIN OFF GOLD. The train was full of campers and staff members, but there were other people. Everybody seemed to be wondering, "What does this mean?" I was going around from car to car giving lectures on what it meant. I'm glad nobody recorded those. It would be embarrassing. I was full of it.

What explanation were you given as to why the Depression occurred?

It would have been basically saving outstripping investment. Investment would include the net foreign balance and so on – it was straight from the *Treatise*. I can't remember anybody on the staff going beyond that at all. There might have been alternative explanations such as money's price had fallen, but that would have been all there was to it.

Was there any fight from the other members of the school, saying, "This is hogwash!"?

No. Not that we heard. But don't forget that the eight-member department included sociology, accounting and auditing, economics and political science. It was very, very tiny. This man Plumptre, though, was really the life of the place, as far as I was concerned. He was a year or two ahead of his time. Chronologically, I was one year ahead, but he seemed younger than any of us. He was small and slight and very quick in movements and had a terribly British accent.

What happened to him?

He died four years ago. He had a fight with Innis, who was the God of Canadian economics. Innis wrote books on the Canadian fur trade and cod fisheries in Canada and so on, using documents, he was an example of a completely different economist. His theory, if he had a theory, was a mix of Marx and Veblen. Innis was Plumptre's senior, probably by ten years, but he didn't have the students flocking to him in the same way that Plumptre did. He didn't like Plumptre's smart-aleck, rather unscholarly ways.

It was Plumptre who actually got me to Cambridge. I had applied for a Rhodes. I was in the finals – there were three of us, and I was the third, as it turned out. But I heard later from one of the judges who was an eminent Canadian economist that I was really the man of their choice, one of the two. But they wanted me to go to Cambridge. Plumptre apparently needled them for this. And if I'd got a Rhodes I couldn't have gone to Cambridge. But Plumptre knew I would get a Massey Fellowship since he was a close friend of Massey's. So I went to Cambridge.

I was able to pay Plumptre back, however: I was one of three people – Joan Robinson was another – who, when we learned that Plumptre was going to visit Cambridge in the spring term of 1936, arranged to have him meet a female Australian economist, who was working on central banking in the British Empire. I thought it would be a match. And it was a match: they were married soon after and remained married till his death.

What can you tell me about Cambridge? Teachers?

I went to Cambridge as an undergraduate because Plumptre told me that in order to be noticed by the faculty I had to be an undergraduate; he said that if I wanted to stay on – fine and dandy, but I would have to have a Cambridge degree. So I started all over again, but I did it in two years.

I don't remember all of my courses or teachers. Some of them are easier to forget. You had Tripos exams and you had tutorials, but the Tripos came only – for me – at the end of my second year. There were no exams and no mid-terms. There was a preliminary, so-called, but I was excused from it. I was glad. So what you did was take those courses of lectures that sounded appealing. Well, I *always* went to Keynes. He lectured on Monday morning at eleven to twelve, and I think that some years there were seven lectures to the term; other years eight lectures. That's all he lectured. The lecture room was pretty darn full. I would guess somewhere between 80 and 120. I never counted, but it was pretty tight.

What Keynes lectured about is in my notes and many other notes, too. I was lucky in being there for four years, between the time he started to give this series of lectures and just prior to the publication of *The General Theory*. At the end he was sending the manuscript in to the publisher, and *The General Theory* came out two months later.

The course was down in the calendar as Theory of Money and Prices, I think, but when Keynes came in the first morning of that first year he announced a change in title, to *The Monetary Theory of Production*. I remember the very first words Keynes said in the opening lecture on October 10, 1932. Keynes came into a room that was pretty crowded. And he said, "Gentlemen, the change in title is significant." That's what I copied in my notes. In a sense that was the opening bugle of the Keynesian revolution.

But the interesting thing is: Keynes was himself not aware of the fact; certainly not fully aware of the fact, that he was leading an intellectual revolution. He backed into it. Richard Kahn and Joan Robinson took a lot of time and effort to persuade him that what he was doing had a significance – I said "revolutionary"; please don't take this to mean Communist or Bolshevik or anything like that – I mean an intellectual revolution of the kind that Darwin initiated when he wrote *The Origin of Species* and Max Planck when he developed the quantum theory – a change in the way of thinking about something that people had taken as true, which had influenced *all* their thinking. It's this that I call the revolution.

I wasn't happy about the change. I was so completely involved in the *Treatise* and I thought all he was going to do was to expound upon the *Treatise*. I couldn't imagine how he was going to give eight lectures, because two hours were enough. The first year I wasn't very excited by the course. Keynes was complaining about his mistakes in *A Treatise* and not making it very clear. He kept referring to the importance of money, but that was perfectly obvious in *A Treatise*.

If you'd asked me at the end of that first year, "What's it all about?" I would say, "Well, I guess he's trying to rewrite *A Treatise* so that people can understand it more readily." An awful lot of the lectures were filled with his fiddling with definitions, trying to get a consistent set. It was also, as he had not been in his *Treatise*, developing definitions, or concepts, that were in a sense usable by the human mind. Remember the funny definition of saving in *A Treatise*. It's not "income minus consumption", it's "income in a special sense that excludes abnormal profits, minus consumption." It didn't bother me at the time. The fact that you couldn't get a statistical or an empirical observation to match the concept "income" in the *Treatise* sense didn't trouble me. I enjoyed the excitement of the lectures, but I didn't feel I was getting much out of it.

I wrote to Plumptre, and I said I thought I'd like to get out of Cambridge because it was a very difficult atmosphere for a colonial in those days, and the winters are terribly long, and it gets dark at 3 o'clock in the afternoon, and it was as gloomy as it could be, and I wrote to this fellow at the University of Toronto where I'd been brought up, and said, "I'd like to get out of economics and do anthropology." Bob Bryce and I wanted to do it in Paris. Both of us had been to Paris and we felt that Paris and French girls had something to offer that we couldn't match in Cambridge. I think we were right, but we neither one of us were allowed to do it. I took my licking, and I found the second year very, very exciting, but the first year didn't turn me on. I spent more time, I'm sure, playing hooky in that first year and enjoying myself traveling in Europe than I did studying Keynes.

How about the other students?

Oh, I'm sure some of them were puzzled beyond belief, because they hadn't read *A Treatise*. Bob Bryce had, although he had not ever had a course in economics, but he was so bright. He was working on the *Treatise* before he came. But there were an awful lot of them who didn't know what it was for.

Were there rumors of the importance of Keynes's lectures?

No, not that I heard that first year. I knew that the faculty were interested, because from time to time I would see some faculty members sitting there; and Dennis Robertson, who was my supervisor, from time to time asked me what Keynes was doing. (I wasn't aware of the fact that there had been a breach.)

Robertson invited a fellow called Sid Butlin and me to tea at the beginning of term the first year, the first term, and he asked me, "Who would you like to meet when you're here?" The first name I mentioned was "Keynes". Well, that wasn't quite the appropriate answer, I guess. Anyway, I had no trouble, because in addition to the lectures I got an invitation to join Keynes's Political Economy Club, which Bob Bryce also got. I know Plumptre arranged it, because Plumptre had been in the Club.

How many were in the Club?

I can't honestly tell you. I've often tried to remember. I don't think there was a set number, but it seems to me there were probably eight or ten undergraduates and a couple of research students, but only those with Cambridge pedigrees; and I suspect that the undergraduates were people who got a First in the First Part of the Tripos. And then maybe somebody who was the son of somebody of influence.

What would happen at the Club?

The Club was really exciting. It met probably three or four times a term. Generally, Keynes would attend. At the very beginning I didn't understand how it worked, but I was invited to present a paper to the Club, and I guess this is standard. I remember a couple of woeful experiences there. It met on Monday nights at 7.30 or 8.00. I'd always walk over with Bob Bryce, who was at St John's College, one further down than mine, Trinity; we'd walk up to King's, and the church bells would be tolling evensong. It was a memorable feeling. It was often raining and windy and godawful. You'd get in, take off your gown (you had to wear your gown, but you could carry your cap). As you went in, Richard Kahn would be at the door with maybe eight or ten slips of paper peeping out from his fist. You took one, but you didn't look at it immediately because you wanted to be sitting when you looked. If it was blank that was fine. If it had a number on it, that indicated the number you had to respond to when you were called to discuss the paper. If it was a one, you were the first person to discuss the paper. You'd discuss it in front of Keynes, Kahn, maybe Joan and Austin Robinson and Sraffa. I guess Keynes's friends on the faculty were commonly invited.

I've heard that Joan Robinson is the only woman who ever attended.

Oh, I can't say that, but she's the only woman I remember who attended. A lot of Toronto boys went over to England, but five or six – probably five – went to Cambridge. Another three or four went to London School. The London School was the center of Hayekian teaching, and some of our LSE friends thought it would be great to have a discussion between the London School students and Bob and me. We met in Soho in an Italian restaurant that is still there, Bertorelli's. We sat down and started to talk. Paul Sweezy, Alan Sweezy and Abba Lerner were in the group; and there were several others.

At the preliminary meeting we were to have a dinner and some drinks, and then go to somebody's apartment to discuss Keynes versus Hayek. Bob and I were representing Keynes and the rest of the cutthroats were representing Hayek. Well, we didn't get far, because Paul, who had a loud piercing voice, had had too much to drink. His father was vice-president, or president, of one of the big city banks in New York – National City Bank of New York, I think it was – and that gave him a loud voice. All I can remember from that dinner is him snarling, "You God damn bastards – you and your Keynes!" in this sort of slurred speech. He still has that snarly way of talking.

We didn't get very far in discussions. Bob and I had to be back before twelve, to get into our Colleges or we'd be fined. So it was broken up because we had to leave. That was my first meeting with Paul, and he was so Hayekian, even Hayek was too far to the left for Paul Sweezy in those days.

I didn't meet Paul again until I went to Cambridge, Mass., to my first job, in 1936. He was then at Harvard, where he'd been an undergraduate, from which he got his scholarship to go to Vienna and then to London. He was a junior member of the teaching faculty and he may have taught a section of economic

history. By then he'd already gone all the way over to Keynes
and a little bit; I saw an awful lot of Paul from then till 1939 or
1940. His wife at that time was a strong supporter of Keynes as
well. I was teaching at Tufts and I lived in Cambridge with my
first wife.

*Abba tells of a group that used to meet halfway between LSE and
Cambridge.*

Yes. That was in my third year at Cambridge. I don't remember a
lot from that year. By Christmas I had fallen in love and the rest
of that year is just a beautiful haze. I went to Keynes's lectures
but I paid no attention. I spent an awful lot of time in London
visiting my girlfriend. I saw Abba quite a bit that year. I can't
remember when I first saw him, apart from that silly meeting at
the Italian restaurant. But in 1934–5 he came up to Cambridge
and we had lunch in my room every week after lectures. He used
to bring a sandwich made of marmite with him, and marmite
stinks. I would usually say that I had to go out, but that I'd be
back as soon as I could, so he would eat his lunch in my room.
Then we would sit down and argue about Keynes. By then I was
pretty much intoxicated by the depth of my understanding – I
don't know that it was all that deep, but at least I could put in an
argument. I remember a fierce argument that went on for a couple of weeks on the subject of saving equaling investment. Abba
could raise more difficulties and, knowing his mind, you can
appreciate the kinds of difficulties. A very important one was to
demonstrate that maybe they didn't have to be equal. I demonstrated that the equality is simply a definitional matter; you know,
in the multiplier process equality is maintained at every instant in
time. Abba told me, when I got to know him in the States, that his
conversion dated from that time.

Let's go back to 1932. When did you get full of Keynes?

When did I get *full* of him? Oh, well, I got full of Keynes from
reading *A Treatise* in 1930, in the fall.

The first lecture, if I have it right, was 1932.

I was impressed with Keynes's lectures. He was so clearly a master of what he was talking about, but I wasn't much interested in the definitions and redefinitions and tentative explanations as to a concept which were the guts of the lectures in the first year. The second year was very very different. The second year I was excited beyond belief. There were a couple of points that he made in the second year that stuck with me. I can still feel the funny prickling-in-the-back-of-your-neck feeling when he mentioned them. One was the distinction between the entrepreneurial and cooperative economy.

My own notes show what happened; I'd been making notes very carefully, but then my notes slide, slacken. I think it was the second, or possibly third, lecture that he said that if we could have a society in which the employer would feel responsible for the employee, whether he was working or not, you wouldn't have to worry about unemployment. If the employer had to pay a worker's wage or salary whether there was work for him or not, he would be working. I copied that down, but I didn't think much about it.

In the second year, he made the distinction between a cooperative economy and an entrepreneurial economy, where the workers were hired for a certain period of time, like a week, for a fixed money wage, and had no sharing profits or tenure. In the entrepreneurial economy unemployment occurs whenever demand falls off for the product of the employer. In the cooperative economy (he also called it a barter economy), by contrast, the worker is hired to share in the profits. In a cooperative economy where money played no significant role – except that of a lubricant – he called that a barter economy, you would also have no unemployment. He mentioned that, in socialist and communist economies, you'd get the same results. He said the real explanation for the failure of the classical economists to have a sensible explanation for the Depression, which was under way, was that they were implicitly assuming a cooperative or barter economy. Even if they had money in it, it worked like a cooperative economy. Workers shared in the profits, but if each worker had a fixed share, say 1 per cent or something like that, if you were unskilled, or 2 per cent if you were skilled, then unemployment wouldn't occur. I thought that so damned exciting. I remember my feeling that "God! You have to listen to this as hard as you can. This is the most important thing you'll ever hear." And I listened so intently that, at that point, note-taking was interrupted.

I used to lecture on this when I was teaching macroeconomics at Stanford. I always used Keynes, and I always distinguished between the entrepreneurial and the cooperative economy. In the third year lectures Keynes dropped the distinction, and there's no reference to it in *The General Theory*.

There is a nice story which is rather revealing about the power of Keynes's arguments and their political content. It is about John Strachey, a Marxist. He was a cousin of Lytton Strachey – they both had the same skill in writing. John Strachey wrote a book called *The Coming Struggle for Power*. In the 1930s this book was so influential in Cambridge, England, that, when I got there, every person had it on his bookshelf, prominently displayed. It was an exciting book, intellectually exciting to read. It was the Bible of Cambridge students. In my last year at Cambridge Strachey was invited by the Marshall Society, which was the general undergraduate society for economics students, to give a talk. In this talk he argued that Marx showed us the way to make the system work, an argument that met a very, very strong favorable response – as his earlier writing had done. I had been asked in advance to move a vote of thanks at the end of the lecture: say a few words, if I could, about his lecture, but essentially to move a vote of thanks.

I did, except I took the occasion to say that there would appear – this was in November 1935 – within a few months a book that would set out a superior method of analysis. It had been written by John Maynard Keynes. I didn't know whether Strachey would know the name. He motioned to me and said, "I'd like to thank you for your vote of thanks," and so on; "I'd like to find out more about the book by Keynes." And I told him, and he took down the name. At the time, I did not realize the connection between Keynes and Lytton Strachey and Lytton and John Strachey.

A couple of years later I received a new book by John Strachey in the mail from the Left Book Club. I was astounded; it was absolutely Keynes. I mean, he was so much influenced by Keynes – he had been so strongly influenced by Keynes that he became an instant, overnight, follower. Strachey really understood Keynes; it's a brilliant exposition and application to the British situation. It's rather more interesting than Keynes and deserves to be reprinted. It shows how Keynes had refuted Communism and how John Strachey, an extreme Marxist whose life up to then had been devoted to Marx and the Marxian course, had been completely changed by Keynes. Given that history, the later attacks on U.S. Keynesians, accusing them of being Communists, were incomprehensible to me.

Who were the top students at Cambridge?

My year must have been a memorable year, because they gave ten Firsts, whereas the usual number was one or two. I understand that ten is still the highest number they have ever given. Among those who got Firsts were Bob Bryce, myself, Reddaway, Champernowne, V.K.R.V. Rao, Dick Stone and, I think, David Bensusan Buck.

Were the students sure this was a revolution?

Oh, God, yes. Bob and I certainly thought it was. Bob was more of a scholar than I, and he did read other things. I was too impatient. I figured, after Keynes, why should I bother reading other things which clearly were wrong? I *had* to read some of Pigou's *Theory of Employment* because I knew it would be asked about on the Tripos, but I couldn't get myself interested in it, except to find stupidities. I looked over my Marshall again, and I checked for unemployment – in the index. "See underemployment" was all the index said. I looked at underemployment and found a silly little statement that said it would occasionally be a bother.

My time at Cambridge was wonderful. The students were bright, and we had discussions all the time. Most of my discussions were with Bob Bryce, but he only stayed for three years. Then he

went to Harvard as a Commonwealth Fellow. Bob Bryce introduced Keynes to Harvard. He was there a year earlier with his
notes on Keynes's lectures and with his own essay on Keynes's
new theory which he'd written to read to the London School.
Bob was still at Harvard when I got there and was the center of
all information about Keynes.

How did you get the job at Tufts?

As I was finishing up my dissertation I put my name in at the
Cambridge University Appointment Centre, and I was waiting
for job offers. I had an offer from Rangoon and another from
Singapore and couldn't decide which to choose. One offered me
250 pounds a year; the other 300 pounds, but the 250-pounder
offered me leave every two and a half years; the other one a bit
less frequently. Suddenly I got a cablegram from Tufts, which I'd
never heard of, offering me a job at $2500 a year. I took it
immediately. I didn't know what Tufts was, but compared to
Rangoon and Singapore and the salaries they offered, I thought
this was a pretty good bet. It turned out to be wonderful for me.
They had just completely cleaned out their old economics department – not quite far enough, but almost far enough. They fired
everybody but one. They brought in a new chairman, and an
older student of Keynes's *Treatise* who had been at Harvard for
several years. So in September 1936 I moved to Cambridge,
Mass. (Tufts was a half-hour walk away from Harvard.)

Was there a group of Keynesians at Harvard?

Yes, in a way, but they weren't ardent. I mean, I'd say Wolfie
Stolper had been very much influenced by Bob. I didn't think he
was very quick. Seymour Harris was certainly sympathetic and
was an ally; he was at least on the faculty. However, he didn't
seem to me to have anything like a full understanding of Keynes.
Hansen was invisible in my first year there; I guess he didn't
come until 1937.

Bob and I talked a lot about Keynes, but it was tough. I can
remember often sitting with these Harvard guys and their sneer-

ing, "Do you mean to imply that workers are subject to money illusion?" I should have said, "Yes – what of it?" But they said it in such a way, I was scared to say "Yes." In those days everyone felt he had to defer to the working man. Really, it was awful. Bob Bryce left Harvard in 1938 when he got a job with Sun Life and a year later with the Department of Finance in Ottawa.

Paul Samuelson was not in the Keynesian group. He was busy working on his own thing. That he became a Keynesian was laughable. In the fall of 1937, Emile Despres and Bill Salant came up for a year at Harvard. They were Littauer Fellows, I believe. They were so fast and they had very quickly become Keynesians: well before anybody else. Once converted, Despres and Dick Gilbert, who was a junior member of the faculty, set out to write a book later entitled *An Economic Program for American Democracy*. Actually, seven of us wrote it, but Despres was the driving force. The others were myself, Bill Salant, Paul Sweezy, Paul's wife Maxine, John Wilson (who had been a student of mine at Tufts before he went on to Harvard for his doctorate) and Bob Bangs. You won't find Emile's or Bill Salant's name on it; they were both in government; they couldn't sign their names. Lauchlin Currie knew about the book and occasionally came to a meeting. We met at intervals, I think in Emile's apartment usually. The book came out in the spring of 1938.

Despres never got a graduate degree, but he was superb. I got him to come to Stanford, and had a fight with the provost to get him because he had no graduate degree. I got Paul Samuelson to write a letter – I bless Paul for this – "Since Stanford cannot hire Adam Smith, I urge it to do the next best thing" is part of that letter. Emile was an economist from the toes up.

Being one of the authors of the book was not altogether positive for me. The president of Tufts thought it was awful. You see, the byline of the book was, "By Seven Harvard and Tufts Professors". He kept sending me reminders of donors who were going to give money to Tufts but who had decided not to, because of the book. In fact, I was regarded as an absolute Red. When you read the damn book now, there's no Red in it! We were trying to save capitalism. The story I told above about Strachey shows you

why it was so difficult for me to understand how that book could
be thought Red.

How about the Hansen seminars?

I attended the Hansen seminars. I remember Hansen sitting there
with his eyeshade down and his eyes closed; you couldn't tell
whether he was listening. Among faculty members who attended
were Seymour Harris, Gottfried Haberler, Ed Mason and occasionally Wassily Leontief.

Being at Tufts was great for me, because I had access to
Harvard. We lived in Cambridge, not far from Harvard Square. I
went to Harvard seminars. Bob Bryce was still at Harvard, so he
helped me to fit in. I was there until the summer of 1939, when I
got a Carnegie Fellowship to work at the National Bureau for a
year; and then I went back to Tufts and stayed there until 1942
when I went to Washington. Actually, I had already decided to
leave Tufts by that time. In 1942 Stanford sent me a telegram
asking me if I wanted a job. I wasn't sure about going to Stanford,
but I decided to go because I was fed up with the politics at Tufts
and wanted to get away. Before I left, though, I got one of these
silly telegrams, signed FDR, saying that my services were ur-
gently needed, and so on and so forth. I had to schedule my
exams two weeks early so I could leave and get down there. I
still wasn't an American citizen but I got a telephone call a few
days later saying "Report to some courthouse in Boston, and
you'll become an American." By then I figured I'd never get an
offer from a Canadian university so I might as well become an
American, which I did. During the war I worked for a year for
the War Production Board. I went to Washington in the late
spring of 1942.

The first year I was in Washington I worked with another
former Canadian who'd been a classmate of mine in Toronto.
The year was awful. I was convinced that I was the most wasted
person on earth. I was writing memos which, in effect, were read
by my roommate and by him alone. While working in Washington I was so damn far removed from economics I never thought
about it. But luckily for me after about eleven months in that

stupid job I was asked by the Pentagon whether I would join a group of young scientists that was to be assigned to an Air Force overseas. I was sent first to Libya, then Tunis, and finally to Italy. When I returned from Italy, I would say in late June of 1945, I went back to Tufts. When I returned, I decided, "Now I have to introduce Keynes to the world." So in the winter of 1945–46 I decided to write a textbook. In the spring of 1946 I signed a contract and then really turned on the steam.

What other books did you have to go by? Were there competing textbooks? Did they use any competing textbooks?

There was one by a man called Myers, and one by Fairchild, Furniss and Buck. But, you know, macroeconomics didn't exist, so I had no model. In the book I gave about as much attention to macroeconomics as I did to microeconomics. The first two sections were standard microeconomics. Book Three was Money and Banking, but that was out of order. I never figured out where to put it. I wanted to separate it from macroeconomics because it dealt essentially with how banks create money and how interest rates are determined. Book Four was macroeconomics. It was very much Keynes. That part was highly successful because it was unique, and even now I run into people who say, "You know, you introduced me to Keynes, and I've never had a better understanding of Keynes than was given me by Book Four of your textbook."

Were the publishers happy to get you to write the textbook?

Yes, they were eager to get me to write it, and then they gave me terrific support. You know, Houghton Mifflin was always known as a very conservative, very proper Bostonian publisher. I took them partly because it was Boston, but also, I must admit, because my first wife's father was an editor at Houghton Mifflin, although he was in trade books, not textbooks.

When the book came out – in probably April of 1947 – I kept getting glowing telegrams from the publisher. I thought, "Oh, my God, this is just beyond belief." The publisher was very happy.

Did you have lots of reviewers?

I didn't have any. The book was done in a rush. I didn't have a sense of competing with anybody, because there wasn't anybody.

What about Abba's book, Economics of Control, *which came out in 1944?*

Well, I didn't use it at all. You see, I'd not been reading any economics during the war, and when I got back I was not reading economics; I was writing. I learned a hell of a lot more from writing than I did from reading.

In writing I relied a great deal on the hearings of the Temporary National Economic Committee and then the National Resources Planning Board materials. They gave me what I needed in the way of statistical material. When the book first came out the book was selling thousands. And then I got a telephone call from Houghton Mifflin that somebody was attacking it vigorously on the grounds that the book was Communist-inspired and so on. What would I say? Well, I couldn't think of any Communist inspiration behind it, but I was worried. And then they sent me the stuff. There was a man called Merwin K. Hart. I'm sure I'm exaggerating when I say he was a member of the Bund, but he didn't sound very different from a member of the Bund. And he saw Keynes behind every sentence that had the word "welfare" in it. He knew that this was Communist.

It never entered my head to be concerned about this, because my whole feeling when I was in Cambridge, England, in the last couple of years (and this continued in Cambridge, Massachusctts) was that, while I agreed with the aim of the Communists in the sense of "Let's do something to get a system that works", I accepted Keynes strongly enough to feel that revolution was not the way to do it. Following Keynes, you could get it to work.

So the irony of it is, I was really, by that time, in the four years in which Keynes was writing at Cambridge, very much affected by Keynes's belief that an analysis that followed his lines – not step by step his policies, that was almost an irrelevancy – an analysis that followed his lines would enable a person to develop the kind of policy that would be needed to maintain the system: not simply to restore prosperity but to keep the system going. I think Bob would remember – I remember quite vividly – that Keynes in those second and third years was very much influenced by what was going on in Germany (he hated it); he was influenced by what was going on in the Soviet Union (he didn't like it) and was scared to death – I can vouch for it – that the young people were turning mostly to Communism or Fascism. He wanted to get his book, his analysis, understood, as providing a viable alternative, a way of maintaining capitalism, maintaining prosperity with the property relations that he knew in a capitalist economy.

I say the irony was that. And I was influenced by that very much. I remember very clearly the feeling that I was given because, unlike a lot of my highly intelligent friends at Cambridge who were moving very far to the left, I kept arguing against it. Not against their aim but against the analysis. And when I wrote my book I was accused by William Buckley, who was a student then at Yale, among others, of being a Communist or at least a crypto-Communist. I was honored by the attack, but boy! did it cost me a lot of money. In the first two or three months in which the book came out I would get letters from my very conservative publisher saying Brown has adopted it, maybe Middlebury adopted it, Yale has adopted it – one place after another had adopted it. Every time I got a letter like this that indicated ten more adoptions or twenty more adoptions, I thought, "Boy, that bank account will be picking up."

Then came the attack. The man who made it went to jail, not because of the attack but because of some financial skullduggery, and the woman who did the legwork also ended up indicted (I think she died before she went to trial). It was a nasty performance, an organized campaign in which they sent newsletters to all the trustees of all the universities that had adopted the book.

How did you answer the criticisms?

Well, I didn't. What could I do about it? Merwin K. Hart organized a thing called "The National Economic Committee". He got

Rose Wilder Lane to write a newsletter for it and he sent copies of this newsletter – I'm pretty damn sure I don't have a copy, but I'm sure the libraries do – to all the members of every Board of Trustees of every university anywhere, including politicians, Republican universities and so on. Then I began to get notices from Houghton Mifflin about "X is canceling its order; Y is canceling its order." Before the summer was halfway through, sales had fallen just as sharply as they had risen. I was at Williams that summer, teaching, and the president of Williams, a man called Baxter – Emile had seen to it that Williams had adopted my book and Baxter was very strongly supportive of the book – wrote a strong letter to other university presidents he knew. But sales, instead of staying at that beautiful peak, went down just like that. The book did all right – I think I sold something like 10 000 copies. But it really died in 1948 or 1949. And then Paul Samuelson's book came out a year later, in 1948.

Why didn't Samuelson's book get hit by the same phenomenon?

I don't know. McGraw-Hill may have been more ready to back it up. Houghton Mifflin was small stuff compared to McGraw-Hill and they were also pretty new to economics.

Paul Samuelson might have had a separate reputation?

Well, he had a reputation, of course. Paul knew how to write, obviously, and his book was used in undergraduate courses in poor colleges to graduate courses in good universities and everywhere in between.

I got all kinds of letters from people who thought my book was great. And then William F. Buckley, the brother of the former Senator, wrote a book called *God and Man at Yale* in which he devotes one chapter to my book, because Yale used it and refused to withdraw it. That bastard Buckley – I get so angry when I think of him, because, you know, he's *still* parading his objectivity and concern for "moral values", and so on. The amount of distortion is enormous. He would pick a phrase and tack it onto a phrase two pages later, another page later, another page four pages earlier, and make a sentence that I couldn't recognize as anything I'd written – I was only able to see it when I had my book in front of me, and I could see where they came from – and make it seem as though I was no supporter of market capitalism, which I felt I always was.

How about at Stanford? Did you have any trouble from alumni there?

Yes, but I didn't personally, because my department chairman sheltered me. I know that from time to time the University had trouble because, after the new president came in 1949, he let me see some of the correspondence. It was villainous stuff. They were after Paul Baran, who was a Marxist; they were after Ed Shaw, who was a monetarist, and me. They thought Stanford should get rid of all of us. Wallace Sterling, the president of Stanford, wasn't as vigorous as I would think the thing deserved, but he would certainly never give an inch.

Were there any fights within the department?

Well, if there were, I wasn't conscious of it. I look back on Stanford, particularly up to about 1968, as about as close to paradise as any place could be. I had incredibly gifted colleagues. The school was excellent; and so too was the department. There were no conflicts about "Should we hire a Keynesian?" "Should we hire a monetarist?" "Should we hire this, that, or anything else?" It was a small department. At first the university, and more particularly the provost, who was an electrical engineer, didn't think well of us, and so we were starved for money, particularly as far as getting support for graduate students and to get faculty. We were a little department; I think we had twelve or thirteen when I got there, and it had risen to seventeen after a few years. We were plagued by classes that were too big.

The provost, I heard, went to the Ford Foundation and he asked, "What can I do to improve this department of economics at Stanford? We want to build a decent department at Stanford." Well, luckily he asked Kermit Gordon (Williams) and Lloyd

Reynolds (Yale), who were the two in charge of the economics program for the Ford Foundation at the time. The answer they gave him was, "You've got the best damned department of economics in the country. Why do you want to improve it?" From then on we got money. We could afford to give scholarships to attract graduate students. As I say, I was in paradise; I thought it was the greatest place on earth. We had Ken Arrow, Tibor Scitovsky, Bernard Haley, Ed Shaw, Jack Gurley, Mel Reder and Moses Abramovitz there. It was just a fine place.

How about your decision to see that you were known for your work? Did you specifically try to publish a lot?

No, I didn't. I don't know; I'm not terribly aggressive. I don't want to sound holy, as though I didn't care – of course I cared. There were people like Ken Arrow who were simply bursting with ideas and would publish ten papers to my one, but I liked to work on things at my speed, and thought I was doing enough. I got tenure when I should have, I became department chairman, and I was enjoying myself and found the place intellectually very exciting.

Did you feel the other Keynesians were pushing to try and get ahead?

No, I never felt that I was being pushed out of the way. I mean, I know that some of them were publishing more than they should. I think that a man like Modigliani, for example, has pushed himself to a point which is sort of absurd, because his ideas are not that revolutionary, you know; his discovery of the life cycle theory of consumption doesn't demolish Keynes; it may throw a bit of light on it, or it may not, but it doesn't do any more than that. I think there are a lot of people at MIT who do the same and push one another, thinking more about the contributions of each than is objectively deserved. I find it distasteful, and I can't see myself doing it.

When did you feel Keynesian economics had pretty much taken over?

Well, certainly by the time Heller and his group and Jim Tobin were running the Council. Even earlier, during Keyserling's period, I knew there were enough Keynesians at the Council, on the staff, so that in a sense it had taken over. But I never felt that Keynes was being followed with full adherence or full understanding of what he'd written. I still feel that way.

4.   Paul Malor Sweezy (b. 1910)

Birthplace: New York

Education:

1931:   B.A. Harvard
1932:   London School of Economics
1937:   Ph.D. Harvard

Significant publications:

Monopoly and Competition in the English Coal Trade, 1550–1850, Cambridge, Mass.: Harvard University Press, 1938.

'Demand Under Conditions of Oligopoly', *Journal of Political Economy*, **47**, August 1939, 568–73.

'Interest Groups in the American Economy', in U.S. National Resources Committee, *The Structure of the American Economy*, Pt 1, Washington, D.C.: U.S. Government Printing Office, 1939.

The Theory of Capitalist Development: Principles of Marxian Political Economy, New York: Monthly Review Press, 1942.

'Professor Schumpeter's Theory of Innovation', *Review of Economics and Statistics*, **25**, February 1943.

The Present as History, New York: Monthly Review Press, 1953.

Monopoly Capital: an Essay on the American Economic and Social Order, New York: Monthly Review Press, 1966 (with Paul Baran).

The Dynamics of U.S. Capitalism, New York: Monthly Review Press, 1970 (with Harry Magdoff).

The End of Prosperity, New York: Monthly Review Press, 1977 (with Harry Magdoff).

The Deepening Crisis of U.S. Capitalism, New York: Monthly Review Press, 1979 (with Harry Magdoff).

Four Lectures on Marxism, New York: Monthly Review Press, 1981.

Post-Revolutionary Society, New York: Monthly Review Press, 1981.

Stagnation and Financial Explosion, New York: Monthly Review Press, 1987 (with Harry Magdoff).

The Irreversible Crisis, New York: Monthly Review Press, 1989 (with Harry Magdoff).

Significant honors:

David A. Wells Prize

Experience:

1937–9:   Harvard
1949– :   Editor of *Monthly Review*

The interview was conducted on 24 September 1987 in Vergennes, Vermont after a symposium on Keynesian economics at Middlebury College with Lorie Tarshis, Robert Bryce and Paul Sweezy.

How did you get involved with economics?

I followed in my brother's footsteps. We were both undergraduates at Harvard at the same time; he was in the class of '29 and I was in the class of '31. We had both gone to Exeter; we both were on the school paper there; we were both presidents of the *Crimson*, which is Harvard's newspaper. As an undergraduate he specialized in history – that was his major; and he then went to Cambridge on a fellowship. I don't know exactly why, but when he came back he was interested in economics. I took the economics course as a sophomore. He came back the next year and his interest influenced me to continue. I had no particular reason for going into anything, so I took economics. He stayed on at Harvard and got his Ph.D. in economics.

In my senior year I took off a semester and went to Europe with my mother, who had been ill after my father died in 1931. So I was a year behind my class. The following year I returned and all of my buddies on the newspaper and various other enterprises, social and otherwise, had left. I had nothing much to do but study, and that was how I got really interested in the subject. I began to do, in effect, graduate work in my senior year.

At the end of that year my brother and I were very closely connected. I believe he was an instructor by that time, but we wanted to go abroad for a year and he went to the University of Vienna to write his Ph.D. thesis on the development of the Viennese marginal utility school. I went to the London School of Economics; there I was exposed to a whole lot of new things, a lot of new experiences, including Marxism, which before that time I didn't know anything about.

Before I went over to LSE, I was relatively conservative, or at least confused politically. I remember very well the first time I ever voted – it was in 1932, and I voted for Norman Thomas. I think it was not because I was a socialist, but it was because I was disgusted with both Democrats and Republicans. If there had been a conservative alternative, perhaps I would have voted for that.

When I went to LSE, I thought of myself as not exactly a follower but somehow very much influenced by Gottfried Haberler, of whom I was very fond. I changed my view considerably at LSE. He got more and more crotchety as he got older and became very intolerant, but when he was young he was an exciting person. I thought of myself within that Austrian mode. So did Abba Lerner and many of the LSE economists. We were a little group.

The only one in that group who was beginning to break away was Sol Adler, who now lives in China. Sol was in Harry White's Treasury group, the Division of Monetary Research. Harry White was a very important figure in the New Deal; he was an economist who negotiated the American position at Bretton Woods and who was Keynes's big adversary. This group was a kind of brain trust for Henry Morgenthau, then the Secretary of the Treasury. I don't think Morgenthau himself knew what it was all about. He was always kind of a conservative fellow. He had good enough sense to appreciate the importance of a brilliant group of advisors and research staff.

What led to your transformation?

What changed me more than anything else were the discussions among the graduate students at LSE. It wasn't only the discussions with economists; it was the extraordinarily lively intellectual environment. I was first exposed to radical ideas at that time; they came as a total revelation to me. There had been nobody, faculty or students at Harvard, who in my experience had anything to do with radical ideas. Veblen would have been about the furthest out that we were exposed to at all, and that was as a sociologist, not as an economic thinker. The students were the ones that radicalized me, not the faculty. I think that may be a general law: "Faculties never radicalize anybody; sometimes students can."

The book that made the biggest impact on me was Trotsky's *History of the Russian Revolution*. I didn't know anything about the Russian revolution, and I was beginning to hear and read Trotsky – it had just come out. It is a brilliant book that everybody ought to have the pleasure of reading. It changed my way of looking about a lot of things.

It took me the best part of the 1930s to acquire a decent education in Marxist thought and economics. It was almost entirely a self-education. There were few people you could go to and get help from. So when I returned to Cambridge from a year abroad at LSE in 1932, I thought of myself as a Marxist and as a radical.

When I came back I became very friendly, socially and intellectually, with Joseph Schumpeter, although this relationship doesn't fit into any of these new grooves. Schumpeter and I were very close friends through the 1930s; I was his assistant in a graduate course in economic theory for a couple of years in the mid-30s. We were poles apart politically and in our ideological stances, but he was the kind of person for whom that didn't make any difference. He had a very sharp mind, and a very provocative way of using it. He liked people who were not dull. He had no patience with dull people and he didn't really mind much about whether they agreed with him on anything. He never tried to create a school. Notice you won't find any Schumpeterians around.

Incidentally, I think one reason Schumpeter didn't like Keynes was that Schumpeter didn't have any followers, while Keynes had so many loyal followers. Schumpeter didn't do anything to overcome that, which I think was good, but it was not good for Schumpeter's ego. I remember, in 1936, the students in the first year theory course sent a delegation to me (I was the assistant at the time). They said, "Look, some of us came here to study economics instead of going some place else because of Schumpeter. We would like to get from Schumpeter his ideas, which we don't get in his course. He never tells us about the theory of economic development or his main theoretical contributions to pure theory." He didn't even touch on these in his lectures or his teaching.

The delegation asked me, "Please tell Professor Schumpeter that we would like him to spend some time on his own ideas." I went to him and I said, "Look, Joe, the students would like you to spend some time expounding your ideas." He mumbled a response – he had a way of kind of mumbling – and he said that he would think about it, but he never did a damn thing. You don't get a following of students unless you cultivate a following. I'm sure Keynes did do that, and therefore Schumpeter is an entirely different kind of a figure in the history of economic thought from Keynes.

Let's go back to 1929. You're in college, taking economics classes. How did people explain the Depression and how did you explain it to yourself?

In 1929 there was no depression; there was a stock market crash. But nobody thought of the crash as anything other than what had happened on a ten-year basis as far back as you could go. It was a long time before it dawned on people that there was something very special going on other than a normal business cycle phenomenon. That's easy to see in retrospect, but at the time it wasn't.

How did you come to learn the ideas in The General Theory*?*

You're asking some question about chronology and I can't sort it out that way. Keynesian ideas began to be influential in the early 1930s in part due to Bob Bryce's missionary work. There was a five-year period there when these ideas were infiltrating around and having more and more acceptance, not specially because they were good ideas, although that was true of many of the younger people, but because the world was operating only in a way that made the older economics look nonsensical. Bob Bryce's reaction to economics of the time was absolutely right. It didn't make sense and there was a feeling that we ought to get back to something that made sense.

In the gap between the *Treatise on Money* in 1931 and *The General Theory* in 1936 Keynesian ideas were around. Keynes wrote quite a lot during this period, books and articles on how to fight the Depression, and the ideas about deficit spending didn't have to wait for *The General Theory* to be known as the Keynesian position. So it's a little hard to determine when that term "Keynesian" became used as general nomenclature. So, by 1932, Keynes' *Treatise on Money* was very much discussed in the graduate curriculum of Money and Banking courses, although not in the general theory courses. Money and Banking courses are also where Hayek's *Prices and Production* was discussed. So that's how these theories began to get into our consciousness and discussion.

Keynesian ideas did not find a fertile ground. I was very properly trained as a neoclassical economist and believed the old economics. It took me quite a few years to get over these ideas, and I ended up a Marxist, but it took me about eight or nine years to understand that the labor theory of value wasn't the nonsense that the orthodox economists said it was. I finally did succeed in understanding that.

But Marxian economics was not a very well-developed set of documents and ideas. Marxism as a radical system of ideas in the more technical economic sense was something else again. But as an analysis of the way the advanced capitalist economy worked it wasn't terribly useful. I don't think that most of the Keynesian ideas are in any way incompatible with basic Marxian ideas, but the Marxian ideas didn't carry a convincing and usable theory of what was happening in the 1930s. Most of the Marxists of the time talked about the collapse of the system and all kinds of things which are very general and, in a sense, true – the system *had* collapsed – but why, and in what way, was not at all well worked out. Keynes came in with a whole set of ideas which were enormously exciting to all of us, Marxists as well as neoclassicals.

Bob Bryce and Lorie Tarshis used to come down to LSE from Cambridge. Do you remember any contact with them?

Keynesian ideas were floating around at both Cambridge and London at the time, although the conversion of any significant amount of London people – Lerner and Kaldor and some others – came, I think, after I left.

Having heard about these Keynesian ideas we sent a delegation of LSE graduate students to find out about them. Our group included Abba Lerner, Ursula Webb, who later married John Hicks, Aaron Emanuel and Ralph Araki, who was very prominent at the time but who committed suicide later. Thinking back, we were a good group. We started *The Review of Economic Studies*, for example. We went up to Cambridge and sat down and had tea with a Cambridge group. The Cambridge group included Joan Robinson and Richard Kahn, and we were introduced to the ideas in *The General Theory* there. I don't know how many times we went.

Do you remember the presentations that Bob Bryce gave in Hayek's seminar or in the Harvard study groups?

I vaguely remember those presentations. There are other seminars and discussion groups that I have been accused of being involved in at Harvard in the 1930s; they probably existed too. Some of the people who were involved in some of these discussion groups later on got involved in McCarthyite attacks. At that time discussion was pretty free. People weren't scared to say what they thought and to associate with people whom they thought were interesting and worthwhile. Later on a lot of that – this is something I think you shouldn't forget – came back to haunt people who weren't careful during the 1930s. They were accused of being Communists and subversives and all the rest of it.

I tried my best to be subversive, God knows, but "spy", "anti-patriot" and all that – that went too far. We were accused of all sorts of things like that. Lorie Tarshis's textbook on Keynesian economics was considered subversive, but it really wasn't a very radical version of Keynesianism.

When was it that people really began to be converted to Keynesian economics?

The General Theory came out late in 1936, and so it was read, probably, in the first half of 1937. I don't think it would have made anywhere near as big a splash if it hadn't been in the middle of 1937, when the bottom went out of the economy.

I don't think anyone who wasn't there really does understand the shock of the 1937 recession. The recovery that began in 1933 and ran to the summer of 1937 was, up to that time, the longest continuous recovery on record. Everyone took for granted that it was going to go on and eventually the economy would get back to normal. Unemployment, which in the depths of the Depression in 1933 had stood at about 25 per cent of the labor force, had declined to about 14 per cent, and everybody thought this was likely to go on and that it would eventually get back up the way it usually does in a business cycle, at the end of a business cycle, which would be around 3 or 4 per cent unemployment. Then all of a sudden in the summer of 1937 – Bang! the bottom went out. Unemployment, which had come down to around 14 per cent – I think that was the official figure – suddenly went back up to 19 per cent in a few months late in 1937.

The New Deal government was in a state of total shock. They didn't know what to make of this. One of the great debates of the 1930s developed between Marriner Eccles, who was head of the Federal Reserve Board, and Henry Morgenthau, who was the Secretary of the Treasury, and inside the administration it was an

extremely confused debate. Suddenly, *The General Theory* became available to us, and it threw a light on what was going on.
We understood *why* the system, after recovering for four years,
got nowhere near full employment and went down again.

So the recession of 1937 was a watershed both in the history of
the New Deal and in the history of economic thought. It was the
beginning of the Keynesian revolution because then, and then
only, did it become clear that things were really different, that
you had something on your hands that was not a normal business
cycle. That's when *The General Theory* seemed to have the explanation, or at least the framework of an explanation, that
standard theory didn't.

It was very liberating in a way. Up till then, even if you didn't
know it, all of us had been very much prisoners of the Say's Law
kind of thinking. It was always a special external situation that
accounted for recessions and depressions. Suddenly *The General
Theory* came along, at just the right moment, and provided a
different way of looking at the situation. It took the economics
profession by storm.

A group of us, including Lorie Tarshis and myself and maybe
seven or eight or a dozen altogether, were involved, got together
in late 1937 and tried to apply these ideas in our little book,
which was published late in 1937 under the title *An Economic
Program for American Democracy*. Seven of us signed it. Others
who partook of the discussions weren't able to sign it, for one
reason or another, because they had government jobs or whatever. So the group that wrote it were not only the people who are
listed in the introduction; there are at least four or five others who
took part in the discussion, not on a continual but on an occasional basis. Emile Despres was one of those; my brother was
one. The group that wrote it was the liveliest around.

Our little book got on the best seller list in Washington for
several months. It's a good little book. It's still worth reading, I
think, if you want a simple exposition of Keynesian ideas as
applied to a particular situation. I recommend it. You want to
look it up in the card catalog under the name of "Richard V.
Gilbert, *et al.*, *An Economic Program for American Democracy*".

And then the ideas in the book began to – not altogether *because* of it, but *with the help of it* – spread in Washington in government circles, in New Deal circles, and of course in the more liberal left-leaning segments. Roosevelt himself I don't think ever had any idea about Keynesian economics. He knew Keynes, of course, but he was not a theoretically inclined person at all. Morgenthau remained a budget-balancer right through the whole bit. Eccles was a practical banker, much more sensible. The Keynesian ideas were identified with some of the things that were done, but that was not a consistent Keynesian program that was carried out by the New Deal at all. It was only the war that brought on the kind of fiscal, monetary and investment policies which broke the back of the Depression in a couple of years. We went from a 19 per cent unemployment rate in 1939 to a 1.2 per cent in 1944. That was really Keynesianism in practice. It could be used again that way, but I hope it wouldn't be due to war next time. But it isn't so easy to put Keynesian ideas into practice because you run up against all kinds of political vested interests. There's where you have the difficulties.

Keynesian ideas have never achieved anything by themselves. They follow along and help us to understand, but they really aren't, and never were, the motivating force for particular economic policies in anybody's program. Later on they played a more important role – but that's a different story. Actually, the ideas are not the basis of any practical program dealing with these economic programs in the 1930s or any other period.

At Harvard what did you specialize in?

The Harvard Ph.D. program at the time required you to have one specialty field and three minor fields. I actually had a hybrid program that I worked out with the department. I specialized in both theory and history, and I wrote my Ph.D. thesis on the history of the coal trade. It was called "The Limitation of the Vend". The Vend was a famous cartel in British history from the late 18th century into the 1830s. It was the subject of many parliamentary investigations. I later modified the thesis into a book called *Monopoly and Competition in the English Coal Trade from 1550 to 1850*.

My thesis was actually related to the other revolution occurring at the time that was the Chamberlin/Joan Robinson monopolistic competition/imperfect competition revolution. I was interested in doing some empirical work on monopolistic or imperfect competition, and the coal trade seemed to be a well-documented case. I spent two or three years studying it. It involved an integration of theory and history. Abbot Usher, who was the economic historian at Harvard at the time, was the supervisor of my thesis. He never did anything to influence it, and never took much interest in it. I wasn't in any way influenced by him. Economic theory I don't think meant anything to him, and I was always convinced that the history and theory had to be done together.

Did you ever accept Keynesian economics, or did you go beyond Keynesian economics and feel his approach had lost the essence of what the problem was?

One thing you should understand is that Keynesian theory permits an enormous variation in political and ideological positions. Later on what Joan Robinson came to call Bastard Keynesianism was the opposite of what I, at any rate, understood to be Keynes's real intentions during the 1930s. Keynes came on not as a socialist – far from that – but as an extraordinarily liberal experimental mind who was prepared to do whatever was necessary – he thought it *could* be done – under the property arrangements and class arrangements that existed at that time. I think he was dead wrong in a lot of the things he advocated, like redistribution of income, social control over investment, which were totally antithetical to the political and ideological structure of the society and would never get through without a very basic change in the nature of the society. I still think that.

But that doesn't mean that, as economic logic, Keynesian ideas weren't miles ahead of anything else available at the time. It wasn't really that they were put into effect as ideas by the New Deal or by anybody else. As a matter of fact, paradoxically, many of the policies of Nazi Germany were very much in line with

Keynesian recommendations for overcoming a depression, and the German depression in general was overcome. Hitler's Germany came out of the depression long before the United States did, and that was because they spent a lot of money, deficit financing, controlled investment, on a war program. As a matter of fact, the Great Depression never was over in the United States until the war. The New Deal did not act on Keynesian policies at all.

The history of Keynesian theory and policy is full of paradoxes. It is important that you really understand the complexities of the history of the period.

In a sense it was possible to be a Keynesian and be much more radical than Keynes. One could use his ideas for much more radical purposes than he had any intention of fostering. Joan Robinson is a good example: she was a Keynesian to the day of her death, but she was one of the most radical people I knew from that whole period. She was far to the left of many of the Marxists, in terms of her instincts and sympathies. So that, when you say you're a Keynesian, it is not exactly easy to see what you're saying; you could be a kind of left-wing socialist Keynesian or a conservative business Keynesian.

As I got to know more and more about Marxism and Marxist ideas, I realized that they weren't at all the sort of simple-minded formulas which get into the textbooks and histories of economic thought – that there was a huge body of ideas that cannot really be systematized into a neat collection of formulas at all. You can fit a lot of Keynesian ideas very easily and compatibly with a much more radical perspective on the political and general ideological levels. I've never really sat down and tried to sort out my ideological perspective. In fact, I don't think I could do so because I've been changing my ideas, and I still do change quite often. I don't know how to fit all the pieces together into a coherent story. I think, if I did, it would probably be made up – imposed from later on. The development of ideas has no coherent structure.

5. Abba Ptachya Lerner (1903–82)

Birthplace: Bessarabia, Russia

Education:

1943: Ph.D. London School of Economics

Significant publications:

'The Concept of Monopoly and the Measurement of Monopoly Power', *Review of Economic Studies*, **1**, June 1934, 157–75.
The Economics of Control, New York: Macmillan, 1944.
The Economics of Employment, New York: McGraw-Hill, 1951.
Essays in Economic Analysis, New York: Macmillan, 1953.
Flation: Not Inflation of Prices, Not Deflation of Jobs, New York: Quadrangle, 1972; Penguin, 1973.
The Economics of Efficiency and Growth: Lessons from Israel and the West Bank, Cambridge, Mass.: Ballinger, 1975 (with H. Ben-Shahar).
MAP – A Market Anti-Inflation Plan, New York: Harcourt Brace, 1980 (with D.C. Colander).

Significant honors:

Won several essay prizes while studying at the London School of Economics
1930: Tooke Scholarship
1937: Rockefeller Fellowship
1966: Distinguished Fellow of the American Economic Association
1980: President of the Atlantic Economic Society

Experience:

1933:   A founder of the new *Review of Economic Studies*; co-editor until 1937
1935:   Began teaching at the London School of Economics
1939:   Came to the United States and moved from university to university. Taught at Columbia, Virginia, Kansas City, Amherst, The New School for Social Research, Roosevelt, Johns Hopkins, Michigan State and the University of California, Berkeley

Alvin H. Hansen (1887–1975)

Birthplace: Viborg, South Dakota

Education:

1910:   B.S. Rankton College, South Dakota
1918:   Ph.D. University of Wisconsin, Madison

Significant publications:

Business-Cycle Theory: Its Development and Present Status, Boston: Ginn, 1927.

Economic Stabilisation in an Unbalanced World, Harcourt Brace, 1932.

Full Recovery or Stagnation?, New York: W.W. Norton, 1938.

Fiscal Policy and Business Cycles, New York: W.W. Norton, 1941.

State and Local Finance in the National Economy, New York: W.W. Norton, 1944 (with H.S. Perloff).

Monetary Theory and Fiscal Policy, New York: McGraw-Hill, 1949.

Business Cycles and National Income, New York: W.W. Norton, 1951; 2nd edn 1964.

A Guide to Keynes, New York: McGraw-Hill, 1953.

Economic Issues in the 1960s, New York: McGraw-Hill, 1960.
The Dollar and the International Monetary System, New York: McGraw-Hill, 1965.

Significant honors:

1928: Guggenheim Fellowship
1937: Vice-President of the American Statistical Association
1937: President of the American Economic Association

Experience:

1916–19: Brown
1919–37: University of Minnesota
1937–75: Harvard

The interview was conducted by an unknown interviewer follow-ing a Boston University lecture on 24 April 1972. Abba Lerner told us of the interview when we were discussing this period with him and the tape of the interview was found in Lerner's files. The speaker is Abba Lerner unless specified.

In 1932 I got my Bachelor degree and became a graduate student at the London School of Economics. In 1933, together with a rather lively group of colleagues, we started a journal called *The Review of Economic Studies*. We did that with the idea that we didn't like the journals publishing long articles, most of which we thought consisted of verbiage. We thought we'd start a jour-nal in which people could say something in one or two pages and wouldn't feel obliged, as we thought was the case in most other journals, to make it into a twenty-page article. We also wanted to translate other things. It didn't quite work out that way but we had a lot of fun with it.

Our first problem was how to raise the money for it. What we did was to ask all the visiting American professors of economics who we thought were very rich. We told them about our program and they were very encouraging. They usually gave us five pounds towards the starting of the journal. Professor Viner was an exception; he was very discouraging and he said there were already so many journals that he couldn't read them, and it was a shame to have any more – but he gave us ten pounds.

Having raised the money, we had to go and get articles. We visited Oxford and Cambridge. We apparently had developed a terrible reputation as being a lot of wild, bright boys, and in Oxford they treated us very royally. They gave us a beautiful dinner; I shall always remember it as the first time I was served sliced grapes as part of the dinner. Unfortunately, you couldn't get them to talk about economics. They spoke about the weather, politics and personalities, but not about economics. We were rather disappointed.

Then we went to Cambridge, where it was completely different. We were taken charge of by Joan Robinson. We began with a few polite words about her book, *Imperfect Competition* with which we were familiar (in fact I had paid my way through college by coaching people in her book). Then we turned to the topic which was really interesting us. We had heard that some very strange things were happening in Cambridge. We couldn't quite make out what it was, something about the elasticity of demand for output as a whole, and we knew that was nonsense, because we were brought up properly on Marshall, and we knew all about elasticity and demand curves. We knew that if you drew a demand curve you had to assume all the other prices were fixed; otherwise you wouldn't know what the demand curve for this item was. If you were to draw a demand curve for another item (for example, say you wanted to look at the consumer surplus which you could enjoy from being able to buy some item for less than you would have been willing to pay) it was your duty to wipe out the first demand curve because the first one was allowing the price to vary. You had to have the prices fixed for everything else if you were going to draw a demand curve. Knowing this, we knew that demand curves and demand and elasticity referred only to partial analysis; and yet, somehow in Cambridge they must have known that and still, very perversely, they were talking about elasticity of demand for output as a whole.

Well, Joan Robinson started explaining it to us, but we didn't understand her and, symbolically, we arranged to have a weekend meeting at a place called Bishop's Stortford, halfway between London and Cambridge. There was a London contingent and a Cambridge contingent, and we spent a whole weekend trying to find out what they were doing. Joan Robinson was in charge. She was aided by a few other people from Cambridge and Oxford. Her husband (Austin Robinson) dropped in for a while; R.F. Kahn came once; James Meade was also there. I think there were one or two others, but I've forgotten now who they were. Mainly, however, it was Joan Robinson in charge and, as we would try to understand, she'd say, "Yes, that's right; now you're getting the idea ... no, now you've gone backwards." When the weekend was over, we still didn't know what they were talking about. However, we were sufficiently impressed to publish an article by Joan Robinson, which we didn't understand, on the Demand for Output as a Whole.[1] This was the first we saw of the Cambridge idea.

The weekend meeting had not been too successful; we still couldn't understand each other – at least we couldn't understand them. They were confident that we were either just very stupid or backward – and we thought they were crazy, obviously doing something that didn't make any sense, but couldn't quite put our finger on what was wrong.

We were not only a very enthusiastic group of young people, we also had very high opinions of ourselves, especially me. I had received a fellowship that I was planning to spend in Manchester because I had been concentrating too much in my economics on pure theory, a subject that interested me very much. I had been shying away from looking at statistics and actual data that didn't attract me so much and that I found much harder. That was the reason why I was persuaded to go to Manchester, where there were a lot of people working hard on real data. I was going to Manchester to dirty my hands. But I couldn't resist the temptation; felt I must spend a couple of months in Cambridge, find out what is this nonsense they are talking, clear it up, and then go on and do my work in Manchester. So we moved to Cambridge (my wife and I and our two little children – twins) and we had a very pleasant time. But instead of being there two months and clearing up the nonsense, I spent six months, during which time they finally persuaded me they made sense.

I enjoyed my time in Cambridge so much largely because I didn't know the Cambridge tradition. The Cambridge tradition is that you belong to a college and you hardly ever bother any don belonging to another college. It just isn't done. But I didn't know it wasn't done, so I went around and spoke to all the professors in Cambridge about everything, attended many lectures, and met them all. They were all too polite to tell me that I was doing what wasn't done. So I gained very much from talking to all of them.

I spent some time doing some of the economics which I was used to and wrote an article together with Hans Singer on spatial competition. This was all in microeconomics and it had nothing to do with what I had come to Cambridge for, but it took up quite a bit of time. We wrote this article which began with my finding that Singer had produced a huge sheet of paper with numbers in every little square. When I looked at it I found that it was a curve, only he didn't know that it was a curve. You could show the curve by just picking out the highest number along each row and drawing a line through them. He was quite excited to find that he had produced a curve without knowing it. We worked on this article for a long time, producing an enormous number of diagrams and having a lot of fun in the process. When we had finished the article and eliminated many of the more complicated curves, the problem was what to do with it. As the managing editor of *The Review of Economic Studies*, I decided against publishing the article. It was great fun to write, but I was afraid it was terribly boring for anybody to read. However, there was a big fat article doing nothing, so we sent it around to some other journals. Professor Viner read it very carefully, improved the notations somewhat, and printed it in the *Journal of Political Economy*. Over the years, I found that quite a number of people have actually read it, which surprised me very much.

The rest of the time I spent in Cambridge finding out what they were talking about. I attended the lectures which Keynes was giving at that time, using the galley proofs of *The General Theory* as the notes from which he gave his lectures. I found his lectures very difficult. The ideas were unfamiliar. I now find it very hard to remember, and to understand, why I found it so difficult.

He was talking a great deal about the consumption function and the multiplier, and I think the essential difficulty was that I had been used to thinking of only two things at a time. On a diagram you had a horizontal axis and a vertical axis, and that was it. Then you could draw another curve on the same diagram. But here I had to think about consumption and investment and the rate of interest and the effect of each on the others; this is what I found very difficult. I think I more or less got it after working hard for a couple of months, but still I was very much disturbed by the continual basic proposition that saving is equal to investment. Nowadays I present this proposition to my students in five minutes, but they don't believe it. I then spend a couple of years persuading them that it is really true, but their resistance is much less than mine was at that time.

I spent a few months writing numerous little notes or short articles, each of them an attempt to provide an example that savings is not equal to investment, and of course each of them was knocked down by Joan Robinson, Robert Bryce, Alec Cairncross or by Lorie Tarshis who had all been in Cambridge a couple of years before and had absorbed it. I think probably it was Lorie Tarshis, more than anybody else, who finally got me to understand what was involved in *The General Theory* and in the equality of savings and investment. I would have thought it to have been a very bad investment on my part to spend so much time in trying to prove that one and one is not equal to two – which is what this really amounts to. However, personally it was a very good investment, because for many years later I could publish articles pointing out how other people kept on making the same mistakes that I had made during that time in Cambridge, correcting their misunderstandings and, sometimes, mistakes about this equality, and explaining how this equality had to be pushed out of the way before you could talk about *The General Theory*.

There was another interesting thing at that time, the meetings of the Political Economy Club which everybody called The Keynes Club. It met in Keynes's rooms in King's College. Only men were invited, primarily visiting professors and a chosen few of the brighter undergraduates who were recommended by their tutors. The only woman, as far as I know, that was ever invited was Joan Robinson, but only when she had to read a paper to them. I don't know if they are still carrying on this anti-feminist tradition. There was also another very interesting phenomenon there; after the paper had been read, Kahn, who acted as an assistant, secretary or minister to Keynes, would go around all the time with thin pieces of paper sticking out of his hands. A student would pick one out of his hand and it would have a number on it; that number indicated the order in which you would be called upon to come to the front of the room and stand with your back to the fire. If the student wished, he could go back to his seat without saying anything, but it was compulsory that he should go up to the front. Of course students spent all their time thinking what they were going to say when they were called upon and then getting very upset when someone who was called before them said what they were going to say. But this, I think, was a very good exercise for them. Every session ended with a summary of the issues by Keynes, which was always the greatest treat of the evening. It was beautifully and masterfully done.

I think Keynes was the best conversationalist I ever knew. The second best one was Alvin Johnson of the New School for Social Research. Once, many years later, I brought Keynes to Alvin Johnson and listened to them both for an hour and a half; I shall always kick myself for not going home immediately and writing down as much as I could remember. Those, of course, were the days before tape recorders were so easily available. And that was a great thing that was lost. (Another great thing that was lost was a discussion that Alvin and I had at Michigan State two years ago when we were talking about the beginnings of the Keynes theory. We did have a tape recorder there, but the man in charge of the tape recorder didn't know how to operate it.)

Well I think that's probably enough of the purely personal reminiscence. Let me just mention one thing that is relevant to recent developments in economics. At one of these sessions at the Keynes Club, Robert Bryce and I (Robert Bryce was a Canadian who was in Cambridge a couple of years before 1935; he was one of the people who helped me get over my pre-Keynesian prejudices) were talking about one of the problems which came up, and we said to Keynes, "Isn't it possible that when you provide enough effective demand to reach and maintain full employment there might be an inflation, and you might find that you have to have this inflation going on as long as you keep on maintaining enough demand to keep to full employment?" Well, Keynes didn't understand that, and Bryce and I tried saying it every possible way that we could. Keynes still didn't understand it.

Keynes was a man who had a limited amount of patience that he used liberally up to a certain point, after which you could hear a sort of click as if he had said: "Well I have listened enough to this and it is not worth spending any more time on it." After we heard that click we must have been so discouraged that for many years later we didn't think about it or talk about it. But I've been talking about that since at least 1958 and maybe earlier, yes, earlier. (In 1951 there are some elements of it in my *Economics of Employment*.) But for many years it was just sort of wiped out by Keynes not being able to see the point and we gave up.

This brings me to a few things about the Keynesian theory and some of the misunderstandings about Keynesian economics. One of the difficulties about the Keynesian revolution was that there were a number of false leads or red herrings, some for which Keynes himself was responsible, as he gave people the wrong impression as to what was the essential element of the Keynesian revolution. The essential element, I think – this is my interpretation and I think Keynes later agreed with it – is a very simple one: mainly taking seriously into account the rigidity of wages and prices. They don't go down when they should do so according to the classical theory. The classical theory was built on thinking about a barter economy in which there is no money and no problems which could be caused by money; then you brought in money and tried to believe, as well as tried to show, that all that money did was oil the wheels, but nothing else, unless somebody did something stupid that he shouldn't have done.

For example, if the government printed enormous amounts of money, this would be bound to upset things. But if you didn't do that and the amount of money had some stability, everything would work out automatically. It was part of the automatic mechanism of laissez-faire and the invisible hand; you never had to worry about either inflation or deflation, because they would put an end to themselves. If for any reason there was more than enough spending to buy the potential output of the economy, prices would rise, the spending wouldn't be too great and then everything would be fine. Or if it was too little, the demand would be less than the supply, you draw the magic supply and demand curve and therefore the price has to fall and at the lower price the limited previously insufficient amount of spending now would be able to buy all the goods we could produce. Therefore there would be no need to worry about this unless somebody was being very mischievous and prevented it from working.

The essence of the Keynesian idea is that this doesn't work downward – that the prices do not fall. Keynes apparently many times thought that he was doing more than that, in that he was departing from the general analysis of the classical economics (he really was a classical economist). He wanted to show that it was not just rigidity because, after all, everybody knew that if you didn't allow the prices to move it wouldn't work, so he tried to give other reasons. He spoke about the liquidity trap, something which corresponds to the collapse of confidence, and other things that required a new theory of what goes on. I think these other reasons are unnecessary and confusing because essentially all they say is that you do not have an adequate mechanism for the reduction of prices which would cure any unemployment automatically. A lot of confusion was caused by a terminological misunderstanding of two meanings of the word rigidity, or the opposite of flexibility. To increase flexibility in a practical manner one would reduce the power of the trade unions, or reduce certain monopolistic situations. I call that practical flexibility. The other meaning of the same word is complete or absolute flexibility: that prices would fall as far as might be necessary, no matter how far it is, to make supply equal to demand.

Keynes said that flexibility is not the issue, and flexibility of wages might make things even worse. He was talking about practical flexibility, the kind of flexibility which one might in fact be able to bring about. But many people said that Keynes is denying that flexibility in the other sense of perfect flexibility would solve the problem; this is wrong. If you did have perfect flexibility, then the classical argument would be correct. Prices would fall until everybody who has a dollar would become a millionaire long before he could go and buy something, and this would solve the problem. But Keynes didn't think it was worthwhile talking about that kind of flexibility. He meant the other thing; this is one of the bases of the misunderstanding.

Another cause of misunderstanding was that in the beginning of his *General Theory*, Keynes said that the trouble is that the workers are not able to lower their real wage. They may try to do so – the unemployed might like to have a lower real wage and get jobs – but they can only bargain about their money wage. There's no way they can bargain about their real wage, so when they lower their money wage, costs go down, and then whatever the existing degree of competition or monopoly is causes prices to go down about the same. Therefore the real wage is not affected and that is why the workers cannot adjust their wages so as to get full employment.

This was a red herring and a slip of the argument that Keynes disregarded later when he pointed out the trouble is not the real wage and the necessity for reducing it; the trouble is that there is no sufficient mechanism for bringing out enough effective demand through the reduction of prices. The method in which it works is to have a sufficient reduction in prices, to increase the real value of the money stock, to provide enough liquidity, so that people will have a lower rate of interest which would cause enough investment to solve the problem of unemployment. What happens to the real wage isn't part of this argument at all. The real wage may go down; it may stay the same, or it may go up. The important thing is the effective demand and not the real wage.

This leads people to another misunderstanding which was discovered only last week, thanks to reprinting of a number of articles by Robert Lekachman in the book on Keynes. Lekachman asked a number of people to write a new article and reprint an old one. I have two articles in there; Professor Hansen has two, as do many other people. There's also two there by Champernowne.[2] (Professor Champernowne, now at Cambridge, was one of the young people who were around at the time when we started *The Review of Economic Studies*, but he was not one of the group who helped start it off. He was one of the brightest boys around there and I remember very clearly some of the work he did. He did a beautiful essay on Marxian economics which was partly due to the fact that he was completely ignorant of Marx and actually went and read the book in order to write the essay, which was very unusual.)

Champernowne had an article on Keynes which, I think, completely missed the point. The article was published in 1936, in which he was fascinated, or hypnotized, by what Keynes said in the beginning (I think about page 4 or 5): that the reduction of the real wage is what workers can't do because they are misled by the money wage, and therefore if they talk about the money wage it is not what really matters; what really matters is what you can buy with the money, not what the money wage is. Therefore he says that one of the two basic differences between Keynes and the classical economics is that, whereas the classical economics said that a supply of labor depends only on the real wage, in Keynes, supply depends not only on the real wage, but also on the money wage. (You make this look more scientific by writing it in algebra and say that N is a function of r, the real wage, and of w, the money wage.) Then he says that, if there has been some change in the price level, the workers don't realize it, or understand it, and they suffer from a money illusion. Therefore they refuse to work, not because they are dissatisfied with the real wage, but because the money wage makes them feel that they are not getting as much as they should get. This is what he called monetary unemployment, which he says is related to, but has some differences from, Keynes's involuntary unemployment. It's all due to the existence of money illusion. Money illusion makes people work either way; it may cause people to work less because they are misled by the money elements into underestimating what the wage really is. It could also cause them to work more by causing them to overestimate what they are really getting, and then you would get what he calls monetary employment, or, if you neglect the differences which I think are not important, in Keynesian language you would get involuntary unemployment in one case, and involuntary overemployment in the other.

I find it extraordinary to read this now, because what it means is there is no involuntary unemployment, because the people who are not working are the people who do not want to work given the money wage and the real wage. To suppose that this is a description of the actual world where we have now six million unemployed, is like saying they are not really unemployed. Now how can you say they are not really unemployed? The explanation is that you don't really look at the individual workers: you look at "the working class", if you like, although Keynes would no doubt shake in horror at the idea of thinking in class terms and not individual terms. But that is what they are doing. They are saying that, since the wages don't go down, and this is determined by the working class through the representatives or negotiators, the workers don't want to work for less money. It is a behavioristic attempt to explain what the individuals feel by seeing what they do as a class, or as a mass. It is a missing of a whole point.

The whole point, as I see it, is that there are people who are unemployed, who would love to get a job on the existing conditions – money wage and real wage. But there's no machinery for lowering the money wage, at least not lowering it to a sufficient degree to make it work. And if you lower it just a little bit, as might be done, you make things worse – Keynes made that perfectly clear – because you establish expectations of still further reductions in wages and in prices and then people will spend less instead of more, because the effects of *falling* wages and prices are the opposite of *lower* wages and prices. And so you get this strange notion of explaining Keynes by defining away, not his theory, but the whole problem.

Champernowne is not the only one, because I think that many people, now, are doing almost exactly the same thing: trying to explain unemployment by saying that the unemployed are *searching* for work. Alchian and others made elaborate analyses, often with a lot of mathematics, explaining unemployment as search – which means they are really voluntarily unemployed. They don't take the job because they think they will get a better one tomorrow. Why there should be a sudden great difficulty in finding jobs, why people should suddenly have become very inefficient in finding jobs now as compared with a few years ago, remains a mystery.

Well, I think I have probably said enough now to start some discussion.

You mentioned at the beginning your role in starting The Review of Economic Studies. *I remember the journal most because the discussion on socialist economics was being published there. What was the role of Oskar Lange? Did you cooperate somehow with him?*

Oscar Lange was in London, I think on the Rockefeller Fellowship, I am not sure, but he was in London; we had lots of discussions. We saw a lot of each other; we liked each other; we became very close friends, and we spoke about it. He was, I think, the more active in the development of socialistic economics. I was reacting more to what he was saying about it, as far as I remember now.

I do know that I first got interested in economics as a socialist. I thought economics should have helped solve the problem of distribution, and I was puzzled by some of the remarks made by Marxists. The ideas attracted me in some ways, but I found them quite unintelligible in other ways. Lange was the one who wrote first. My contribution consisted of essentially one article in which

I corrected a slip which he made, which he immediately recognized. He had said that, in a socialist society, if you paid each worker his marginal product, this might call for more or less than is needed altogether. There's no guarantee that the sum of the marginal products will add up to the total amount. He said, in that case, what you should do is to pay them all the same fraction of their marginal product. I thought this was a mistake and said you should do anything except that. You should give them some more money, or take some money away from them, but you should not tie this to their wage because that would make the higher-paid wage workers relatively too high, and the lower-wage workers relatively too low because they would depart from their marginal product. He even incorporated this argument in his later work. (Incidentally, I just got a letter from his wife; they are publishing a collection in his honor and they want to reprint this article of mine in this collection.)

Oskar Lange, then, also somehow moved to Keynesian economics. What was his role?

He was one of the people who did a lot to help make it clearer. He had an article that, I think in a very effective way, pointed out that there might be a positive or negative relationship between consumption and investment. The classical approach was that the given volume of output – determined by the size of the population, the skills and their endowments – determined the T in the $MV=PT$ equation, and that was equal to the sum of the investment and the consumption. So if consumption increased, investment would have to decrease and vice versa. The Keynesian argument was to say "Nonsense". You can increase both together – which is what a multiplier is – if there are unemployed resources.

Lange wrote a very effective article saying that, in certain situations, a certain amount of saving would set free resources which would increase investment and that's the classical argument. But if you had too much saving, then, although the setting free of resources would have the effect of making more investment possible, the decline in demand for consumption could work the other way, and it would at a certain point overcome the tendency for the savings to increase investment and, if it discourages investors enough, you could actually decrease the amount of investment. It's really the Keynesian proposition from a different angle. It is possible that not all of it came from Keynes. Lange was very familiar with Kalecki, and Kalecki had a number of very similar notions to Keynes.

Would you like to comment on Hicks' contribution? You recently suggested that Hicks put Keynes back into general equilibrium analysis, and this was not what Keynes was trying to do at all. It was essentially disequilibrium, not equilibrium, analysis. And yet Hicks with his IS/LM...

I don't think that there's any disagreement; the IS/LM curve accurately describes what Keynes had in mind. Nor is the idea of disequilibrium a point of disagreement. The IS/LM curve gives you an equilibrium without full employment, which before Keynes was never called an equilibrium. Maybe it shouldn't be called an equilibrium. It doesn't matter what you call equilibrium; I myself think it should be called equilibrium because, to me, equilibrium means a situation which tends to stay where it is. And unemployment does tend to stay where it is for the reasons given by Keynes, although it wouldn't stay where it was if you had a perfect flexibility of prices. But you don't have perfect flexibility, and so it's equilibrium. I prefer to call it equilibrium, but it is a matter of language. There are people who say Keynes shouldn't have called his situation one of equilibrium; rather they should have called it disequilibrium. All this means is it is not the same as the classical story. Well, it isn't the same. And the reason for it is rigidity.

Now, on what I am going to talk about this afternoon, I want to say that, for Keynes's purposes, for dealing with unemployment and depression, this argument is sufficient. The wages don't go down. He didn't explain why they don't go down, but you don't need to do so. That's interesting and becomes important for other problems, but for Keynes's purpose it doesn't matter. Given that it doesn't go down, we get stuck, and then you can argue forever whether it is equilibrium or disequilibrium. Is it equilibrium if you get stuck on the way to somewhere? You can say it is, or you can say it isn't; it is not of any interest, or of any importance. You got stuck if you think you could go on further. On the other hand, if you recognize that the stickiness is going to keep you there for a long time, what's the use in saying you could have gone further if you hadn't got stuck?

How do you explain the link between unemployment and inflation, the sort of thing that's dealt with in the Phillips Curve? Can that not be done within the Keynesian context satisfactorily?

No. Not within the Keynesian context. You must go further, and that means some developments. Keynes did not deal with the problem of inflation and depression at the same time. This was the point of the question which Bryce and I asked him – which he wasn't able to deal with. If you look through *The General Theory*, and you look very closely with a bit of a magnifying glass, you will find that there are references to this possibility – to what happens when the wage unit increases. He didn't want to go into that; it wasn't a problem of practical concern. In order to do this you must go into the question of why wages are sticky.

I have to say that Keynes was really making a bigger revolution than he was willing to admit to himself. He was, in fact, saying that the market doesn't work. He only half recognized it. He said the market doesn't work on the one side. If you remember, he says the classical theory has two equalities. The first is that the wage is equal to the marginal disutility of labor. This one, he says, doesn't work because workers would like to work but can't find jobs. This throws out at once theories like "search" or Champernowne's. Keynes says they do want to work, so they are not on their marginal utility curve.

Keynes kept the other equality. He said that the price is equal to the marginal product of labor. This is possibly an explanation of why he didn't want to bother with imperfect competition or monopoly, although he said you could easily make an adjustment, because what you need to do is not really an issue between perfect competition and monopoly. You have to deny the market, that the price is determining the sales, in the same way he had in mind the prices determining the employment. This didn't fit into his scheme; he was much too good a Marshallian economist to admit that he was really moving into a realm of what he might have called, and what I used to call, institutional economics – which was used as a pejorative term.

We used to think of an institutional economist as a man who talks about institutions because he doesn't understand economics. But here it is really an institutional matter of what it is that happens. When Keynes said that when you are off the supply curve of labor, but are still on the demand curve, that means you have unemployment. But you don't have depression in the sense that every businessman wouldn't want to sell any more than he is currently selling. The businessman is on his demand curve. He can't sell any more at the same price.

Now it seems to me one of the most obvious things about any depression is that almost all businessmen are only too happy to sell more at the same prices at which they are selling now. But this doesn't fit in the Keynesian theory. So I say he is describing the situation in which you draw the supply and demand curve, and there's a point on the demand curve where he says you are, and that is not on the supply curve so you have involuntary unemployment in-between. Now, that would mean that you would have unemployment but you don't have what I want to call depression. Or you could do just the opposite; you might be stuck on the other curve. Then you would not have depression, and you don't have any unemployment because the workers are doing all the work they want to do. But you would have a tremendous depression because they wouldn't be able to sell all they want to sell.

Actually, we are somewhere in between because we have some depression and we have some unemployment. And this was done very much later by Patinkin. What Patinkin did was argue that, and this is really the very central point of the whole thing, the whole classical difficulty arose from their not having money in their story. They left it out. Patinkin very elaborately and very ingeniously put it back in again through the cash balance effect.

All this complex work of Patinkin wouldn't have been necessary if they hadn't left money out in the first place. You can start off by telling the whole story with money in, and then all Patinkin's work would not be necessary.

What kind of remedy would you suggest if there is unemployment and inflation and no depression whatsoever?

Well, then we have a depression, only we are very polite about it; we call it a recession. You have unemployment and you have inflation at the same time. If you have unemployment, it means you don't have too much spending and therefore it can't be true that the inflation is due to too much spending. It is a tragedy that our government has been operating until very recently on the assumption that the inflation must be due to too much spending and that we must cut down on the spending. To cure the inflation. Nixon believed that, because Milton Friedman told him that. But, then, he stopped believing that on August the 15th; he did something else.[3] That is to say that, since the inflation is not caused by too much spending, it must be caused by something else. It is really due, not to people trying to buy more than is available, but to the various contributors to production, trying to get or demanding as their share for work, or for capital, its profit, more than 100 per cent of the total product. Of course, they can't succeed in that either, and so you have a pressure; what you must do to deal with this pressure is more difficult. It is not a market but is an institutional problem of the power of labor to raise wages and businesses to raise prices, each blaming the other, perhaps quite honestly, for having to do it, and the government increasing the amount of money or spending so that this doesn't lead to too catastrophic a depression. So we are stuck with some inflation and some unemployment and recession and not depression. What you must do is deal with this institutional problem by institutional technique.

Does that include price and wage controls?

Regulation. I object to the word "control".

We have Professor Hansen here as a guest. We learned from Lerner about how Keynesian economics started in England; we would now like to hear how the Keynesian economics started in the United States. Could you tell us, Professor Hansen? Would you say it was fully accepted by 1938?

Hansen: No it was not. The American economists were all dead against it. J.M. Clark was always a very generous and accommodating person, a fine personal type; he, more for that reason than anything else, was friendly, but he wasn't really intellectually friendly to Keynesian economics. All the American economists were against Keynesianism for quite a number of years. I went to the Federal Reserve as an economist in 1940, and then the war came on. This, of course, stimulated a lot of discussion, but the discussions that went on were much more applied and less theoretical than the kind of thing that Abba has been talking about. They were related in this country very much to the matter of the public debt. There was violent opposition to, for example, my views on the public debt. I gave lectures all over the country and was always nicely received, but the press was very critical and, in general, all of the economists were critical. I can name people who have been ardent Keynesians in recent years who were very strongly anti-Keynesian in earlier years. Not people like Viner and Frank Knight who remained opposed to Keynesianism all the way through, but there are a number of people I could mention who have become important leaders of the progressive Keynesian movement who were very strongly against it. There was practically nobody in the United States who accepted Keynesianism up to and as we got into the war. And *The General Theory* was written in 1936.

I think it was the war, rather than Keynes, that changed opinion in the United States – well, it didn't change opinion much because there was no good development of thinking about the problem, but it changed the atmosphere in the country. My gracious, here we had a third of the labor force unemployed, and we see what the war has done; it's made everybody prosperous. Now they didn't go from there to analyze Keynesian economics or to perhaps change their ideas, but, anyhow, something had happened – the world hadn't all disappeared just because there was a slight increase in the public debt. It was a new experience. Just talking about a billion dollars of increase in public debt was viewed as being *tremendously* dangerous.

When you saw the huge issues associated with the war, you began to think that these issues were wrong. But, early on, opinion changed in a practical way about very practical problems, but it wasn't until 1956 in the Economic Report of the President – 10 years after the Full Employment Act of 1946 – that any congressional committee accepted the practical applications of Keynesianism in terms of employment policy. There was a controversy between the minority report that year and the majority report. The majority report was Keynesian; they had other things too: it was really half baked, but nevertheless it took the practical position that fiscal policy is an important part of how to run an economy. This was as late as 1956.

There was a meeting celebrating the tenth anniversary in Washington; the audience including a good many members of Congress. I was the principal speaker; Arthur Burns was then on the council and he also spoke at that occasion. I would say this was a milestone, in a way, in this development of the general opinion among economists. It is a very slow process, an incredibly slow process.

Lerner: Alvin, did you know that you were ahead of Keynes on the question of the national debt?

Hansen: Keynes was never interested in the national debt; he never really gave any serious systematic discussion, as far as I can remember, to the debt. He took a practical English position. My gracious, Englishmen had behind them more than a hundred years of the British debt being two and a half times or three times the national income. Well, with that experience behind him, public debt looked a little different.

Public debt never disturbed Keynes very much. Moulton, who was chairman of Brookings, had published a little book about the public debt. It made all the arguments against me, all the way through: what a terrible thing the public debt was. One of my students (I can't think of his name) who was very conservative, and now dead unfortunately, wrote an article showing how Moulton's arguments were completely fallacious.[4] It was a very good article. Moulton was going to answer it, but (I heard it through the grapevine) he finally concluded his answer wouldn't get any place anyhow, so he withdrew it. That book, which came quite late, also shows how slow opinion was in the United States, how very slow.

Then came the Committee for Economic Development that took the position that what goes up must come down; if you first increase the public debt, you must repay it all in the next expansion. I don't know if anybody took that seriously but it was a sugar-coated way of being prepared to do something on the public debt. Yes, Keynes is quite surprising in a way, there was very little discussion by Keynes about the public debt.

Lerner: Let me tell you one of the discussions. About 1943, I was in Washington visiting and there was a meeting at the Federal Reserve Board in which Keynes came to speak.

Hansen: I was the one that organized that meeting.

Lerner: You've forgotten what happened there?

Hansen: No, I don't think so. Was this a dinner meeting at the hotel or was it the seminar at the Federal Reserve?

Lerner: It was a seminar at the Federal Reserve.

Hansen: Well, I'm sorry, but I think you're wrong, and I'll tell you why I think you're wrong.

Lerner: You haven't heard the story yet.

Hansen: What I'm now going to say has nothing to do with the story. It is good preliminary, though. I had been in London in

1941, and we had seen Keynes practically every day at the Treasury and to discuss post-war problems with different people. He came to Washington, shortly thereafter, you said 1943, didn't you, it's about right. Well, I arranged a dinner at one of the hotels and about 40 economists were there; you were there; Mason was there; Chamberlin was there, and a good deal of the economists around Washington were there. You were sitting in the corner of the room – I don't know why you always want to sit in that corner over there. I introduced Keynes and he was, since there were no newspaper people present, at his best; namely he looked to be responsible on occasions like that and say funny things. In the discussion you raised the question – this is your question – you said, "Mr Keynes, why don't we forget about all this business of fiscal policy, public debt and all those kinds, and have some printing presses?" To which Keynes made this reply: "It's the art of statesmanship to tell lies, but they must be plausible lies." This was supposed to squelch you for the evening and, as a matter of fact, you said nothing more.

After that, we had a seminar: it's still running at the Federal Reserve Bank. Keynes spoke but was very tired, and Stone really did most of the talking. Goldenweiser and I had dinner with Keynes and we took him – he was very tired – to the hotel. This was actually the last time I saw Keynes, as far as I can remember. Now for some reason or another on the way the name, Abba Lerner, came up. I don't know exactly why, but Keynes said to Goldenweiser and me, "Have you seen Lerner's book that's just out?" I don't remember which one it was.

Lerner: *The Economics of Control.*

Hansen: At that time, he said he had been reading it and that there are some things in there that are very important and that we should get into our mental furniture. It didn't sound like the attitude he took towards us when you were asking questions about the printing press, but he was very high in his praise of you. He said, "We should have him back at Cambridge, England

– we brought him up; we need him and we should have him back.' I don't think I ever told you that.

Lerner: No, you did not.

Hansen: Keynes said this, and it could well have happened, I think, if Keynes had lived on. Instead, you remained in the United States and you've been spreading Keynesianism over, how many, sixteen universities, I think you said, but this was about the story.[5] I permit you now to tell your story, with this important background that I've just given.

Lerner: I'm very glad that you did that because it does fill in some things. On the other hand, there are still some important discrepancies. Now, of course, my memory is beginning to fade, I don't remember the meeting you talk about. And the meeting I'm talking about is one which took place earlier – before the one you are describing. This was a meeting at the Federal Reserve. It was not a dinner because I remember I was standing in back of the hall; Evsey Domar was standing on my right. I was in the middle of the back of the hall. I hadn't been invited; I happened to be in Washington by accident and somebody told me about it, so I turned up. This is a seminar at which Keynes gave a lecture, and he was very much concerned about what was going to happen after the war, when he thought people might want to save too much and then there wouldn't be enough investment coming. ...

Hansen: It was a small group of about twelve, right?

Lerner: No, there were about a hundred people there.

Hansen: We're thinking of two different things.

Lerner: It's a different meeting. There was no sitting at a table; I was standing right in the back.

Keynes was worried about there not being enough investment or – he put it in his language – too much saving. I asked why we should have to worry about that: if you give people enough money they will spend more and then there will be enough spending; there's no need for any depression if you're prepared to give them more money. So he asked where would you get the extra money and I didn't say, "the printing press". I said you could borrow it. He said, you mean the national debt will keep on growing, and I said yes. "What would happen?" I said – nothing. So we talked for a moment and he said: "No, that's humbug" – that's the word he used, humbug – "the national debt can't keep on growing." And that was again when we had the same sort of "click" I was just talking about; that was the end of his discussion. (I want to say this, when he said that, Evsey Domar, who was standing next to me, said he ought to read *The General Theory*.)

Hansen: This chap who attacked the Brookings book attacking me on the public debt got a letter from Keynes which praised him very highly for his article.

Lerner: I was told that a month later there was another meeting of the same seminar at which Keynes appeared – I was not there – and at that meeting Keynes withdrew his criticisms of me and said he thought I was right after all. And then I got a long letter from Keynes in which he told me that he read my *Economics of Control* on the boat on the way back.[6] It must have been after that he spoke to you about it in your meeting. He read this book and had some criticisms of a philosophical kind, but he said that it was a grand book. He said that when he got back he would make the heads of the Treasury read it – and then he said no, that won't do. He would make their sons read it and have their fathers promise to accept what their sons told them.

Hansen: That sounds like Keynes all right!

Is it fair to say that, in England, the Keynesian views were accepted because of their intellectual stimulus and that, in the United States, Keynesian views were accepted because a sub-

stantial proportion of American economists were on government payrolls and that these people in Washington acted as catalysts for future acceptance of Keynesianism here? In other words, if it hadn't been for so many economists working during the war in Washington, would Keynesian views have been accepted subsequently? Would the business economy, in other words, have prevented Keynesian ideas from spreading the way they had?

Lerner: I don't think that this was the reason. There are two kinds of acceptance. I think one of the important reasons for the acceptance of Keynesian thought, even by those people who call themselves anti-Keynesian now, is not so much because they were originally persuaded by Keynes's arguments. When he came and spoke to Roosevelt, Roosevelt didn't understand him. Rather, it is because the war demonstrated how an enormous increase in spending would do what Keynes said it would do; that was a demonstration. The actual application of it in the New Deal was on much too small a scale to do any good. But I think the general acceptance was due more, not to the economists in Washington, but to the economists in the universities who spread it among the people who then later became the other professors and later became economists in the government. It was the spreading of ideas and teaching of economics by Keynesian economists in the university which spread the idea far and wide.

Hansen: I agree with that.

Lerner: People often ask me, do our ideas ever get across? I'm sure Professor Hansen has the same problem. And my general answer is, yes, they work; they influence society but only when we have forgotten where they came from. People think that it is their own idea and then they follow it.

How would you explain, Professor Lerner, the fact that Keynesian ideas have been so warmly received in the Anglo-Saxon world and that there have been criticisms leveled at Keynes in Western Europe? It was hard to sell these ideas to some people who wrote roughly simultaneously to when Keynes made his contribution.

Lerner: I think it's because Western Europe economically is a backward country. I remember going to a conference in Paris long before Keynes; they were discussing the gold standard in Paris. I was there with a group of students and professors from the London School. When we listened to what they were talking about in Paris, it reminded us what we were told was debated in 1890. I think this is true, and even more true of Germany, where the war interrupted the development of thought. They're just behind, and there are very few people there who are genuine economists. It is now improving very much. They were just backward; they didn't know.

Wouldn't you say that they don't consider their economy to be as vulnerable to the pressures to which the Anglo-Saxon economies were exposed? They simply don't have the need for the Keynesian medicine and the Keynesian prescriptions?

Lerner: They may have been luckier sometimes; they had depressions too. There were very bad depressions in Germany. In Germany, for example, the Keynesian ideas were put forward before Keynes by a number of people, among them Woytinsky, the Social Democrat, who tried to persuade the Weimar government that they ought to do something about employment. But they were too strong believers in sound finance and they wouldn't do it. And it's one of the more important reasons why Hitler came to power.

Notes

1. See Joan Robinson, 'The Theory of Money and the Analysis of Output', *Reivew of Economic Studies*, October, 1933, 22–60.
2. See Robert Lekachman (ed.), *Keynes's General Theory Reports of Three Decades*, New York: St Martin's Press, 1964.
3. On 15 August 1972 President Nixon instituted a modified plan of wage and price controls.
4. See David McCord Wright, 'Moulton's *The New Philosophy of Public Debt*', *American Economic Review*, September 1943, 573–90.

5. Early in Lerner's career, Lionel Robbins wrote Keynes to ask his advice on hiring Lerner at the London School of Economics. That letter and Keynes's response, both of which Don Moggridge was kind enough to forward to us, are reprinted in an Appendix to this interview.
6. The letter is printed in the Appendix to this interview.

Appendix to Lerner–Hansen Interview

1st May 1935

Dear Keynes,

Have you had any opportunity of observing the habits and intellectual qualities of Abraham Lerner during the time that he has been resident in Cambridge? As you know, he was foolish enough to refuse the opportunity of taking the job for which you were so kind as to support him last year, and as his scholarship comes to an end in July of this year the question of his future becomes very acute. There may be vacancies at the School here, and it is pretty clear that we should have to consider him very seriously. But as you will easily realize, there are snags. He is exceedingly highly specialized in a field in which we are still very strong. He is not a British subject and we already carry a very high complement of teachers of foreign extraction. Moreover, some doubts have been raised about his general suitability as a teacher in our particular *milieu*.

I have been talking to Beveridge about this, and he agrees with me that if you have had the opportunity of seeing anything of Lerner during the last few months your judgment would be especially helpful to us.

I am so sorry to bother you about this. You were so sympathetic and helpful in the business of the Chair of statistics that I am tempted to ask for more.

Yours sincerely,

Lionel Robbins

May 2nd, 1935

Dear Robbins

I have seen a good deal of Lerner during his time in Cambridge and have much respect and affection for him. But the problem of his future is exceedingly difficult.

He is very learned and has an acute and subtle mind. But it is not easy to get him to take a broad view of a problem and he is apt to lack judgment and intuition, so that, if there is any fault in his logic, there is nothing to prevent it from leading him to preposterous conclusions.

Personally he has been extremely successful at Cambridge, getting on very well indeed with the other research students and playing quite a part in the common intellectual life. He is generally liked.

As it happens, he has very lately sent in to me a heavy article for publication in the Journal. I have declined it, but you may find it instructive to read the letter which I enclose giving my reasons why I cannot take it. (This letter is addressed to A.W. Singer, a young German refugee student with whom Lerner has made great friends, and with whom he has collaborated in this article, though I suspect it to be mainly Lerner's work.)

On the one hand, therefore, one feels that Lerner deserves every encouragement, but, on the other, that it is very difficult to make proper use of him. I should doubt his general suitability as a teacher to elementary students. Much the best use of him which could be made would be to help with research students and their dissertations, and to give advanced lectures on special problems of modern theory. If you had room for him to help the professors in handling research students (the sort of post which is now becoming very necessary), I believe he might play a valuable part. The integrity and high disinterestedness of his character make him a very admirable intellectual companion for young researchers.

In thinking over the problem of Lerner's future, I feel in my own mind that the really right solution would be to make him take up some manual craft of a kind which would not exhaust him and would leave him free to pursue his own studies in dialectic in the evenings. I should like to see Lerner as a printer's compositor, or as a cobbler, or grinder of lenses like Spinoza; – free from 5 or 6 o'clock onwards to discuss high subtleties with his friends and to pursue, like the Talmudist that he is, the curious aspects of truth which appeal to him.

Yours sincerely

JMK

Source: King's College, Cambridge, UK. Unpublished writings of J.M. Keynes copyright The Provost and Scholars of King's College, Cambridge 1996.

At sea Septr. 1944.

My dear Lerner,

Your book arrived in London whilst I was away at Bretton Woods. But now again I am on the sea for yet another visit to the U.S.A., and the sea voyage has given me an opportunity to read it.

It is a grand book worthy of one's hopes of you. A most powerful piece of well organized analysis with high aesthetic qualities, though written more perhaps than you see yourself for the cognoscenti in the temple and not for those at the gate. Anyhow *I* prefer it for intellectual enjoyment to any recent attempts in this vein. A few observations in detail for what they are worth. I wish you had not begun quite so near the beginning of things, for it delays you very long from your most original and characteristic contribution. In truth you have written two books, the first 227 pages and the rest – two books largely distinct, the first of which has but a very tenuous connection with your ostensible theme. Moreover in this part of the book you are largely re-organizing in your own setting what is already familiar, and it is only in the second book that your real stuff and proper theme begin to emerge. It is in this first part too that there is the only chapter, chapter 3, where you fall flat-footed to the level of the vulgar. The whole complication and fascination (and truth) of the ethical doctrine of organic unity passes you by, and you accept uncritically the Benthamite arithmetic which I thought had been riddled to death forty years ago. It is one more proof of the grievous deficiency in the Cambridge curriculum as it was in your days with us (won't you return some day?). For I, two generations before, had been properly brought up and had spent endless hours on all this.

In the second of the two books which you have placed within one cover, I have marked with particular satisfaction and profit three pairs of chapters – chap 20 and 21, chap 24 and 25, and chap 28 and 29. Here is the kernel of yourself. It is very original and grand stuff. I shall have to try when I get back to hold a seminar for the heads of the Treasury on Functional Finance. It will be very hard going – I think I shall ask them to let me hold a seminar of their sons instead, agreeing beforehand that, if I can convince the boys, they will take it from me that it is so!

Two points on the last two chapters-probably quite wrong since I have not persevered to think this through, but I should like to know from you what is right. P. 376 you give the critical point beyond which there is a perverse movement. Is there a simple formula for the optimum point for maximizing a favourable balance of trade? e.g. is it the point where $e_s + e_d$ is a maximum? My second point is similar. On p. 382 et seq. you give the formula for the optimum tariffs for exploitative purposes. Can you work out the optimum rate of exchange for exploitation purposes? Is it the rate at which $1/e_s - 1/e_d$ is a maximum?

On p. 387 you say that depreciation is a species of 'beggar my neighbour' game. So, of course, is appreciation. As you point out earlier, to let the exchange find its own level is the only policy which is to the general advantage. But is it not reasonable to allow any country which is suffering from balance of payments difficulties to use any of the possible devices, regarding this as the right criterion?

Yours ever,

Keynes

6. Walter S. Salant (b. 1911)

Birthplace: New York

Education:

1962:   Ph.D. Harvard

Significant publications:

Important Liberalization and Employment, Brookings Institution, 1961 (with Beatrice Vaccara).

Indonesia: Perspectives and Proposals for United States Economic Aid, Yale University Southeast Asia Studies, 1963, (with other members of U.S. Economic Survey Team to Indonesia).

The United States Balance of Payments in 1968, edited with L. Tarshis, E. Despres and A. Rivlin, Washington: Brookings Institution, 1963.

Money in the International Order, Dallas: Southern Methodist University Press, 1964 (contributor to book edited by J. Carter Murphy).

International Monetary Arrangements: The Problem of Choice, Princeton: Princeton University Press, 1964 (contributor to book edited by F. Machlup and B. Malkiel).

Maintaining and Restoring Balance in International Payments, Princeton: Princeton University Press, 1966, (contributor to book edited by W. Fellner, R. Triffin and F. Machlup).

International Reserves: Needs and Availability, New York: International Monetary Fund, 1970 (contributor).

European Monetary Unification and Its Meaning for the United States, Washington: Brookings Institution, 1973 (edited with Krause and contributor).

Worldwide Inflation: Theory and Recent Experience, Washington: Brookings Institution, 1977 (edited with Krause and contributor).

'Rationing and Price as Methods of Restricing Demand for Specific Products' in M. Boskin (ed.), New York: *Economics and Human Welfare: Essays in Honor of Tibor Scitovsky*, New York: Academic Press, 1979.

Experience:

1934–6:	Treasury Department
1938–9:	Securities and Exchange Commission
1939–40:	Department of Commerce
1940–45:	Office of Price Administration, and predecessor agencies
1945–6:	Economic Stabilization Office
1946:	Price Decontrol Board
1946–52:	Council of Economic Advisors

The interview took place at Brookings Institution in 1985. During the interview Robert Goldsmith stopped in. His comments are noted. All other comments are Salant's.

How did you become interested in economics?

My father was by nature a scholar, but by force of circumstance a businessman; and he encouraged me. He was something of an amateur economist so I had a good background in economics before I got to college. For example, I understood multiple expansion of bank deposits, which was much talked about in the late twenties.

I went to Harvard in 1929 as an undergraduate, and concentrated in economics. I graduated in 1933 so I often say that I came in with the stock market crash and came out with the bank holiday. Given the events of the time, as you can imagine, I was one of many of my classmates who was interested in economics.

What type of economics were you taught at the time? Did it explain the crash?

Not really; economics then was well described by Tibor Scitovsky when he said that it was bifurcated. Prior to the *General Theory*, there was no framework for discussing business cycles. Business cycle theory existed but it was not at all integrated with what was called "principles of economics", which consisted almost entirely of what we now know as micro, although it didn't have that name at the time. The areas covered – allocation of resources, price theory and the theory of distribution of income – contributed absolutely nothing to an explanation of the depression.

Didn't students ask?

They asked, but nobody was really able to give satisfactory answers. They didn't, however, ask what the relationship between these two separated subjects was. There was no theory of total output. In John Williams's popular course, "Money Banking and Business Cycles", we studied Robertson, Hawtrey and Keynes of the *Treatise*, but none of these had an explanation of the depression.

At Harvard did they try to use rigid wages as a reason for unemployment?

There was a book written by members of the Harvard Economics Department called *The Economics of the Recovery Program*, which is a good illustration of the conventional pre-Keynesian view of the unemployment problem. It was that there would be no problem if money wages would only decline. Schumpeter was the most famous contributor to this book.

After I graduated from Harvard, I went to Cambridge University for a year, having been fascinated by the idea of studying where Robertson, Pigou and Keynes were. I attended their Cambridge lectures. This was 1933–4, which was two years before the publication of the *General Theory*. Keynes was lecturing on what he called a Monetary Theory of Production, which became the *General Theory*, so I was in on it at an early stage and knew the general ideas of the book before it came out.

Who were the other people at Keynes's lectures?

I only remember some of my good friends. One was Lorie Tarshis, who went to the same set of lectures for three years; his lecture notes are referred to in *Keynes, Cambridge and the General Theory* (edited by Don Patinkin and Clark Leith of the University of Western Ontario). Bob Bryce was another; he attended for two years and occupied a unique position as propagator of Keynes' ideas because of a remarkable paper he wrote expounding them in early 1935, over a year and a half before the *General Theory* was published. Bryce's paper was prepared for delivery at a seminar at the London School of Economics. Although he distributed the paper in March 1935, it was never published until 1977, when it was included in the book I just mentioned. Others I remember include Alec Cairncross (now Sir Alec Cairncross) and an English economist named Stanley Dennison, who works on industrial organization problems. There were, I guess, forty to sixty people in attendance.

Keynes' theory was so attractive because it provided a theory of aggregate output. It is impossible to imagine what it was like when there wasn't any theory of output.

At Cambridge I decided I wanted to be an economist, but I also decided that I didn't know where to find a single fact. So I decided that I'd better get some acquaintance with statistical sources, and a year or two in Washington seemed to be a good way of doing that. I looked for a job in Washington when I came back, and, on the day of my arrival there, I was hired by the U.S. Treasury, which was one of many departments in Washington that was expanding its staff. I worked there for about a year and a half; then I went back to Harvard and did two years of graduate work. Bob Bryce, who served as a Keynesian emissary, was still there. He was regarded as an almost official Keynesian emissary to spread the word.

As I understand it, Harvard was really the one place where Keynesianism developed in the U.S. Was there a fight at Harvard?

There was a cleavage all right – between the junior faculty and graduate students on one side and what I then regarded as the senior faculty members on the other. (When I stop to think how old these senior members really were, it shakes me a little. Take, for example, Gottfried Haberler. We're talking about almost fifty years ago. He wasn't even forty.) Because I then considered some of the more senior people so backward I remember thinking that faculty salaries should be automatically reduced with age unless people did something to justify maintaining them.

Evidence of the split is that soon after the publication of *Economics of the Recovery Program*, a counter-book in support of New Deal policy was written in 1938 and published in 1939. It was called *An Economic Program for American Democracy* and was known as written by seven Harvard and Tufts economists. The fact is that there were eleven authors, but four did not sign because they had government jobs, or would have by the time the book was published. I was one of the four. The Tufts economist who signed was Lorie Tarshis; the other six acknowledged authors were Harvard graduate students or instructors. This book had great popularity in Washington, where it sold out. In Roosevelt's public papers, there is a story that, when his son Jimmy was away from Washington and asked, "What was the name of that book you mentioned that I should read?", FDR wired back the name of that book.

After going back to Harvard, I did graduate work for two years (1936–8). My second year was also the first year of the Littauer School and the first year that Alvin Hansen was at Harvard. It was an exciting period because you had an open and intellectually honest atmosphere. For example, when Hansen came in September 1937, he was not a Keynesian. In fact, he had written an adverse review of the *General Theory*. He switched upon coming to Harvard and he was the only senior member of the faculty who was sympathetic with the *General Theory*. He ran a seminar jointly with John Williams on fiscal policy at the new Littauer School of Public Administration.

Keynesians had their own problems at that time. The recession that started in 1937 was intellectually very upsetting to the Keynesians. The decline in industrial production from 1937 to the first quarter of 1938 was as steep as any we have ever had. The Fed's index of industrial production went down some 30 per cent in five months.

I left Harvard in 1938 and returned to Washington. Raymond Goldsmith was at the S.E.C., where he was in charge of economic research. He was working on a new method of estimating annual individual saving by estimating net increases in assets and liabilities of individuals, and I was his research assistant.[1] I next went to the Department of Commerce. Harry Hopkins, the Secretary of Commerce, was pretty ill but had asked Willard Thorp to organize a group of economists for the Office of the Secretary. A little group called the Division of Industrial Economics was formed under Richard Gilbert, a brilliant, although non-writing, economist. I had known Gilbert before; he had taken over John Williams's course at Harvard when Williams had gone to Geneva; he was teaching at Radcliffe and Tufts also. I worked with him during the war until April 1945, when I became economic advisor in the Office of the Director of Economic Stabilization. Dick Gilbert was the O.P.A.'s broad policy man; he was not concerned with operations. Ken Galbraith was director of price operations.

Were the economists working in Washington at the time generally Keynesians?

I guess the leading people who subscribed to the theory that is labeled Keynesian (I put it that way for reasons that will become clear in a minute) included Lauchlin Currie, first at the Fed and then the White House; Mordecai Ezekiel of the Department of Agriculture; Richard Gilbert, Harry White, Gerhard Colm, Alan Sweezy, Leon Henderson, Isador Lubin and just shortly before World War II, Emile Despres. Most of them had ties to Harvard. Lauchlin Currie was the section head in Williams's course at Harvard that I mentioned earlier. He had come to Washington as the assistant director of research at the Federal Reserve Board. Although Goldenweiser had a firm grip on the directorship of the

Research and Statistics Division, Currie was really the chief personal advisor of Eccles.

Currie was a highly original economist. During the McCarthy period aspersions were cast on his loyalty and he went down to Colombia, where he has been ever since. I'm not sure when he first read *The General Theory*. He seems to have developed similar ideas by himself. That's the reason I referred earlier to people "labeled Keynesians". I think he figured it out for himself, but I'm not sure. I was at the O.P.A. from the time price control was introduced until near the end.

Do you consider O.P.A. as much of a success as Galbraith does?

Yes, I think so.

At the time were people thinking of inflation?

Yes, the government did as soon as the war began or was seen to be inevitable. They felt that the public needed to be educated to things they are not fully educated to, even now, but that are commonly known in the profession, namely that excess demand is not the only cause of inflation. Some prices go up because other prices have gone up.

Was there any concept of what full employment was?

Even in the early 1940s there was recognition that a change in the composition of demand will cause inflation. The government economists were way ahead of academic people at the time. That's an unwritten part of history, I guess. At an early stage I wrote a piece called "The Strategy of Price Control under the Defense Program". An analysis of a model of a price-controlled economy came to my attention in a paper by Jacques Polak. (He was Eddie Bernstein's successor as the Director of the Research Department and Economic Advisor of the International Monetary Fund until he retired in 1979 or 1980 when his country, The Netherlands, and several others elected him their Executive Director of the Fund.) He showed me that paper in 1942; it worked out the consequences for the price level in a model in which prices were all determined by cost plus markup; excess demand had nothing to do with it. Our ideas about price control in O.P.A. were based on the assumptions that such a model described a large part of the actual economy. You can have the price level rising for that reason as long as demand isn't so restrictive as to prevent it, but without any substantial excess demand. Polak's article was great; Seymour Harris, editor of *The Review of Economics and Statistics*, published it in 1945. It is still a superb article.

I worked in O.P.A. until Fred Vinson was replaced as Economic Stabilization Director by William H. Davis, who had been chairman of the War Labor Board and who had a justifiably great reputation as a labor mediator. (That was in April 1945.) I was asked to become his economic adviser. The Office of Economic Stabilization was a small agency of ten to fifteen people, which sat on top of the Office of Price Administration, the War Labor Board and the War Production Board. Its duties were mainly to coordinate wage and price stabilization, which were the direct responsibility of the first two of those agencies. That's where I remained, until after Truman moved that agency's functions into the Office of War Mobilization and Reconversion, displacing Davis and appointing Judge J. Caskie Collet in his place. In June 1946, by which time Bowles had become Stabilization Administrator, there was a big fight in Congress over renewal of the price control legislation, which kept coming up for renewal every June 30th. At this point the war was over and there was such a fight over extension of the legislation that Congress couldn't agree over whether some sectors of the economy should be exempted from the control. They delegated the decision about those sectors to a new agency created by the Act mainly to perform decontrol functions, called the Price Decontrol Board, and I became the economic advisor to that Board.

Just before the 1946 election, Truman took all the price controls off. I was then invited to join the Council of Economic Advisers, which was just being organized. I went over there in 1946 as the senior staff member responsible for international economics and that's where I remained until 1952.

*World War II is taken as the event that convinced most econo-
mists that Keynesian economics worked. There were also wage
and price controls, but after the war almost all economists seemed
to agree that they had to come off. Did anyone interpret the
experience as implying that Keynesian economics only worked
because the expansion was accompanied by controls?*

I can't recall that anyone said that you wouldn't have gotten high
employment and high output without the controls, but I think
everyone acknowledged that price controls were important in
holding the price level down.

Ken Galbraith may have said the controls were needed to
obtain high output and employment in his book, *A Theory of
Price Control*, but I can't remember now. I had a private reaction
when I read it: Ken finally has absorbed what we were trying to
teach him all those years since Richard Gilbert had been pushing
all those ideas. But after the war I found that Ken had written up
some of the same ideas independently in an article. I think the
article is excellent and the book, too, is right on nearly all important points.

Gerhard Colm is the only person I can remember – apart from
the laymen who always worried about inflation when the budget
had a one-dollar deficit – who, as early as the first few post-war
years, really worried about inflation and whether you need price
controls under normal peacetime conditions. He worried about
that a lot. Richard Gilbert had left Washington by that time; he
could well have had the same view.

*[At this point Raymond Goldsmith phoned to say that he was
stopping in to visit.]*

*Tell me about Brookings at the time. How conservative was it
then?*

Brookings used to have seminars, which included mostly conservative types. That's where I met Raymond Goldsmith, who
just phoned to say he was coming up, and he could tell you about
Brookings in those days better than I could. Moulton was the first
President of Brookings and he was here until 1953. He ruled the

place with an iron hand. This was the time when Brookings was particularly famous for four books which came out during the 1930s: *America's Capacity to Produce, America's Capacity to Consume*, and – I can't remember the titles of the other two. These books were not terribly sophisticated or pioneering; they were for the interested layman. Moulton was very conservative and because he was dictatorial the outlook of the whole place was conservative. *The New Philosophy of the Public Debt* was just one example.

In an interview Alvin Hansen said that he was intending to write a reply to The New Philosophy of the Public Debt *but that a conservative student had written such a good reply that he didn't need to.*

It was a very big thing for Alvin Hansen to come out and say that the debt doesn't matter.

Would you say that the debt was the issue that differentiated people in Washington?

It was part of the whole spending issue. I don't know whether the debt aspect was more conspicuous than the deficit. (I'm thinking of the stock versus flow question.)

How about Ken Galbraith's book?

He was one of the several original deputy administrators under Leon Henderson in the Office of Price Administration, the one responsible for price control. He wasn't in that position for most of the war; he was in it only for a year and a half. As a matter of fact, Galbraith left shortly after Leon Henderson left. The idea that he had more experience with price control than anyone else is certainly questionable. I can name three other people who had much more experience. For example, Gardner Ackley, Griffith Johnson and the late Harold Leventhal, all of whom had experience with it during the Korean War as well. Gardner was very young – in his mid-twenties during the war. But Ken had greater responsibility for it during the short time he held that office than any of these three did. Galbraith had written what he referred to in his autobiography as a design for price control and he stated that it was one of the reasons he was appointed. I was not aware of that article when in 1941 I wrote something called "The Strategy of Price Control under the Defense Program" of which I've been able to find only one copy. It was published by O.P.A.

[At this point Goldsmith enters the room.]

What was your relationship to Abba Lerner?

Goldsmith: I met Abba Lerner in 1933; I was a graduate student at the London School of Economics and he was there for the second or third year; he was winning all the prizes. He ran around in sandals and open shirts but nobody doubted that he had an extraordinary mind. He was older than the other students; before he entered L.S.E. he had been a printer and had failed. In his attempt to find out why such things happened he went to school. He was married at the time and had two children. He was also on the first board of the *Review of Economic Studies* which was founded in 1933 by a group of graduate students primarily at L.S.E. Ursula Hicks was one of them; I was the first treasurer the first year I was there. Lerner was recognized as a coming man and history has borne it out.

A lot of Keynesians had written that they expected that inflation would no longer be a problem – that World War II was a perfect demonstration of Keynesian economics. During that time there were wage and price controls; was there a feeling at all that the only reason Keynesian policies succeeded was that the price controls existed?

Goldsmith: I think it was a combination; there was a large degree of underutilization at the beginning of the war which permitted expansionary policy to work for a while without extending controls. However, you couldn't have carried it beyond 1941 or 1942 without controls. That was halfway toward Keynes's basic views but halfway toward the suggestion that you couldn't do such a thing without controls. You figured that, in the normal business cycle, there would be such a rapid expansion that it would be necessary to have controls. It was conclusive in the first sense that when output is extraordinarily low you can have an expansion of demand without inflation.

Was there any concern that the average level of unemployment that could be maintained over the cycle was much higher than what the political structure had in mind? I know there were debates in 1945 about the employment bill.

Goldsmith: One thing that I was pretty positive about (I used to work at the planning committee of the War Production Board at that time) was that everybody expected that there would be a great slump after the war. There was a man named Fred Cone, who later worked for many years in the Department of Commerce; he was on the Planning Committee and he dissented; he said no, there wouldn't be any slump. I regret to say that the majority held the otherview and the reports of the Planning Committee were based on the assumption that you would get a slump unless the government took action. As it turned out, Cone was right.

Salant: At the war's end when everyone was thinking that way, Vit Bassie was also disagreeing.

Goldsmith: Yes, that's right, and he is still around. (He's now retired, but he had worked closely with Lauchlin Currie at the Federal Reserve Board.)

Note

1.   An official series was subsequently developed and published by the S.E.C. The original estimates are published in Volume Three of *Studies in Income and Wealth*, published by the National Bureau's Conference on Research in Income and Wealth. These measurements are now done quarterly. They have been taken over by the Department of Commerce.

7. John Kenneth Galbraith (b. 1908)

Birthplace: Ontario, Canada

Education:

1931: B.S. University of Toronto
1934: Ph.D. University of California, Berkeley

Significant publications:

Modern Competition and Business Policy, Oxford: Oxford University Press, 1938.

A Theory of Price Control, Cambridge, Mass.: Harvard University Press, 1952.

American Capitalism: The Concept of Countervailing Power, Boston: Houghton Mifflin, 1952; 3rd edn 1962.

The Great Crash 1929, Boston: Houghton Mifflin, 1954; 3rd. edn 1972; Penguin, 1961.

The Affluent Society, Boston: Houghton Mifflin, 1958; 3rd edn 1976; Penguin, 1962.

Economic Development, Cambridge, Mass.: Harvard University Press, 1962.

The New Industrial State, Boston: Houghton Mifflin, 1967; 3rd edn 1978; Penguin, 1969.

Economics and the Public Purpose, Boston: Houghton Mifflin, 1973; Penguin, 1975.

Almost Everyone's Guide to Economics, Boston: Houghton Mifflin, 1978 (with N. Salinger).

The Anatomy of Poverty, Boston: Houghton Mifflin, 1983.

Significant honors and awards:

1946: Presidential Medal of Freedom

1972:   President of the American Economic Association

Experience:

1936:	Harvard University
1937:	Cambridge University
1938–41:	Harvard University and Princeton University
1941–3:	Office of Price Administration
1943–9:	US Strategic Bombing Survey, Fortune magazine
1949– :	Harvard University
1961–3:	Ambassador to India

The interview took place in August 1986 at John Kenneth Galbraith's summer home in Newfane, Vermont.

When did you become interested in economics?

I started college in the fall of 1926, but I didn't have any thoughts on economic matters until some time in the early 1930s. I was an undergraduate for five years because I had to make up some high school deficiencies. Along about 1930, the crunch came in Canada. I was studying agriculture, and the thought occurred to me that there was very little purpose in achieving more efficient production of crops and livestock if they couldn't be sold for a fair price. So I shifted my attention to agricultural economics, which at the time was a very primitive, neglected, subject at the Agricultural College of Ontario. I confess I didn't learn very much that satisfied me.

Do you remember anything about what they taught you about why the Depression occurred?

My memory doesn't go beyond the impression that it was inexplicable – an act of God, modified possibly by sunspots. It wasn't until I went to the University of California at Berkeley in 1931 that I began serious study. Berkeley was much more eclectic. The mainstream of the Berkeley department, both in economics and agricultural economics, held that the Depression was an exceptionally severe manifestation of business cycles, which would correct itself in time; and the department certainly believed that what would now be called modern macroeconomic steps would be unsound. You certainly didn't deliberately unbalance the budget as an act of fiscal policy – that was out of the question. There was some debate on whether it made sense to reduce interest rates. Otherwise the mainstream attitude, reflected by people like Carl E. Plehn, who was the dominant figure in the department at that time, was negative as regards any activist policy.

Outside the mainstream, there was a younger, more alert and aggressive group of teachers – one was Leo Rogin – who introduced us to a range of thought, including some of the very early expressions of Keynes, long before *The General Theory* was published. Thorstein Veblen, who had died a couple of years before in Palo Alto, was also still influential in the Berkeley community at that time. This view was that depressions were inherent in the business system, that there was a repressive business hold on production that offset the natural productive tendencies of the engineers. Veblen's views were broadly expressed in *The Theory of Business Enterprise* and *Engineers and the Price System*. We read these with great attention.

A third current of thought was well expressed in Robert Brady's work. It held that big business and the liberal tendencies of the corporation were responsible for the Depression. In terms of policy this view called for – vaguely speaking – enforcement of the antitrust laws and the restructuring of the business corporation.

Finally, there was a strong student commitment to the belief that the system was basically at fault and that only radical – very revolutionary – changes could improve the situation. This was essentially under the influence of Marx, although I've always had some doubt as to how much Marx was actually read. Quite possibly he was more discussed than read at the time.

So all of those currents were in competition at Berkeley. I was not strongly committed to any one of them. I was in the Giannini Foundation of Agricultural Economics, a little outside the mainstream, to some extent a bystander – a very much interested bystander. I involved myself with the particular problems of agriculture. So far as I had an interest in policy it was not in macroeconomic policy but in what might be done to restore agricultural prices and control agricultural production.

I suppose to the extent that I was influenced by anybody, it was by Veblen. Not in terms of specific recommendations but by his general attitude of suspicion of orthodox doctrine and by the notion that orthodoxy, to a substantial extent, is in the service of economic interests.

At Berkeley in the 1930s there was a large and active graduate body and a great reluctance to take one's Ph.D. because then one was unemployed. Better be doing some teaching or working on a thesis. I taught at Davis the beginning course in economics, the basic course in agricultural economics, and a course in farm accounting, and I was the full staff of all those departments. Then, in 1933, the emergency agencies opened up in Washington, particularly the Agricultural Adjustment Administration, but also the National Recovery Act and the relief agencies. All of them had to have economists. There was a rush to turn in long-delayed Ph.D. theses and a further rush to Washington – a reverse gold rush. Or to local branches of the new Federal agencies. I was a part of this reverse gold rush.

In 1934 I took my Ph.D. and went to Washington to work at the Department of Agriculture, where I stayed for the summer and all the following year. At that time the Department was the very heart of the economic discussion. No other part of the New Deal could boast of anything like the intensity of economic and political debate. Unfortunately the people who were engaged in that discussion were at a level above me – Rexford Tugwell, Henry Wallace, Jerome Frank and Adlai Stevenson. I either didn't know them, or saw very little of them. I was assigned responsibility of seeing what could be done with all the tax-reverted land in the country. I traveled around to Michigan and New York, talking to people who had ideas of how the Federal government might be the recipient of all this land that had reverted for tax purposes. If I had had my way, there would have been an enormous increase in the public domain from taking over the land. Among the people who shelved it was Rex Tugwell himself.

How did you, an agricultural economist, come to get an offer from Harvard?

At that time there was a chair at Harvard that was given to agricultural matters, held by John D. Black. He, in turn, had an assistant but his then-assistant received a Social Science Research Fellowship in 1934/35 and Black needed a replacement. I was recommended. I also taught in the beginning economics course.

Do you remember what text you taught from at Harvard?

At Harvard there was never any question. One used Taussig's *Principles of Economics.*

At that time, were Keynesian thoughts being discussed at Harvard?

No. The nearest that one came was in John H. Williams's Money and Banking course. To everybody's surprise and slight shock, he repeatedly said there was something in the work of Foster and Catchings and that it could not be dismissed. This precipitated a certain discussion of Foster and Catchings and made respectable what would otherwise at Harvard have been considered an outrageous aberration – slightly respectable, but not fully so.

There was one other development before I got there. Lauchlin Currie had written *The Supply and Control of Money*, which had Keynesian overtones. At least, it was an activist economic tract. It was considered suspect, radical – not so much radical perhaps as irresponsible – and it probably was one of the reasons that Currie was not taken on to the Harvard faculty. Instead he went to the Federal Reserve and, in company with Mariner Eccles, became one of the two leading Keynesian intruders upon Washington. Currie's book was a matter for some comment when I went to Harvard. There was no faculty discussion of Keynes at that time, and very little student discussion.

Do you remember the first time you heard about The General Theory *being written?*

I don't know that I heard about it before it was written. I have no recollection that I did. One of the reasons that I didn't hear about it was that I was working on my own explanation of the Depression. Why we had this enduring misery: it was the great transcendent fact of one's life.

I was attracted by the notion that the problem lay in the nature of the price structure, that we had moved from competition to a structure of rigid, restrictive prices with competitive energies going into things like advertising. In this view I was somewhat influenced by Ed Chamberlin and his *The Theory of Monopolistic Competition* and Joan Robinson's *The Economics of Imperfect Competition*. I developed a theory of unemployment and aggregate performance, based on the idea of an imperfect market structure and what should be done about it. I wrote a long paper on this which attracted attention during the summer of 1935/36, about the same time that Keynes's *General Theory* came out. I had a temporary assignment to work with a group of New England businessmen who were convinced that something had to be done about unemployment and had broken with the ranks of the conservative business apparatus and were supporting Roosevelt.

The leader of the group was Henry Dennison of the Dennison Manufacturing Company. Dennison was an instinctive Keynesian, who had the view that all flows of income were on the way to saving, which didn't get spent, or on the way to consumption, which did get spent, and that one could do something for unemployment by taxing savings and releasing consumer expenditure. I came up with the notion that the problem was in the price structure, and persuaded Dennison sufficiently so that the two us wrote a book, which I've always recommended that people not read (I don't know that I have a copy of it left). It was called *Modern Competition and Business Policy*, published by the Oxford University Press, which must have been hard up for material at the time.

While that book was going through final revisions I read *The General Theory*. The terrible thought developed in my mind that I had been wrong in persuading Dennison as I did, that he was instinctively right, and I told him so. I got the disconcerting answer that, "Indeed, I always thought that among economists Keynes made more sense than most." Unfortunately, the book had gone so far it couldn't be stopped,. It was well received by some of the orthodox of the profession.

I then wrote another book for the three businessmen of this same group. It was called *Toward Full Employment*, and it embraced Keynesian ideas to a much larger measure. One of the businessmen was Ralph Flanders, who was later Senator from Vermont; one was Lincoln Filene of Filene's in Boston; and the third was a manufacturer from Philadelphia, a good Quaker, Morris Leeds. I put together their ideas with, as I say, a heavy Keynesian overtone. My name doesn't appear on the title page. It had no effect. But that was the process by which I became attracted to Keynesian ideas.

Enthusiasm for *The General Theory* at Harvard was prompt and very great. Copies of the book were actually shipped over from England before it came out in the United States. We younger economists were, as I've said, all looking for an escape from the commanding horror of the times. We were comfortable, and we believed others should be too.

Robert Bryce played an important role in bringing Keynesian ideas to Harvard. He came for the academic year of either 1935/36 or 1936/37, fresh from Keynes's seminars and willing to resolve all of the ambiguities of *The General Theory*, of which there were many. Joseph Schumpeter once said in a half serious manner, perhaps more in amusement than anything else – he wasn't capable of anger – that at Harvard, "Keynes was Allah and Bryce was his Prophet." But Schumpeter, while he didn't like Keynes and deplored Keynesian economics, also could not disassociate himself in the discussion as some of the others did. The younger people, many of whom had been moving to the left, moving toward Marx, found Keynes a very agreeable alternative to the protection of a system which, as I've noted, we all, personally, enjoyed.

Alvin Hansen came on the faculty a year or so later, in one of Harvard's more unexpected steps. He had achieved his reputation as an exponent of liberal trade and what we now would call neoclassical economics. He had co-authored an impeccably liberal orthodox book, sympathetic to needed government intervention but basically a mainstream volume. Hansen had had a dispute with Keynes over a set of equations in *A Treatise on Money*, Keynes's set of equations, and had corrected them – Keynes had admitted the correction. Hansen's first review of *The General Theory* was far from favorable. But in the process of reviewing it and defending it he had, like others (myself included), the same tendency to move to acceptance. Presently his seminar was the official, as distinct from the unofficial, center of Keynesian discussion.

There were lots of unofficial centers. Two or three of us ran a seminar in the evenings on Keynes. By the autumn of 1936 the Tricentennial Celebration, the 300th anniversary of the University, was in prospect and, in a tolerant mood, the professors in the government department asked the young government teachers for their suggestions as to honorary degrees. They considered the names that would be most embarrassing and came up with Leon Trotsky. We were similarly asked, and came up with the name that we thought would be most embarrassing, which was John Maynard Keynes. Both names were righteously rejected; instead in economics they honored Dennis Robertson, a critic of Keynes, who would not now be thought to rank with the master.

In 1937 I received a Social Science Research Fellowship to study abroad. It would have been eccentric to go any place but Cambridge, where I stayed through 1938. My time there was fascinating. That was the year that Keynes had his first heart attack, so he didn't show up at the University at all that year. The Keynes seminar was not held, but that didn't make much difference because R.F. Kahn, Joan Robinson, Michal Kalecki and Piero Sraffa were all there. We met in the afternoons in the Marshall Library and held a discussion, almost always on Keynes. The intensity of this discussion with my contemporaries was the reward of that year. I can't think that there were many ideas of Keynes that weren't discussed at length at one time or another. All the ambiguities of *The General Theory* were also resolved.

When I finished my year there, I came back to Harvard and then in 1938/39 went to Princeton. Princeton was an unsatisfactory place at that particular time for economists of my generation. There was, first, the fact that the war was coming – and had come in Europe. This made study anywhere difficult. Second, at Princeton I felt that I was living in an academic backwater. Harvard, by this time, had very close associations with Washington and in 1938/39 you could have held a Harvard faculty meeting on the Federal Express going from Boston to the capital. There was nothing like that at Princeton. Most of all, Keynes had never come to Princeton. There were open-minded figures, like Frank Graham and Ray Whittlesey, but they hadn't embraced Keynes. For others, Adam Smith was still a mentor figure.

In the spring of 1940, I was asked to go out to Chicago and organize a research department for the Farm Bureau Federation, which I did. Then after the fall of France things began to look serious in Washington, and an Office of Price Control was organized under Leon Henderson. Henderson's reputation at the time was that of one of the old New Deal trust-busting types. The New Deal always was split between those who thought that a restoration of competitive markets would be the salvation (going back to my earlier position) and the Keynesians. Lauchlin Currie called me from Washington to say they had to have a Keynesian with Henderson. I got the train the next night. Initially, there wasn't much to do on price stabilization, and I worked for much of the rest of that year (commuting back to Chicago at times) on some matters having to do with plant location. This work was very interesting and very important. We had a plan, more than a little successful, for getting the defense plants out of the Northeast and into the South and West. Then, in the spring of 1941, I went back to Henderson and was put in charge of price control.

Was the theory of price control a Keynesian idea or was it a general economists' idea?

There is always the danger of exaggerating one's particular role. I think it is probably fair to say, though, that I was more a source of the ruling ideas there than anybody else. It would perhaps have been agreed at the time. I wrote a paper in late 1940/early 1941, setting out the basic changes for price stabilization. At or approaching full employment you stabilized the economy by controlling the flow of aggregate demand. And you identified and acted on shortage areas with price control and perhaps rationing. I wasn't this precise but such was the general scheme. The paper had a large and interested reception in Washington. It probably led to my appointment to head price control operations.

I was basically responsible for guiding the operation from the spring of 1941 to the summer of 1943. Unfortunately, when I took charge, I discovered that picking out and acting on the individual areas of shortage and price inflation was not practical. Indeed it was administratively impossible. So that plan was set aside. Instead, we placed a ceiling over all prices, and then released or adjusted those that were too low under price regulation.

My design was the right one; however, my political management of the situation, particularly my relations with Congress, was less than perfect. The only real applause I had from the Congress was when I left in 1943.

In 1951 you wrote A Theory of Price Control. *As you reflect back, would price control have been needed at full employment if Keynesian economics was valid?*

This was the beginning of something which I have argued and I have since argued. One must not separate macroeconomic and microeconomic effects. In the absence of price control and wage restraint, there would have been a microeconomic dynamic that would have been disastrous even though one had managed to have some kind of an equilibrium, some kind of macroeconomic equilibrium of full employment.

Going back to 1937, the inflation of 1937, how did Keynesian economists explain the inflation that occurred in 1937, and then the recession again?

Well, there was no real inflation. The movement of prices was to some extent a recovery from the extreme deflationary pressure of those years. The signal feature of that time was the paranoia about inflation. In World War I prices about doubled, and this left a grave fear of inflation in the minds of the older generation of economists and businessmen. They believed that if somehow inflation became ingrained in the system it couldn't be ameliorated or stopped. This attitude was responsible for the restrictive steps that had already been taken in 1936 and 1937. When the economy was expanding you had the fully unjustified fear that there was going to be some great inflationary surge.

As you look back, what was the thinking of the business writers of the time? Were they influenced much by Keynes? Were they Keynesians?

When I left the Office of Price Administration in 1943 I went to *Fortune* magazine, and the first piece I did was on the establishment of the National Accounts system. No history of Keynesian economics should ever be written without giving nearly equal credit to the scholars who took Keynes out of the realm of theory and into the real world. The numbers in the National Accounts made it impossible for the practical man to deny the validity of Keynesian thinking. In this article I set up a model, it would now be called, of the economy for the post-war years, showing what would be required in production, investment, wage income and so forth – the whole Gross National Product and National Income – and it showed very cautiously that a deficit would be required to maintain full employment.

The January 1944 issue of *Fortune* was just about going to press when this manuscript came along. It was halted; the lead article was torn out, and this article was put in and featured on the cover.

Was that at Fortune *or was that more in general? I guess I've heard a lot of stories about Alvin Hansen going around, and any time he mentioned "deficit", he almost got thrown out. This seems to contradict your story.*

Fortune at that time was way ahead of the crowd, there's no question. Harry Luce had had the idea in the 1930s that it was far better to have a readable journal published by liberals and socialists who could write, than a nonliberal one published by less literate conservatives. He had brought in a whole range of people – Archibald MacLeish, Dwight MacDonald, James Agee – and put them to work on business stories, sometimes with disastrous effect. There was an open mind there that caused me to be taken on.

I do think you are right – and it's an important point – that the wave of business opinion, the respectable corporate opinion and the establishment, was still strongly anti-Keynesian. So too was the establishment position in the academic world, but that was a diminishing sector of that world. The Keynesian community was year by year getting a much larger foothold. In the department of economics at Harvard, by 1948 the Keynesian structure was accepted with few exceptions. On the other hand, there was a very adverse reaction from Harvard graduates. The Veritas Foundation was organized to oppose Keynesian economics. And the Board of Overseers held my appointment up for a year partly because I was thought to be too Keynesian.

Who called you too Keynesian?

The Veritas Foundation. There were also other factors holding up my appointment. I had had a terrific row with the Air Force over a report of the U.S. Strategic Bombing Survey, which demonstrated beyond the shadow of a doubt that the Air Force had greatly overclaimed what it had accomplished in World War II. That report struck at the very heart of the establishment. But my Keynesian reputation was a primary factor. There was, to repeat, a split between the academic community where Keynes was acceptable and the larger business establishment. This split, I think, partly disappeared with the Eisenhower Administration, which in a backhanded way accepted the overall management of the economy.

When did you see Keynes?

I first met Keynes in the summer of 1941 after I'd been put in charge of price control, and I was still deep in the job of getting the basic organization established. On a really hectic day my secretary came in and said, "There's a Mr Kines who would like to see you." I told her I couldn't see him, but she responded, "He gave me the impression that he expects to see you – and asked if you had received this." She then handed me a paper; it was by John Maynard Keynes on the pricing of hogs. The title is vague in my memory, but it was something like "The Pig/Pig-Fodder Relationship". Keynes had a pig farm in the south of England, as you know. That was my first encounter with Keynes. It was the Holy Father dropping in on the parish priest!

Keynes was quite frequently in Washington during the war on some negotiating mission. Anybody who's had experience with diplomatic negotiating matters knows that it's an exercise in idleness. You're waiting for instructions from your government, you're waiting for the others to be instructed; you're waiting for a meeting. Keynes filled in those times by moving into the American government. By this time there was a sizable group of younger people, of whom I was one, who were devoted to his ideas – a much larger group, as he has said, in Washington than he had in London. His vanity was not above being touched by this effect, so he brought around him a group of younger Washington people for discussion of wartime policy, and I was naturally in that group. The person who saw most of him, and with whom he communicated most, was Walter Salant. I was less involved, because I was much more actively engaged in creating the whole price control operation. I started with seven or eight people, something like that (including the rationing and rent control staff) and finished with around seventeen thousand.

8.   Paul Anthony Samuelson (b. 1915)

Birthplace: Gary, Indiana

Education:

1935:   A.B. University of Chicago
1941:   Ph.D. Harvard

Significant publications:

'A Note on the Pure Theory of Consumers' Behavior', *Economica*, Feb. 1938.

'Interactions Between the Multiplier Analysis and the Principle of Acceleration', *Review of Economics and Statistics*, May 1939.

Foundations of Economic Analysis, Cambridge, Mass.: Harvard University Press, 1947; 2nd edn 1982.

'International Trade and the Equalisation of Factor Prices', *Economic Journal*, June 1948.

Economics, an Introductory Analysis, New York: McGraw-Hill, 1948; 12th edn 1985.

'The Pure Theory of Public Expenditure', *Review of Economics and Statistics*, November 1954.

Linear Programming and Economic Activity, New York: McGraw-Hill, 1958.

The Collected Scientific Papers of Paul A. Samuelson, vols I–V (various editors).

Significant honors:

1941:   David A. Wells Award (best thesis, Harvard University)
1947:   John Bates Clark Award

1953:   President, Econometric Society
1961:   President, American Economic Association
1965–8:   President, International Economic Association
1970:   Albert Einstein Medal
1970:   Nobel Prize in Economics

Experience:

1940– :   Massachusetts Institute of Technology

The interview was conducted in Samuelson's office at MIT in August 1986

I was born in Gary, Indiana. My father was a pharmacist. My family was lower middle class, made up of upwardly mobile immigrants who had prospered considerably in World War I because Gary was a brand new steel town when my family went there. By the 1920s, however, already my father was engaged in losing a good deal of his net worth, so I was a premature sufferer from the Great Depression. When I was eight-and-a-half we moved to the Chicago region; and later I spent a couple of years in grade school in Florida. Then I went to Hyde Park High School in Chicago. One thing I remember about high school is the stock market boom. I remember helping my freshman algebra teacher pick out her stocks: Hupp Motors and some other losers. My Aunt Sophie was caught in the last of the new issues of the boom, the Ford Limited issue of Canada.

Just before I graduated from high school – in the middle of the year – I went on to the University of Chicago. I started at the University January 2, 8 a.m., 1932, when I attended a lecture by the sociologist, Louis Wirth, on Malthus. Before that lecture I knew nothing of economics, even though we had the *Harvard Classics* in our home, that five-foot shelf has *The Wealth of Nations* in it, but it would never have occurred to me to pick up *The Wealth of Nations*. Except for a Virgil poem and one boring look into *Two Years Before the Mast*, that opportunity for culture was completely wasted on me. Because I became a Freshman in the middle of the year, I missed the new economics part of the compulsory Social Science Survey course, which Harry Gideonse, as colonel in charge of the staff, had lectured on and assigned readings in. As it turned out this was very fortunate, because I was put in an old-fashioned elementary economics course taught by Aaron Director that was being phased out and had all upperclassmen in it. My first textbook at Chicago, which was also Jim Tobin's first textbook at Harvard, was Sumner Slichter's *Modern Economic Society*. It was kind of an Institutionalist textbook, and was pretty good – very full of the data of the 1920s. (His publisher begged him to keep it up to date, but he wasn't hungry and he let it go. Because it had been in date, it went out of date – most textbooks were never in date and so don't get out of date.)

I had a very strong grounding at the University of Chicago, where I took a record number of economics courses and did well in pre-Keynesian economics. My second teacher, under the quarter system, was Lloyd Mints, who used Ely's *Outline of Economics* – I think maybe the 7th edition – the theoretical parts of which were written by Allyn Young. I also took Statistics and Labor Problems from Aaron Director, and labor again from Paul Douglas. Henry Simons was very influential at Chicago. I took Public Finance from him. I knew Simons quite well, and talked to him a lot, so I knew about his 100 per cent money proposal and about his positive program for laissez-faire.

During this time (and this is what is not sufficiently in the record), there was a lot of dissatisfaction, even among orthodox economists, with the simple notion, "Let prices fall enough and there will be equilibrium." Simons already had the notion: what good does it do to have open market operations when short-term interest rates are already infinitesimal? Short-term bonds, Treasury bills, are then very close substitutes for money. What's the advantage of issuing new money and retiring an equivalent amount of a close money substitute when the efficacy of monetary policy per unit is very low? You begin to see here liquidity trap notions of later date.

Although the term "macroeconomics" had not yet come into use, we had a kind of macroeconomics before 1936. It was mostly taught in Business Cycles and Money and Banking courses. There wasn't very much relationship between the Business Cycles courses and the Value Theory that Jacob Viner and Frank Knight taught at the University of Chicago. There was a kind of schizophrenia. In the Business Cycles courses, people were very sensible; they talked about unemployment, and increases and decreases in unemployment. But when you studied Walras or a rigorous course in Value Theory, markets cleared and there was no unemployment. It wasn't that Say's Law was invoked – it wasn't necessary, because by definition of a market clearing system there was no unemployment problem. (People didn't worry about the niceties of existence and uniqueness; in those days they were taken for granted.) This was being taught while in South Chicago, not all that far from the University of Chicago, everything was closed down most of the time. In the early years of the Depression, you could have bought *anything* merely by assuming the mortgage.

Frank Knight wrote some polemics against Slichter's textbook in *The Journal of Political Economy* in the early 1930s. He smelled some kind of heresy in Slichter. But Knight's discussion was methodological. He argued that old Slichter was a do-gooder who thought he could change human nature, and that governments can do some good. Hardened, experienced people, by contrast, know that people are cussed. I think there's a lot of merit in Knight, but a lot of demerit, too. Whether his total effect on me was more bad than good I'm not sure. But from 1932 to 1936 I was besotted on Frank Knight.

It's not true, I'll say categorically, what Milton Friedman at one time tried to sell: that there was a very subtle Chicago oral tradition on the demand for money and monetary theory. Read Robertson's handbook on *Money*, and you will have plumbed the depths of Chicago's monetary sophistication.

I left Chicago in 1935.

How did your teachers explain the Depression?

Well, I got the impression from Aaron Director and Henry Simons and maybe Lloyd Mints that it was the tariff. The Smoot–Hawley

Tariff had been a bad thing. We were also taught the ups and downs of the money supply and the banking system, the Phillips multiplier, expansion of bank credit. During my time at Chicago I was a believer. Just to give you an example of how brainwashed I was by my Jesuitical training, I found it incomprehensible that Jacob Viner, who'd been away when I first came to Chicago, refused to sign a petition in favor of 100 per cent money. By 1934 I thought that, if only we had 100 per cent money, then no leverage between bank reserves and total money would ever be variable because one is a constant number, and if you didn't have variability in the money supply you wouldn't have the ups and downs of the dollar.

I think Frank Knight himself, by the time the Great Depression had dragged on for a long time, remained with the conclusion that in all ordinary times it's only frictions that cause depressions, and sometimes you get a double whammy or a triple whammy. If you read *The Economics of the Recovery Program* (it's a terrible book) by what was called the Harvard second team (Schumpeter, Leontief, Mason, Chamberlin, Harris, Douglass V. Brown), you will see the argument that depressions are inevitable and are even a little bit healthy. They're catharsis for the system. But the Great Depression was a particularly bad one, Schumpeter thought, because you got the Kitchen–Crum 40-month cycle interfering with the eight-year Juglar cycle, which interfered with the long-wave Kondratieff cycle. The ham bone was attached to the shin bone, and so you got triple whammy, and once it got itself spread out the market system would be okay.

The exception to this schizophrenia at Chicago was given by Paul Douglas, who was a reflationist, and not on very good terms with Simons and Knight; they regarded him as a power-hungry do-gooder. Jacob Viner actually appeared as a moderate in that environment, although I would say that he was on the sagacious conservative side of the ideological spectrum in economic doctrine in general.

Books that I remember include D.H. Robertson's little Cambridge handbook, *Money*, which was used in my Money course with Mints. The other book used in that course was *The Banking*

Process, written by an undistinguished professor at the University of Michigan. In it I was taught $MV = PQ$. I think I also was assigned – but I can't think in what course it would have been, but maybe it was a supplementary reading – Currie on *The Supply of Money in the United States*. According to my best recollection it was not a precursor of the Keynesian analysis. In that book he's worried about the instability of money supply, but that was because the non-member banks and the small banks have a different reserve ratio from the member banks; therefore when you get a change in the ratio of relative reserves in different parts of the banking system, the resulting volatility in the money supply exceeds the volatility in M reserves.

Did the explanation of the Depression convince the students?

Yes, but remember: in all these courses we didn't much address the underemployment problem, and we didn't primarily address the Wesley Mitchell fat years/lean years problem of being above some norm and below some norm. It was just a way of talking about past inflations and panics.

Did the students talk among themselves and say, "What explains the unemployment in the economy?" Or did they just not deal with that issue?

I would say that there was some preoccupation with things such as were propounded in William T. Foster and Waddell Catchings who published, I think even before the mid-twenties, two or three different books in which they argued the underconsumptionist view. Now, it's obvious to me, since I knew Catchings in his old age around 1950, that Foster must have been the brains because extrapolating backward age-specific qualities, Catchings was not. Waddell Catchings was head of Goldman-Sachs when they were bankrupt in the twenties. Earlier he was part angel in setting up the Pollack Foundation which helped support Irving Fisher's *The Making of Index Numbers*.[1]

Well, Foster and Catchings had a challenge or contest. You got $5000 or $10 000 if you could find a flaw in their theory. That was quite a lot of money then, and a lot of economists joined in. The guy who won was something of a nut, named Souter, a New Zealander or Australian. If you looked up the series of Columbia theses that were published in those days, there's one called *Prolegomena to Economic Science*, or something. It's a very mystical book, dedicated to those anti-Marshallians who think they have replaced the master but haven't. I don't know what the quality of his critique was or whether he patted them on the back, but Alvin Hansen entered the contest and did not win, although he might have been second or third and gotten some prize money.

Hansen was most famous in my year for Garver and Hansen, and he had done, from what I understood, the macro primarily, and Garver had done the micro part. It was an interesting textbook because, unlike most American economists, Hansen is in the Spiethoff, Wicksell, Cassel, Schumpeter tradition, arguing that it is technological change and things like that, the external shocks, that mainly cause the business cycle.

The Foster and Catchings theory, like that of Major Douglas and so many of the underconsumptionists, is really quite obscure: and therefore specifying just what's wrong – or right – with it is not easy. I want to emphasize that because I think that either Foster or Catchings might have been a student of my Harvard money teacher John Williams, or his contemporary, at Brown University many years ago. John Williams himself was a fairly conservative fellow, but enough of an iconoclast to devote class attention to the Foster and Catchings book. If a student said, "Say's Law is exactly right," he'd say, "Well, wait a minute! There may be something in Foster and Catchings. And if there is something wrong with it, I can't tell you exactly what that is." That's as near to a Keynesian influence in the early Harvard environment as you could find.

Did the students talk about Foster and Catchings and say it didn't make sense? Was that the general consensus?

No, probably some of us students and some of the graduate students flirted a little bit with [Gesell-type] stamped money, or scrip. You know, there was scrip being issued in the Great Depression, since a lot of towns couldn't pay their teachers and police in cash. And there were notions afoot that if you could only date the money it would lose value unless you spent it, and that would make the money be spent. There were even floating around – I can't date exactly when this was, but I'm inclined to think before my June 1935 commencement day – stories like the following. A counterfeiter comes to town, creates some fake bills, buys a suit of clothes; the tailor uses the money to go to the baker – and finally the money comes back to the counterfeiter, who tears it up. Who lost? Everybody gained because there was extra production. In other words, there was a very strong notion – which I probably heard Stuart Chase orally espouse, maybe in my last months of high school – that we lived in poverty in the midst of plenty.

Even somebody like Princeton's Frank Graham, who was a pretty orthodox economist, had a scheme. He argued, "Why can't we organize all the unemployed people and the unemployed plants and have a dual economy alongside the market economy which can pay for itself; have everybody take in each other's washings and enjoy its extra employment?" There was a strong feeling in most of American academia, probably stronger outside the economics departments than in, and probably stronger in most economics departments than in the University of Chicago economics department, that something should be done.

But the students didn't really force the professors to deal with those plans and say what's wrong or right with them – is that a fair statement?

Yes. It's a bit curious because I don't remember in economics classes the loud radical who interrupts things, asks the questions that shouldn't be asked or that are hard to answer. Also, by the time I finished my undergraduate work, and up to that time, I met almost no communists. If you read memoirs, honest memoirs, of the various New York colleges, Columbia or NYU or CCNY in the period from 1930 to 1940, you would find either a tremendous antipathy or attraction towards communism. Communism didn't seem to loom large at the University of Chicago in the

1931–1935 period. But maybe as a commuter I was oblivious to it.

Keynes wasn't discussed much either, except by an instructor named Eugene Staley, who was a student of Viner's. I remember asking him, probably at the end of my freshman year (about 1932), "Who's the greatest economist alive?" He replied, "John Maynard Keynes." This was on the basis of Keynes' *Treatise*, which I had sampled, and *Monetary Reform*, which I probably had read. I wasn't assigned these books by Mints, Director, Simons or other undergraduate teachers.

Who else was there at Chicago?

Well, Jacob Mosak was my undergraduate colleague, and we were in friendly competition for prizes and honors. He probably is now retired from the United Nations, where he's been for many years. He wrote a classic book on trade theory for his Chicago Ph.D. Mosak played a key role later, in World War II, when he was chief macro expert for Richard Gilbert at the OPA, the most Keynesian shop in that town in the war's last months.

At this time Mosak was very much in the camp of Henry Schultz's econometric researches. Schultz was an object of derision to Frank Knight and maybe Henry Simons, and this was picked up by George Stigler and Allen Wallis, who were graduate students. I was an undergraduate student, but I came to know them pretty well. And I knew Albert Hart and Milton Friedman, but not quite so well. About that time Milton Friedman married Rose Director, Aaron Director's sister. The Knight crowd didn't need much to get an attitude of derision towards people and theories. Schultz was a self-trained mathematician and econometrician and a little unsure of his ground. He was a student of H.L. Moore's, and I would say a somewhat limited man, but he did perform a valuable role at that time. Wallis and Stigler used to make him nervous by trading on his insecurity.

In "Succumbing to Keynesianism", I wrote of the frustration that I felt of not being able to rationalize what was going on in the world around me with what I was being taught. I remember arguing with my parents. My father thought that Father Coughlin, who spoke frequently on the radio, was great. He would declaim against the bankers and against "fountain pen money". Only as certain anti-Semitic undertones began to appear in his addresses broadcast from Detroit did my father begin to lose enthusiasm for him. I couldn't really explain why Coughlin was wrong. I remember my mother saying to me, what would have been regarded as great heresy in the classroom, "Don't you know that times are only good during war?" (She had World War I in mind and the Gary steel boom.) And I had to admit there was some empirical basis for that.

So you did have a certain amount of internal confusion?

Yes. But my friends who were not economists regarded me as very conservative, a person who would debunk schemes for reform and things, because the system would take care of itself, or you would only make things worse. On the other hand I became very enthusiastic for Franklin Roosevelt. It was a little hard to explain how I could rationalize that.

Despite any doubts, I thought Chicago was wonderful. The only reason I left was that I won a fellowship from the Social Science Research Council for my entire graduate study. This fellowship had a requirement that you could not stay where you were. Were it not for this fellowship I would not have left the University of Chicago; I thought it was perfect. But I had to leave. I'm not sure whether or not it was open to me to go to the London School or Cambridge, which might have tempted me; and I wouldn't for an instant have thought of going to Oxford. That left the realistic choice between Columbia and Harvard.

There was a strong connection between Columbia and Chicago in those days because people like Allen Wallis and Milton Friedman had studied under Hotelling. Because of this connection most of my advisers – and I was on quite good terms with the Chicago faculty – thought I should go to Columbia. Harry Gideonse said, "How could you go to Cambridge if you could go to Morningside Heights?" (He came from Columbia.) I was warned that Schumpeter was kind of a crank, who believed in a zero interest rate. I was warned by Lloyd Mints that Seymour

Harris in macroeconomics was an inflationist. This is interesting, because if you read *The Economics of the Recovery Program*, 1934, you'll see that Harris, not yet having tenure at Harvard and still under the influence of Harold Hitchings Burbank, is a stout reactionary. Lloyd Mints must have had some keen sense of smell, because after Harris did get tenure he became a flaming Keynesian.

Despite these urgings I chose Harvard, but for the wrong reason. I thought it was going to be like Middlebury or Dartmouth – a green common and a white church – nice quiet surroundings. My irrational expectations were frustrated when I saw Harvard Square. One reason I chose Harvard was because Edward Chamberlin was there. I had looked into *The Theory of Monopolistic Competition* and Joan Robinson's *Economics of Imperfect Competition* as an undergraduate. They weren't assigned but were discussed vaguely in the advanced undergraduate theory course given by Paul Douglas. At the very end of the class he said, "This is the best class I've ever had. Because you're such a wonderful class, I'm going to give you something extra." That something extra was the following. He put a U-shaped average cost curve on the blackboard, and he drew a marginal cost curve and said, "For reasons I can't quite explain, that marginal curve must go right through the bottom of the average curve." A graduate student from the business school who was in that class told me that Joan Robinson had proved that in equilibrium you've got to be to the left of the bottom of the curve. But I drew lots of equilibria which proved to me that this wasn't the case. What he hadn't hold me was that it had to be an equilibrium with a downward-sloping demand curve and *no profits*. As you can see, it was a pretty primitive state of affairs.

Thomas Nixon Carver had an article – I can't remember whether it was in the *Quarterly Journal* or where it was – that if you get the real wage down to the intersection with the supply curve of labor, there will be no unemployment problem. It was much the same argument that was in Pigou's *Theory of Unemployment*. Finally, old Edwin Cannan in *The Economic Journal* had an article in 1932 in which the market got cleared at the right low-enough real wage.

We spent a lot of inconclusive time, wasted time I would say, on stuff like this: if you cut the wage and the demand for labor is elastic, then you really will be dealing a benefit to the laboring class as a whole because it will get more income. On the other hand, if you cut the wage and the demand for labor is inelastic, then there will be a loss in total purchasing power. Just what this general demand for labor was that we were talking about, and what these sterile totalities were, never got clarified; all this wasn't any statement about the real world, it was just a statement about what is meant by the elasticity of demand being above or below unity.

There is quite a lot of this type of argument in a book authored by Douglas and Director: it seemed to be a book concerned to reduce the seasonal fluctuations of employment. Director appeared ashamed of his earlier collaboration with Douglas. He probably was making a living, just barely keeping on good terms with Douglas, for whom he had some contempt as a sentimental, empty-headed do-gooder.

There was some dissatisfaction with these Say's Law views. Earlier I mentioned that Simons had the beginnings of a notion of the liquidity trap. I also remember that John Williams, who gave the first graduate course in Money that every graduate student took, was by 1935–1936 not a Keynesian – the *General Theory* book was hardly out; it *hadn't* been out; and it took him time to get up to speed (I don't know whether he ever got up to speed) on the Keynesian system, but he certainly did a lot better than, say, Schumpeter did in learning what Keynes's system was all about. Williams would say things like, "You can pull on a string but you can't push on it." By my Harvard entry, we were ready for public spending and budget deficits, and not just monetary policy, even though monetary policy was the principal thing taught.

I should also remind you of the Harris Foundation Lectures, a subsidized series at the University of Chicago, which had John Maynard Keynes as a visiting professor around 1931, and published a volume. That was before my time and I never met him. If you read that volume carefully (as I did only after 1945), there is already a notion that the flow of income is the primary determinant of saving and, when income falls enough, then the saving falls to equality with the reduced investment. Keynes' *Means to Prosperity* came out in 1933, although I was never assigned that, I believe, in any University of Chicago course.

To give you the Chicago flavor, once around 1944 or 1945 I wrote in *The New Republic* an article in favor of the Bretton Woods system. In it I had as a final sentence something like this: "History will learn who's the better friend of the capitalistic system, Alvin Hansen or Henry Simons." After I'd written this, I sent Henry Simons, who was a friend, a postcard and I said, "You and I come from a part of the country where if you call a man a son-of-a-bitch you'd better be smiling. Well, I was smiling when I wrote that." Henry Simons wrote back and said, "I took no offense but I want to remind you that I had no wild oats of deflationism to live down, as Alvin Hansen did." And I say that because in Alvin Hansen's business cycle book, written in 1929, he argues that the business cycle may be a thing of the past, it may be just part of the growing pains of capitalism. He also argues that in the debate between Malthus and Ricardo on whether mass unemployment is possible, because of ineffective demand, no one who thinks it through could fail to realize that Malthus was wrong and Ricardo was right(!). Up until, I would say, as late as 1932 or maybe even later, Hansen is still espousing sweating it out. Henry Simons, on the other hand, was part of the University of Chicago group which was in favor of deficit spending when that was still unfashionable.

Once Arthur Burns, after he'd been at the Council of Economic Advisors, to boost himself in the history of thought, said to me that he was one of the deficit financiers, that he had written a letter to *The Herald Tribune* in 1931 or 1932. I said, "Yes, Arthur."

You went to Harvard in 1935? How did Harvard differ from Chicago?

A lot. In Chicago everybody knew the answer; economics was a completed science. Allen Wallis never got a Ph.D.; Homer Jones never got a Ph.D.; Al Hart had terrible problems in getting his

Ph.D. past Knight because he wrote about the period of production. George Stigler told me that everything good in economics was already in Frank Knight. His thesis was essentially on Menger; he argued that there's a lot of good stuff in Menger, but it's all better in Frank Knight.

Actually, this is a bit strong. There was this three-way split at Chicago. Henry Schultz was an empiricist and empiricism was looked down on very much by Knight and Viner, although Viner's position was more complicated: in principle he did not look down on it; in fact he did, because all the models that were being measured were more abstract than any sensible man could believe in. Then there was this little wing of Paul Douglas liberals, liberal in the American sense. Even Frank Knight was never your simple conservative in the sense that Milton Friedman was, or even in the sense of Henry Simons. He just was against any government action, but he really was also cynical about the market at that time. Williams, who was a very good teacher, was certainly very open-minded.

Mathematics, which I was beginning to get interested in, was laughed at by the Knight wing. Chicago was happy when the Cowles Commission left Chicago after the war, and they left because they felt that it was a hostile environment.

At Harvard there were lots of different viewpoints. There wasn't homogeneity. Schumpeter made economics seem a very developing subject. *You* would be doing great things, everything was left to be done. If you'd asked me five years after I went to Harvard, in 1940 when I left Harvard for MIT and after being a Junior Fellow for three years, I would have said, "Thank God I left Chicago. Because the three biggest things in economics have been the Keynesian revolution, the monopolistic competition revolution, and the mathematicization of economics", and Chicago was against all of these things during that period of time.

When did you first hear of The General Theory?

I first heard of *The General Theory* in the academic year 1935–1936 from the Canadian Bob Bryce. Bob Bryce, fresh from Cambridge University, was in John Williams's graduate class. Bob

Bryce arranged for *The General Theory* to be available to us as soon as it was published. I don't know whether I still have my copy. It cost five shillings. But before it came out he wrote up a summary of it. I still have a copy somewhere in my files, but I don't know where I can put my hands on it.

I heard Lorie Tarshis and Bob Bryce at London, Ontario, at the conference that Patinkin and others held, and I found it disappointing. That is, I could not learn from their accounts just what parts of *The General Theory* they were able to acquire from Keynes's lectures. I'm not sure that it all came from lectures. It may have come from what we would call research students, talking among themselves. I don't know, if I were to read Bob Bryce's memorandum today in the Patinkin fashion, exactly what it is I would find.

Even after I read *The General Theory* I resisted. In a sense I was sampling the whiskey and finding it unpalatable. Leontief was my teacher then and Leontief, in his way, which has not changed at all, was derisive. He argued that the ideas in *The General Theory* were nonsense, and that he and I know better.

I took my general exams in my first year, which was a little unusual, around May 15, 1936, so I was either twenty or twenty-one. On the whole, they were a breeze, but there was one question asked me by Seymour Harris which I thought was off limits and I felt uneasy about it. He asked me about the leakages in the multiplier. Of course, that was too soon for me. *He* knew about the leakages in the multiplier, but I didn't.

What I resisted in Keynes the most was the notion that there could be equilibrium unemployment. I'd argue with Bob Bryce, and discuss with Leontief, that first chapter where workers react differently to an increase in money wages from the way they react to a change in real wages that comes from inflation. The way I finally convinced myself was to just stop worrying about it. I asked myself: why do I want to refuse a paradigm that enables me to understand the Roosevelt upturn from 1933 till 1937? It's not sufficiently realized – I don't know why people don't discuss this – that money supply did not grow according to Friedman formulas, it had much more rapid rate of growth during this period; and it's completely untrue that the New Deal didn't work until World War II came and bailed it out. Some of the highest rates of real increase in and highest levels of plant and equipment capital formation are in the period 1934 to 1937. I was content to assume that there was enough rigidity in relative prices and wages to make the Keynesian alternative to Walras operative.

Another thing, of course, that confirmed me much more, and this is where Hansen had an influence on me: it was so patent in the last part of the thirties that monetary policy had little potency. When I came to Harvard I could not get a bank account. Neither Cambridge Trust nor Harvard Trust would take my account. They didn't want students' accounts, and they didn't want them because they only got a fraction of a per cent on Treasury bills. By 1938, Treasury bills would pay less than three-eights of a per cent. There were times in the year when they'd go negative. I once asked someone at the Treasury, "I understand a lot of million dollar Treasury bills are not turned in. How come?" And he said, "Do you know a better way to hold a million dollars?" I had to use the Postal Savings system. It's gone now. It also had the advantage that you could go there later in the day.

What happened with the Keynesian revolution and the monopolistic competition revolution? Did the Keynesian revolution just wipe out the monopolistic competition revolution?

I don't think there was any direct competition between them. When I wrote to Jim Tobin – he asked me for any comments [on his interview] – I said, "I want privately to correct you on one matter. You said that for the most part we early Keynesians were satisfied to assume perfect competition as an understructure." And I said that that was not my feeling about myself, and I've checked it with Bob Bishop. We always assumed that the Keynesian underemployment equilibrium floated on a substructure of administered prices and imperfect competition. I stopped thinking about what was meant by rigid wages and whether you could get the real wage down; I knew it was a good working principle, a good hypothesis to explain that the real wage does not move down indefinitely so long as there is still some unemployment. Thus I assumed a disequilibrium system, in which people could not get on the supply-of-labor curve.

I worried most of all in my Chicago years and the first part of the time I was at Harvard. You know, I was like a tuna: the Keynesian system had to land me, and I was fighting every inch of the line. I was worried about the micro foundations. I had worked out in my mind naively that one of the reasons that you could have unemployed people who wanted a job alongside people who were employed was the people who were employed would be damned unhappy if they lost that job. My answer to the question: "Why don't firms cut the wages of the people who are at work?" – was that if employees developed rents of special knowledge then it wouldn't be good economics for the employer to cut the wage rate on the differentiated specific factors.

I guess I should emphasize this: I spent four summers of my college career on the beach at Lake Michigan. I did not have a wealthy family and they could have used the income that I would have produced if I had worked, but it was pointless to look for work. I didn't even have to test the market because I had friends who would go to 350 potential employers and not be able to get any job at all. I was very conscious that the unemployed had no way of going to General Motors and offering to work for less than those who were already working there, no way of displacing already employed workers. Moreover, the question would be: why didn't little firms take over the automobile industry, or the steel industry, by starting up in Tennessee with low wages? And the answer to that was we thought of the Fortune 500 companies as requiring a tremendous amount of capital. Free entry was not a feasible thing and there was overcapacity in all lines. This goes back to the system being floated on imperfect competition and increasing returns technologies.

But that was never really formalized?

There was no need to.

What do you mean, "no need to"?

I think that I took a positivistic attitude that we know that there are ups and downs in the degree of utilization, and the Keynesian model has given us an apparatus that moves up and down to explain this. Just because I don't understand the process of digestion, should I refuse my beefsteak? Actually, the opposition of somebody like Schumpeter to the Keynesian system was rationally based. He couldn't see – in fact he found it very disappointing – that Larry Klein could write (under my direction) the thesis *The Keynesian Revolution* in which there existed in the market system a mismatch of supply and demand for labor. How can that be in an equilibrium system? The underemployment equilibrium system lacked the properties of full equilibrium, but the real world behaved in that way.

It's a modern desire to have impeccable micro foundations for macro. You see, the original people, like Leontief, Taussig and Viner, who criticized 1936 Keynes in the *Quarterly Journal* – his homogeneity axiom, for instance – were worried about this sort of thing. I decided that life was more fruitful not worrying about it. You weren't making any progress on it. Moreover, the search today for micro foundations for macro does not have a rich set of results. It's a methodological principle with me that in the longer run people will find more ways of getting around the disequilibrium. For instance, if union wages are too high in the steel industry, somebody will be working on electric furnaces, which don't require that you replicate the size of Bethlehem Steel, and you can begin to chisel away on the market. It's because I get a better positivistic macroeconomics to do some worrying about the micro foundations that I do that worrying, and not because I have a conscience that everybody's micro foundations must be tidy.

But your work in mathematical economics and foundations is tidying up enormous amounts of confusion at the same time. Is there schizophrenia there?

Remember that I was able (in *Foundations*) through the correspondence principle and other things, to take systems like the simple multiplier system and work out what its comparative static properties were, and how you were able to predict them in advance – even though the full Walrasian equilibrium was not realized. I also probably had in mind, if you want to know why my conscience wasn't worse, the lectures I had in mathematical economics from Old Edwin Bidwell Wilson. He started life as a mathematician and mathematical physicist and was Willard Gibbs's last protégé. He would describe equilibrium like this: You leave your car in the MIT parking lot overnight. The rubber tire is a membrane which separates the inside of the tire from the atmosphere, and because of this stiff wall there's an equilibrium difference in pressure. Wilson would say, "Come back a thousand years later, and that tire will be flat." That was not strict equilibrium. It's just a very slowly adjusting disequilibrium. The time period was involved.

It was a model that worked. I should also say that I was very much influenced – moving to the 1935–1937 period – by Schumpeter's off-the-cuff general methodological remarks. Schumpeter was Kuhnian in Tom Kuhn's sense long before Tom Kuhn was in high school. He always said, "You never in economics kill a theory by fact; you kill a theory by a better theory." L.J. Henderson, who was the chairman of the Society of Fellows, head Senior Fellow, was very anti-economist. (I was a Junior Fellow from 1937 to 1940 and was really the first proper economist: I got elected because I was a mathematical economist. Henderson was in favor of Pareto, but he thought all the rest of economics was no good.) He always emphasized, probably derivatively from Pareto but also from his own methodological work, that you can't be a pure empiricist; you've got to have a systematic way of thinking about things. So the Keynesian system gave one a systematic way of thinking about things.

I don't think it's systematic if your great uncle was a heretical underconsumptionist and then said, "Look, Keynes stole my stuff. I already had it way back then." There was a German banker named Albert Hahn who was a refugee in this country and who turned very conservative. In the 1920s he'd been an underconsumptionist. He'd always say, "Keynesian notions are all wrong but I had them first." That's why I think that Leijonhufvud's interpretations are a complete distortion of how it happened and what happened. Keynes versus the Keynesians gets it all wrong. Keynes the master was supposed to have very subtle, deep insights which he can hardly articulate – those are the good things. Then you have this terrible Keynesian cross – we can draw it all with the Hicks–Hansen diagram. And that's a perversion. Well, about eight different people *independently* discerned in Keynes' book that Keynesian system. Six, at least, of those eight were close friends of John Maynard Keynes. Keynes read them in his lifetime, had plenty of opportunity to disclaim them if that was not what he had in mind. But more than that, I go to the positivistic fact that what counts in science is not your vague inarticulations. It's what you can write down, what you can use, what people do use; it's really even what people *mis*-use, the things that don't fit.

Who else was there besides Bryce, among the students?

Well, I would say that people who became early Keynesians would be Paul and Alan Sweezy. Jay Raymond Walsh of the Walsh–Sweezy case was also there. J. Raymond Walsh and Alan Sweezy were popular undergraduate teachers, but they did not have great claims to tenure at Harvard. And they were radical.

How about Lauchlin Currie?

He was gone before 1935. If you had asked me in 1937 or 1936, "Is Lauchlin Currie a leading Keynesian?" I would have said, "I'm not aware he's a Keynesian at all." If you'd asked me in 1938, I would have realized he was because he was at the Federal Reserve and influencing fiscal policy. I should also tell you that I didn't myself quite realize that the Roosevelt New Deal Administration was not Keynesian until about 1937. The early, first-term Tugwell, Moley, Kirkland, Kahn group were really Veblenian. They were in favor of restructuring American life, and they ended up being enemies of Keynesianism. For them, Keynesianism was a palliative.

Most economists – you could have said this up to 1962 or 1963 – thought that it was a crime that Franklin Roosevelt jettisoned the World Economic Conference in 1933 by devaluing the dollar. (Fritz Machlup, as late as 1962 or 1963, spoke of that as a crime.) In 1935 I probably thought it was a crime – in 1933 John Williams was on the boat to Europe and the rug was pulled out from under him. But later I became convinced, as Seymour Harris became convinced, that, although America didn't have to devalue, it gave us extra leeway, and that Belgium was very smart to devalue in 1936 – it should have done it earlier; and France was very stupid never to have done it. The way that Britain and Scandinavia came out of the Great Depression earlier – by 1932 they were on their way up – was not by beggaring-my-neighbor devaluation, but it gave them the room to expand so they made an impact on their neighbor in a neutral way at worst. That was somewhat in Seymour Harris's book of 1936 on currency depreciation.[2]

What about the Hansen seminars?

Hansen came to the Littauer School in 1937 before the school had any students. That's when I met him; he was never a teacher of mine. In 1937 I became a Junior Fellow, so I had a generous fellowship and no classes. I wasn't allowed to work for a degree, but I was able to drop in on Alvin Hansen's seminar. By then I had finished my graduate course work. But I often attended his and Williams's seminar the next year, 1938. Hansen would try out his new books. The seminar had a lot of important visitors.

When would you date your conversion to Keynesianism?

I was already a Keynesian at the time of the Hansen–Williams seminar. If you think of Michael Farraday as the fellow who measured electromagnetism, and Maxwell as the theoretician who took the insights of Farraday and made models of them, in some ways that was my relationship to Alvin Hansen. I remember being proud that I got him to put the income on the horizontal axis and not on the vertical axis. If you put it on the vertical axis, when you have an increase in the propensity to consume, there's a rightward shift, just like your demand curve, Hansen protested. And I said, "Just like the demand curve; and the demand curve's been wrong because of Alfred Marshall these fifty years. Why should we get off on the wrong foot again?" I formalized the Keynesian cross, where you add the investment to the consumption function and look for the forty-five degree line and I worked out the mathematics of the accelerator/multiplier model. I simply took a numerical model of Hansen's, from which he was drawing over-strong conclusions, and showed that if you actually carried it further it would come back and you'd have self-generated cycles.

Then there is the story about how the original theorem of the balanced budget multiplier originated independently in four or five places. The first I knew about were I, Bill Salant and Alvin Hansen – this at a time when Perloff and Hansen were writing their book. Also the B-B-Multiplier Theorem is to be discerned in the speech which Keynes wrote for the Chancellor of the Exchequer on financing the British war, and possibly – although this was a little later – in Nicholas Kaldor's exercises in alternative means to full employment.

I waited a long time to publish the theorem because Bill Salant and I were going to publish it together and he was engaged in public service. Also Hansen had found a different way of looking at it. He was quite intrigued when I was able to show that the Keynesian cross measure of the stimulus would not be a correct stimulus. The miracle to me was not that several discovered this balanced budget multiplier with the remarkable feature of the multiplier being exactly one; it was surprising that everybody didn't see it earlier. And the reasons we didn't see it earlier were completely accidental. It was primarily taxonomic. When Kuznets first measured national income, he did not include in national income government expenditure financed by a deficit – something strange like that. His definition would have been absolutely impossible once the war made the government fully half of the GNP and half of that financed by fiscal deficit. People realized they couldn't live with that definition and it was rightly dropped.

So I realized that I'd actually had the balanced budget multiplier back in 1937/1938 in earlier papers, but it was not counted as kosher income. [A rise in government spending with taxes unchanged gave no first-round increase in old-Kuznets income. With no rise in income, no secondary multiplier effects would follow.]

I should also say that the majority of the able students by 1937/1938 were Keynesians. I may be off a year, but I don't think I am. Emile Despres came to Harvard in 1937 as a senior civil servant, and Walter Salant stayed a second year. I thought of Richard Gilbert as a Keynesian, but I don't remember why. James Tobin thought that maybe Richard Gilbert was influenced a lot by Hansen, but I don't remember much interaction between Dick Gilbert and the rest. At Harvard he was having to teach and lecture outside to support his family. He had no tenure. Phil Wernette at the business school was a heretical underconsumptionist. He, in my time, didn't teach on our side of the river. I was impressed by Sumner Slichter, whom I didn't particularly like at that time – I thought of him as a conservative. He had some University of Utah lectures in which he said that consumption is passive and investment is active; and, years later, I said to Alvin Hansen that I thought there were some good notions in Slichter. He said, "Well, to tell the truth, I always thought of Sumner as a closet Keynesian, who wouldn't admit it." I suspect that Sumner Slichter was kidding himself; that he didn't really face himself in the mirror and perceive that a lot of his notions were Keynesian.

The two books which show the change in viewpoint in the Harvard community are *The Economics of the Recovery Program* – the stupid book I already mentioned by Schumpeter, *et al.* – and *An Economic Program for American Democracy*. I once said to Alvin Hansen years later that I thought that *An Economic Program for American Democracy* in program and analysis was most like what went on in the next twenty years. I had the opportunity to be one of the members of that group but I wasn't much of a joiner. Hansen replied, "I never thought it was very original. I thought it was just about what was in my lectures." Hansen was not a terribly vain man, as scholars go. He surprised me a few times. Practically everyone speaks well of Allyn Young. Allyn Young was the great theorist at Harvard in the twenties. When Edwin Cannon retired from the London School, Young answered a call to a chair there. He was only there a year or two when he died of pneumonia, at about the age of 50. He never wrote much, but was one of America's leading economists. He was a great teacher who supposedly didn't publish because he knew so much. Supposedly Young was just ready to publish when he died. But Alvin Hansen said to me, uncharacteristically, "You know, I always thought he was a stuffed shirt."

You asked me about other people in the seminar. Always things looked different to people on the scene. For example, at that time we had Richard Musgrave (the quintessential Hansenian) down as an anti-Keynesian. The same with Benjamin Higgins, if you know that name. Soon Musgrave left Harvard – went to Swarthmore, I think, then to the Federal Reserve, then to Michigan, Hopkins and Princeton, and finally to Harvard. I would judge Richard Musgrave became number one of his generation in the field of public finance and in the top few in the field of money and Keynesianism. But that seemed not yet the case in the Hansen seminar days. The same thing about Higgins. But Higgins was in Washington only about three months when he told me at the Christmas AEA convention, "We're going to spend three billion here and 17 billion there." I concluded, "Boy! Marx was right. The job makes the man."

To a degree what I'm saying is also true about Henry Wallich, who was of a slightly later period. I always thought of Henry Wallich as trying to be conservative. He was an intelligent critic of Keynes's system, but also a good practitioner of that system. There was a little bit of a Williams camp at Harvard, and a Hansen camp. It was kind of embarrassing because the Williams camp was so skimpy compared to the Hansen camp. Gabriel Hauge of Eisenhower White House prominence was in the Williams camp.

Ken Galbraith has written of his role as an early American Keynesian. In the Hansen seminar group Ken was not thought of as primarily a macroeconomist at all. We were bigots.

In 1940 I became an instructor and tutor, but got a better offer at MIT and I decided to take it. When I came here our department was a service department and there was just beginning to be a labor economics group and an industrial relations section. A year after I came here we started a graduate program and we started to acquire people like Bob Bishop and Dan Vandermeulen. And then, after the war, we began to acquire people like Cary Brown, Charlie Kindleberger, Max Millikan and Bob Solow.

During the war, how would you characterize most people's beliefs about Keynesian economics?

I would say that within university life, if you tried to get a job for somebody in 1938, you had to suppress that he was a Keynesian. Roland Robinson, a name you would not know, was at the Federal Reserve for some years. He was a pretty good money economist and he went from the Federal Reserve to be the chief economist for the main trade association of the banks, or saving banks. He had some interesting ideas. Somebody once said to him, "Whose idea is that?" and he said, "Well, it's Keynesian." And he said the temperature went to zero in the room, and he finally decided he couldn't live in that environment and went to Michigan State University.

However, I would say that Keynesianism at the beginning of the war was a majority view among the active young people at the elite universities, with some exceptions like maybe Chicago. By the end of the war the entire academic profession was Keynesian.

Did you ever meet Keynes?

No. Keynes knew about me because he told somebody – I can't remember who – that I was a comer. He never lectured at Harvard in my time; I think because he was not invited. I have to be careful, because in an earlier period, before my time, he was invited and didn't come. He definitely was blackballed shamefully when Harvard passed him by for their 1936 Tercentenary gathering of great world scholars.

You can see that the profession was Keynesian by the success of Lorie Tarshis's 1947 textbook and my post-1948 textbook. One of the reasons for the triumph was that during the war the Keynesian wing of the U.S. civil service had been vindicated. This was actually supply-side economics, not aggregate demand-side economics. Most of the business civil servants, called to the War Production Board and so forth, believed that the expandability of production was very limited. People like Richard Gilbert at OPA argued that there was big room for further expansion. I remember being told that Keynes came over and was asked his opinion. He said, "Well, how much was 1929 real output over 1913?" He was given the numbers. He said, "Well, that was a 15-year period and it's been 12 years since 1929. So let's take 12/15 of that increment, and I think that that would be a reasonable goal for potential GNP." That crystallized the problem. And that was about the number that Gilbert and others of that Keynesian wing had chosen. It turned out that they were right. Of course there was no problem of explicit inflation because of price controls.

"Keynesianism" was a naughty word politically outside economics long after the war. Inside the profession it was another matter. Fiscal policy dominated monetary policy. One interesting exception was Clark Warburton, who antedated Milton Friedman as a monetarist. But he got little attention.

Why did Keynesianism sweep everything?

Because it seemed to work on war finance. Nobody cared a rap about money. The head of the Federal Reserve, Mariner Eccles, felt guilty that while boys were dying in the field he was fiddling at the Fed. A rumor went around Washington in the early forties that the Federal Reserve was going to lose its air-conditioning system. It was going to be transferred to WPB, OPA, or some other important wartime agency. You can't transfer such units. What's interesting is two things: one, that someone would contemplate doing this; and the other that everybody would believe such a rumor.

De facto, government spending became half the GNP by the late war years. Rationing and shortages kept people from consuming much of their incomes; perforce they saved, at banks and buying government bonds issued to mop up excessive income and finance the deficits that matched the tax share of the public spending. The need for high interest rates to confine private spending was thus minimal. Such a disequilibrium system might not have lasted for a long war; but it did set the stage for a postwar reconversion and boom fed by cumulative private liquidity and cumulative longings for consumption.

There's another reason, I think, why Keynesianism swept the field. It's the same reason rational expectations attracts people today. It provided a lot of Ph.D. fodder, a lot of clever models to work on. An example is an issue of *Econometrica* on the balanced budget multiplier, the first time it surfaced belatedly in print, in which Musgrave, Haberler, Hagen, Haavelmo, Goodwin and Arthur Smithies could spin their elegant theories. Theory is the lifeblood of science: if that's decadent, well that's the way it is.

Tarshis's textbook lasted for one year. He said that the reason for that was that the publishers got scared, everybody started calling it Commie, and an enormous amount of hate mail.

It's true. Two things: he had a very good first year, and then – do you know Hope Ingal's and Rose Wilder Lane's children stories, *The Little House in the Forest* and *The Little House on the Prairie*? They are novels, semi-true family stories. The daughter is Rose Wilder, and she wrote a well-received novel, *Let the Hurricane Roar*, about some Swedish immigrants in the northwest fighting snow blizzards and so forth. She later turned semi-Fascist and jumped on Tarshis and his books as being Marxist–Keynesian poison. There were many others, too. Young William Buckley, just grinding his baby teeth, wrote a hatchet job called *God and Man at Yale* on my book. (Part of the indictment is there's a Protestant minister at Yale and the other is Yale's bad economics.) The criticisms my book got pale against those leveled against Tarshis. I don't quite know why Tarshis got those undeserved calumnies. In fact, the Tarshis book was stopped right in its tracks. But I think what's important is not its being stopped in its tracks, but the resonant response that the Keynesian approach met with in the universities. My *Economics* generated a lot of imitative clones.

What kind of attacks did your book get and how did you deal with it?

For some reason that I have no understanding of, the virulence of the attack on Tarshis was of a higher order of magnitude than on my book, but there were plenty of attacks on my book, and there was a lot of work done by people. Also I wrote carefully and lawyer-like so that there were a lot of complaints that Samuelson was playing peek-a-boo with the Commies. The whole thing was a sad scene that did not reflect well on conservative business pressuring of colleges.

Why did you decide to do the textbook?

I started the textbook because the head of my department, Ralph Freeman, came to me and said, "I'll give you half time off: write a textbook so that our juniors, who have economics only as a compulsory subject, will like it, and believe in economics." He said, "It doesn't have to be long; there are no topics you *have* to cover. Just make it interesting." So I undertook to do it. I was very conscious of the lack of a text. I didn't know the Tarshis textbook then; I knew Lorie, but I didn't know he was writing a textbook. I was very sanguine that the field was waiting for a modern book, and that this would be a good seller. I didn't know it would be a good seller over forty-five years! I didn't know it would be as good a seller as it was, but I thought it would do very well. Writing the book took a lot longer than I thought it would. Instead of taking a semester, it took about two or three years. In the interim I had mimeographed preliminary chapters to try out on MIT classes.

Was your book the first to use the term "macroeconomics"?

No. In the 1960s Edwin Nourse, who was the first Chairman of the Council of Economic Advisors and a distinguished agricultural economist at Brookings, wrote to Alvin Hansen and said, "Who invented the word 'macroeconomics'?" Hansen sent me a card with his answer. He said, "I don't know – probably Samuelson." But I was pretty sure I hadn't. When I did some research for Hansen, I found that the terms "microeconomics" and "macroeconomics" do not surface early in the literature. Even at the time of my first edition they're not in my index. I looked in the index of *Econometrica* because I thought it was Frisch and Tinbergen who'd first used "macroeconomics", but what they had used in the early thirties was "macro dynamic systems". "Macroeconomics" appears in the *Econometrica* cumulative index, but that was some editor's afterthought.

The earliest case of the word "macroeconomics" that I could find was by Larry Klein, but his usage is somewhat different than normal. You and I think of macroeconomics primarily as involving effective demand, total amount of unemployment, the rate of inflation, and such. But the other sense in which "macroeconomics" has been used is a J.B. Clark aggregative model, which is a black box, with one output and two or three inputs. And that's the sense in Larry Klein's 1946 *Econometrica* discussion. (Hendrik Houthakker later found for me this 1941 *Econometrica* reference by Pieter de Wolff: "Income elasticity of demand, a micro-economic and a macro-economic interpretation.")

How about full employment after the war? Was there a big concern?

The general profession, I would say, and particularly some leading members of the profession, laid a big egg for which they paid in acclaim, dis-esteem, recrimination. That is the famous prediction that there would be mass unemployment after the war unless the government slowed down the return of soldiers and did a lot of deficit spending. This culminated in an official governmental estimate of all the agencies. The titular author of it was Everett

Hagen, my late MIT colleague who I believe was on the War Production Board; but Dick Gilbert's stalwarts David Lusher and Jacob Mosak and Arthur Smithers of Budget were also very important. They went public, around the spring of 1945.

I can remember being told by Roy Blough, the head of economics at the Treasury, about a famous meeting. I wasn't in on this because I was at the Radiation Laboratory doing mathematical wartime work. This was a meeting at the Treasury where William Fellner, an eminent anti-Keynesian, gave a talk arguing that there would be a big boom after the war. His argument was the same as W.W. Woytinski's and Sumner Slichter's. He said, "There's a tremendous post-war nest egg that's been accumulated by the American people because of deficit financing and swollen liquid holdings. The counterpart of that is a tremendous built-up hunger for durables and other consumption items and vacations that people couldn't have; and the juxtaposition of these two things will mean a tremendous period of buoyant demand." Probably he added in the accelerator, that the wartime step-up in the real income which would remain would require new equipment. You couldn't work the factories three shifts and expect that to last forever. Roy Blough told me that the seminar was a slaughter, with Jacob Mosak leading the assault: "Do you think that housing can go up three years in a row by such-and-such?" Fellner said, "They tore me to pieces every way." Yet as we look back now, that's much what happened. Fellner was very near the mark. I would say that the Keynesian branch of the profession was tarred very much with this gizmo prediction, which was quite wrong. I do not absolve myself from this error; I did allow for secular shifts in the saving function but I failed to anticipate the Friedman–Modigliani–Duesenberry–Kuznets–Dennison analyses of how much long-run saving patterns could fall below short-run extrapolations.

But it didn't seem to hurt them.

Oh, it did. It slowed down the spread of Keynesianism. By the end of the war Keynes was a very respectable figure in Britain, an establishment figure, but that still was not the case here. Now, there were some exceptions. In the Department of Commerce there were rosier post-war forecasts. Paul McCracken and Dick Bissell were working on viewpoints that would later be espoused by the Committee for Economic Development. Dick Bissell was the effective person running the Marshall Plan. And he was head of the CIA at the time of the Bay of Pigs fiasco. His career was ended by that. They and the C.E.D. believed that, if all businesses knew what the post-war GNP would be and made their investment plans conditional upon that, then all of them doing that would create a boom. (This does resemble De Gaulle's *Le Plan*.)

I might mention that Alvin Hansen was not a believer in post-war unemployment. He said, "There'll be a big restocking boom." Alvin Hansen also – because I've heard Alvin Hansen rationalize – said that one of the reasons there wasn't a problem of effective demand stagnation after the war was that economists had warned so against it. For example, he said that his wartime projections of what the budget should be post-war were the highest by far of anybody's and, he said, "I was a piker; the reality was way ahead of what I had, and that's what made the difference." By and large, the error was something to be expected occasionally in any inexact science. There was an extrapolation of short-run saving habits that was both unwarranted in terms of long-term history and implausible when you really think about it, and which, by hindsight, was very wrong. My contribution in Seymour Harris's book, *Postwar Economics*, argued that there would be no secular increase in the savings rate at full employment. So there was nothing in my toolbox that required me to help lay a big egg, but I did. My brother Bob Summers asked me, oh, maybe five years after the war, "Paul, were you right or wrong about the post-war thing?" and I said, "I was wrong." But I didn't, until I looked it up, realize *how* wrong in the stuff I'd written, some of it unsigned in *The New Republic*.

How did that hurt the Keynesian revolution?

Principally because it seemed to suggest that macroeconomic models are all wrong. However, it was Keynesian macro modelers like Lawrence Klein who made their reputations correcting those models that had wrongly predicted unemployment. Not until after Camelot, when stagflation persisted and monetarists offered their alternative *theory* to Model T Keynesianism, did Keynesianism lose its glamour.

Still, in terms of the development of the field, Keynesian economics ruled.

Well, yes. It's like rational expectations. I get maybe fifty yellow-jacketed National Bureau papers a year that have a bearing on the rational expectations model. Of that fifty, maybe fifteen are actually tests of the model, one form or another of it. Of those fifteen, about fourteen out of fifteen are rejections of the model, using ordinary statistical technology. Still I don't see much of an effect on what they'll be discussing at the Kansas City Federal Reserve meeting at the Tetons today. All the young bloods will be there. But it does have an effect in the long run; and actually, rational expectations is not doing as well in the mid-eighties as it was in the late seventies because it hasn't worked very well.

In science there is always cultural lag. A lot of people were just catching on to Keynesianism in the first post-war years. Remember, a whole new generation was being born who had just learned it, who didn't know what pre-Keynesian life was like. If you look at my textbook you can see that it starts out – because all textbooks simplify – mostly with flow models. There is a little chatter about the money stock having an influence, but it's never really in the early editions given very much emphasis. You have to realize that it was about 1950 before American Keynesians, to say nothing of the anti-Keynesians, began to realize that the quasi-liquidity trap behavior of 1938 and the artificial wartime situation were things of the past. Model T Keynesianism, in America, but alas less so in Britain, was evolving into its Post-Keynesian emphases on wealth stocks and money stocks. The Hicks–Keynes diagrams could have served a Fellner as well as a Hagen or Mosak!

I think Howard Ellis used the expression "the rediscovery of money". Money was rediscovered by Keynesians, American

Keynesians, as well as by anti-Keynesians. The money was already in the Keynesian system. You also have to emphasize, if you want to be fair, the Pigou Effect began to be perceived in the literature, after about 1940. So Keynesianism was already becoming eclectic, and moving beyond what I call Model T Keynesianism – which is just the one-variable system with $Y = C + I = f(Y) + g(Y)$. When you remember to include the interest rate and money supply, i and M, as variables and remember to write liquidity preference as $PQ = Y = MV = Mv(i)$, then you realize that Friedman's monetarism of 1955 and beyond is agreeing with rather than debunking the Keynes–Hicks diagrams. I consider it a great advance when monetarist anti-Keynesians can share with Keynesians the post-1936 paradigms. It's a bit like bipartisan foreign policy in politics! The New Classicists are something else again.

There are some stories I've been told about the Lerner/Keynes exchanges. Can you shed any light on them?

Keynes gave two famous Federal Reserve seminars, which I was not able to attend. However, from accounts at the time – probably from Hansen – I know what happened. At the first one he was utterly charming but was kind of reactionary and, in particular, he jumped on Abba Lerner, who had written about functional finance. One of the things he said – and I can never remember whether it was Aristotle or Plato – was, "Plato said, 'The art of politics is the art of telling plausible lies.' But you know, Abba, those lies have got to be *plausible*", implying that Lerner's weren't. He must have felt, maybe at the time, that Lerner had overdone it; or maybe he came to feel that. But anyway, in the meantime, Lerner's *The Economics of Control* came out. He must have paged through it – he was a very quick reader – and in the second seminar he made redress and went out of his way to say nice things. How Lerner happened to be in Washington on these two occasions I don't know. Lerner was a brilliant mind, and only his lack of *gravitas* limited his influence on actual policy.

Notes

1. Samuelson elaborated: "By this time Fisher was a wealthy man twice. He'd married the chemical heiress and he invented a visual filing system which became Remington Rand, or something like that, and that went way up in the stock market. It kind of pleased him that he could do it on his own. And so he undoubtedly subsidized a lot of his own research. There are a lot of formulas in that book, and you didn't have giant computers in those days – they were probably computed by his assistants in his New Haven basement.
2. Jeff Sachs has gone back to review the period in National Bureau papers. Before I read his paper, I wrote down what my bunch thought in 1936, to see how we came out. I think we came out pretty good, first rate.

9. Evsey David Domar (Domashevisky) (b. 1914)

Birthplace: Lodz, Russia (now Poland)

Education:

1930–31: State Faculty of Law, Harbin, Manchuria
1939: B.A. in economics, University of California, Los Angeles
1941: M.A. in mathematical statistics, Michigan University
1947: Ph.D. in economics, Harvard

Significant publications:

'Proportional income taxation and risk-taking', *Quarterly Journal of Economics*, **58**, May 1944, 388–422 (with Richard A. Musgrave).
'The Burden of Debt and the National Income', *American Economic Review*, **34**, December 1944, 798–827.
Essays in the Theory of Economic Growth, New York: Oxford University Press, 1957.
'The Soviet Collective Farm as a Producer Co-operative', *American Economic Review*, **56**, September 1966, 734–57.
'The Causes of Slavery or Serfdom: A Hypothesis', *Journal of Economic History*, **30**, (1), March 1970, 18–32.

Significant honors:

1965: John R. Commons Award of Omicron Delta Epsilon
1970: Vice-President of the American Economic Association
1970: President of the Association of Comparative Economics

Experience:

1943–6:   Economist, Board of Governors of the Federal Reserve System
1946–7:   Carnegie Institute of Technology
1947–8:   University of Chicago
1955–8:   Johns Hopkins
1958–84:   Massachusetts Institute of Technology

The interview was conducted in Evsey Domar's office at MIT in 1983.

Tell me about how you got into economics.

At the end of the last century, when the Russians were building the Trans-Siberian Railroad towards Vladivostok, they faced the choice of two routes: (a) around the bend of the Amur river or (b) straight across Manchuria, then a province of China. The second version would have saved them several hundred kilometers. They "persuaded" the Chinese government to give them a long-term lease on a ribbon of land all the way from the north-west to the south-east across Manchuria. For all intents and purposes, this ribbon became part of Russian territory, particularly after the suppression of the Boxer Rebellion (1900). It had Russian troops, police, courts, administrators, etc., with the city of Harbin as the center. Later on, the Russians built an extension of this railroad south to Dairen and Port Arthur. The major part of this extension was lost after the Russian–Japanese War (1904–5), but they kept the rest and maintained a commanding position in Northern Manchuria until after the Revolution.

I grew up in Harbin, a Russian city (though with a sizable Chinese population), originally built next to a Chinese city. Our language was Russian, our schools were Russian (there were separate schools for the Chinese), the street names were Russian (later Chinese names were added). Harbin was probably the only place in the world where old Russian measures were still in use at that time.

In 1934 I went down to Dairen, then a Japanese colony, to work as an accountant in a chocolate factory. (Our high school in Harbin offered good training in accounting. I found it very helpful later in my college accounting courses.) In 1936 I crossed the Pacific and entered UCLA.

How and when did you decide to study economics?

First, my father was an importer; conversations about letters-of-credit, exchange rates, custom duties, prices, competition were our daily fare. Second, Harbin was "blessed" with two currencies – the Japanese yen and the local dollar. Retail trade was forced to use the latter, but many contracts were made (surreptitiously) in yen. Small Chinese exchange shops were all over. If you received a payment (for tutoring, for instance) in yen, you had to decide whether you should convert them into local dollars right away or hold on to the yen and exchange them as the need arose. (Later on at UCLA, international economics was an easy subject for me.) Third, I took a year of economics at a kind of a partial university called the State Faculty of Law. One of its three departments was called "The Economic Faculty". Its economics program contained a good deal of law, European history, elementary statistics and – rather surprisingly – calculus, but no economic theory. I also felt, perhaps under some Marxist influence, that economics held the key to the understanding of a society and its history.

At UCLA, where I spent three years, 1936–9, there was no shortage of economics courses, but the only thing I had found out about Keynes before graduating was that such an economist did exist. This I learned not from my professors, but from a graduate student. This was in the first three years after the publication of *The General Theory*!

What happened when you studied the aggregate economy?

There was really no macroeconomics in the modern sense then. Lewis Maverick (a cousin of the well-known liberal Texas congressman), who taught Intermediate Theory, attributed unemployment exclusively to high wage demands. As a proof, he offered to relieve unemployment by hiring a secretary if he could find one at half the existing wage. That a general reduction of wages would pull down prices as well he did not mention. This was typical.

Did you question it?

I don't think so. One of the two liberal members of the Department of Economics, Gordon Watkins, was also the Dean of Letters and Science. He had a working background; on arrival from Wales, he had worked in Montana steel mills. He did not advocate cutting wages. But his only answer to the marginal productivity theory of wages (which, in a micro context does suggest that lower wage rates would lead to greater employment) was the insistence that this theory was not precise. But he had nothing positive to offer.

In 1939 I graduated and went to Michigan where I took a course in macroeconomics (I don't think it was so called then) from Arthur Smithies. He was an Australian who had spent some time at Oxford and received his Ph.D. from Harvard. He used parts of *The General Theory* as a text. It was hardly an appropriate one, but there were no others. The course was a revelation. At last, economics began to make sense to me.

Did the students agree or disagree with Keynes?

Neither. It was a big class and we had little discussion. I don't think we knew enough to argue.

After two years at Michigan I decided to move on and almost landed at Chicago. But on Smithies's insistence, I went to Harvard instead on a teaching fellowship (in 1941). For that I have been ever grateful to him. Almost as soon as I arrived I made a fool of myself. At the first departmental dinner (to which teaching fellows were invited) I found myself sitting between Harberler and Leontief. My attempt to participate in their conversation was a disaster.

My second (or perhaps that was the first) *faux pas* was to tell Schumpeter (to whom Smithies had written about me) that I wanted to study fiscal policy. The narrowness of my interests shocked him. He must have wondered how Smithies, his own favorite student (who used to visit him every summer) could have recommended such a *Dummkopf*. But my relations with Schumpeter blossomed when and after I took his Advanced Theory. It was neither advanced, nor theory, but fascinating. I regard Schumpeter as one of my two best teachers. The other was Jacob Viner.

Was Hansen running the Fiscal Policy seminar?

That seminar was the highlight of my stay at Harvard. It was run by Alvin Hansen and John Williams, an expert on finance and banking. The two were extremely different persons but they got along well. I never took that seminar for credit, but I hardly missed a meeting. It was attended by some young faculty and many graduate students, including the late Lloyd Metzler. Paul Samuelson, who had just moved to MIT, also came frequently.

As usual, student presentations were rather dull, but outside speakers were fun. Hansen and Williams had many connections in Washington. One visitor from the Federal Trade Commission told us how he, at the request of one Democratic and one Republican senator, had written two papers on each side of the protection issue and then enjoyed hearing both presented in the Senate. That in writing these opposite papers he had acted like a member of the oldest profession must have never occurred to him.

The seminar was mainly concerned with policy, but theory also appeared from time to time. A paper given by Lerner on some fine points of Keynesian economics provoked a long discussion.

Teaching at Harvard in those days (only in those days, I hope) was rather relaxed. The course on macroeconomics, which for some reason was called Money and Banking, was usually taught by Hansen in the fall and by Williams in the spring. But in the fall of 1941, when Hansen had gone to England on some government mission, the fall term was begun by Williams. He lectured on the British foreign exchange experience in the 1930s. When Hansen returned he did not bother to ask Williams what had been already covered and gave us the same story again. When the spring term began, Williams had forgotten what he had done in the fall and we heard it for the third time!

After some eighteen months at Harvard, I went to Washington, in February 1943, to work at the Federal Reserve Board as Hansen's assistant. He was the "Special Adviser to the Board", but really did what he wanted during his two or three days a week in Washington. I think the presence of such a distinguished adviser enhanced the position of the Board – so long as Hansen remained popular. Later on (probably in 1945 or so) conservative winds began to blow harder and Hansen was asked to leave. (At least, this was my understanding.) During his stay at the Board, Hansen tried, among other things, to have Congress pass a housing bill. It did not.

Fresh from the Harvard seminars, I suggested to Hansen to organize one at the Board. On hearing that Keynes was in town, we invited him to be our first speaker. Keynes agreed. But now an unexpected problem arose: if the audience was to be limited to some thirty persons, who should be chosen? Our first inclination was to invite the most prominent economists in Washington. But this idea backfired terribly: if a person was not invited, not only did he miss hearing Keynes, but he was also told that he was not prominent, a double punishment. In a couple of weeks, I made more personal enemies than ever before or after in my life. Eventually, we decided to invite only Federal Reserve economists, plus a few outsiders. Nevertheless, several others crashed the gate.

Lerner told me that he wasn't invited; that he just happened to be in Washington and showed up.

Lerner was certainly there. I don't remember now whether he was one of the outside invitees or one of the gate crashers. Probably the former. I don't recall what Keynes talked about. It was not a formal presentation. But I do remember (as a matter of fact, this is the only thing that I do remember) his nasty comments on functional finance. Someone asked Keynes about it. In response he said that you could fool all of the people some of the time, etc., but you could not fool all of the people all of the time. He probably used the word "humbug" or something equally strong. I sat next to Lerner at the end of the table (with Keynes and Hansen at the head) and recall very vividly how red was his face. No one defended him.

Why do you think Keynes said that?

Taking into account that a year later he praised functional finance to the skies, I have to conclude that Keynes either had not read it and didn't want to admit it, or that he had read it and had not understood it. He had plenty of company. Functional finance shocked everyone. Imagine a true believer being told that God does not exist!

Did Keynes's response stimulate your thinking and your work on the debt?

I don't know about Keynes's response, but Lerner's functional finance certainly did. Richard Musgrave and I must have read it (the article, which appeared before the book) at the same time. Our excitement was so great that we dashed to each other's office and met in the hall. We decided to prove that Lerner's assertion that income taxes do not discriminate against risk taking was all wrong. We ended up proving that not only had Lerner been right, but that he had not gone far enough. (Our paper was published in *QJE* in 1944.)

Did Keynes's remark concern functional finance or did it concern the possible excess of savings after the war?

Those remarks were about functional finance. As I said, Keynes was not the only one who had suffered a shock. Just think about the main points of functional finance. I'll list several of them. (1) There is no greater virtue in having a surplus (in the Federal budget) than in having a deficit; it all depends on the state of the economy. (2) Taxes should be collected *only* to prevent or to reduce inflation. (3) A government could function without imposing any taxes so long as there was no threat of inflation. Has a greater heresy ever been propounded? Even Musgrave, with his wide experience and liberal outlook, had a hard time accepting it. He thought that it might be all right for Lerner to utter such heresies, but not for the more reasonable and practically inclined people.

Lerner was famous for his outlandish schemes. During World War II he wanted to distribute men and matériel among the various field commanders in Europe and the Pacific by means of the price mechanism: each general was to be given a certain amount of purchasing power and each unit, such as a battalion, a plane, a tank, etc., was to have a price tag. Then the generals would order what they wanted within their budget constraint. Prices would be adjusted from time to time to equilibrate the market for each item. [*Laughter.*] You laugh at it at first; then you ask why? Without such a scheme, one commander undoubtedly got too many tanks and too few planes; another, exactly the opposite. Why not let them order what they need provided they were subject to some constraint?

Do you think functional finance makes practical sense or is there something missing in it that causes practical people to be against it?

If you consider taxation by the central government from a theoretical point of view only, then you can say that taxes are imposed for the following purposes: (1) to prevent or to reduce inflation; (2) to redistribute income and wealth; (3) to discourage the consumption of things which some people do not want other people to consume, like alcohol and tobacco. Functional finance is concerned only with the first reason. At least I do not recall anything said about the other two (though I may be mistaken now). The reason why the general public (and MIT undergraduates) have such a resistance to functional finance is the lack of understanding of *macro*economics. Everyday experience gives us lessons in *micro*economics, but none exposes us to macro. You can see this in pronouncements of high government officials fresh from their corporate jobs. It takes time and effort on the part of their subordinates to teach them even the elements of macroeconomics.

There is also another and a deeper reason for the opposition to both Keynesian economics and functional finance. Both teach that there is no great virtue in saving; that, depending on economic conditions, savers can do more harm than good. Since most saving is done by corporations and upper-income groups, this denigration of saving undermines a major justification for the unequal distribution of income and wealth. Both results are revolutionary.

Was there any concept of an optimal level of the debt?

I don't remember what Lerner said about it. I would prefer as small a debt as possible. Not because a large debt will bankrupt the government, but because of the friction that tax collection creates (assuming that interest payments must be covered by taxes). But as I recall, Hansen was fond of quoting Hamilton's ideas on the Federal debt. It seems that Hamilton welcomed it. Perhaps Hansen was also influenced by Charles Beard's ideas (*The Economic Interpretation of the American Constitution*). Beard asserted that a wide distribution of the ownership of Federal bonds strengthened the Federal government because all bond-holders had a vested interest in supporting it.

You could also make the argument that, in order to conduct monetary policy, you need a debt.

Well, perhaps you could, although you could probably buy and sell bankers' acceptances and bills of exchange. I don't remember if Hansen was concerned with this aspect of the debt.

Moulton, who was at the Brookings at the time, wrote a very negative little book about Hansen's position on the debt. Do you remember that?

I remember that such a book was published, but I don't remember the details. Brookings was a very reactionary place at the time; it has changed a good deal since.

I'll illustrate how business people felt about Hansen. In connection with my work on post-war taxation (that I was doing for him), I wanted to hear the views of the U.S. Chamber of Commerce. They were delighted to talk to an economist from the Federal Reserve and practically rolled out the red carpet. But on being told that I was Hansen's assistant, they shut up like oysters. Talking to an assistant of a radical was obviously repugnant to them.

What were the views on Keynesianism by business?

Very unfavorable. An incident at the University of Illinois around 1948 (I believe) will illustrate this. A new liberal university president (whose name escapes me at the moment) appointed Everett Hagen chairman of the Department of Economics, much to the distress of the old guard in the department and of some local businessmen who were suspicious of Keynesianism and of deficit financing. Presently a member of the old guard received an offer from some university in Florida, I believe. He took the offer to Hagen, as it is customary to do, and asked him whether the department would match it. Hagen should have gone through the usual act of promising to try to do something about it; but instead, he congratulated the man and wished him *bon voyage*. The man went to Florida, but his friends in the department, together with the local business people, staged a revolt and eventually got rid of both Hagen and the president. Some accountant, I believe, was appointed chairman; the business people were reassured that he was opposed to deficit spending. The best people (among them Modigliani and Patinkin) left and a good department was destroyed.

How many economists at the time would you say were Keynesians?

Samuelson put it very well: he said that those who were over forty at the time remained untouched and those below forty were never the same. So if you can look up the age distribution of our economists at the time you'll get the answer.

How did Keynesianism spread?

There was a lot of writing. Both Hansen and Seymour Harris, for instance, were very prolific. But the real reason for its spread was a beautiful empirical demonstration that it worked: as the defense spending went into high gear, unemployment gradually disappeared. Thus it was established that sufficient government spending can increase demand and lead to full employment.

During the war wasn't inflation a serious concern?

During the war, yes. That war and inflation come together was accepted by everyone.

Wasn't there some concern that, as time passed, if government kept stimulating demand, inflation would become more of a problem?

During the war we had wage and price controls. We tried to raise taxes but never enough.

Why didn't people see that the war had demonstrated that high demand could cause inflation?

The Keynesians thought that so long as unemployment persists the increase in demand will affect quantities (output, employment) rather than prices. But as Keynes himself had said, once full employment is achieved, classical economics takes over. But until then, there was no danger of inflation. My generation really did not know what to expect under full employment. We had so little experience with it.

How did you come to leave the Fed?

My position at the Fed was rather unusual. From time to time I was called upon to do some practical work, such as helping Musgrave prepare the Chairman's testimony on the taxation of farm co-ops. (Now, having constructed a model of a co-op, I would love such an assignment.) I hated such assignments because my mind, at the time, was on growth models. In the meantime, I developed a guilty feeling that the Fed was paying my salary without getting much in return. If this happened now (after my experience at RAND), I would not worry about it because ideas are most important and I think that every large organization should have several persons who do not participate in everyday work but think out new ideas. But at the time I felt uncomfortable, even though the people at the Fed, much to their credit, never said a word about it. So in 1946 I decided to leave and to get a job at some university where I could build my models without feeling guilty. Unfortunately, I landed at Carnegie Tech (with Mel Reder and Bill Cooper). Everything there, including the library and housing, was in such bad shape that Reder and I, who shared an office, spent the whole year complaining ("bitching" was the correct word) and did little work. I did manage to finish my thesis, however, and receive my degree in the winter or spring of 1947. But both Reder and I hated the place so much that we left after one year. I hear Carnegie Tech (the Carnegie-Mellon University) is quite a place now.

From Carnegie Tech I moved to Chicago. I need not describe Chicago, except to say that there was little interest there in growth models. I presented my model at a seminar which turned out to be the most unsuccessful presentation I ever made. The formal structure of the model turned them on, but its content – not at all. They never let me finish.

Fortunately for my self-confidence, I visited Harvard (probably at Hansen's invitation) and suddenly realized that my models had aroused a good deal of interest, at least there. The *AER* copies in which they had appeared had a worn-out look. Every young man should get such a boost.

You had written a couple of articles on the public debt?

Yes, one was published in the *AER* and the other in a paperback published by the Fed.

What stimulated your thinking on the debt?

It happened when I was still at Harvard, getting ready for my generals. Browsing through Hansen's *Fiscal Policy and the Business Cycle* I noticed a diagram, on page 272, I believe, showing the effect on national income of a recurrent stream of government expenditures, say one hundred (million) dollars in each time period. As you know, at first national income rises, but gradually it reaches an asymptote. It looked strange to me that these expenditures, which could have been investment, were presumably increasing the stock of capital and therefore our productive capacity, and yet resulted, after a while, in a non-increasing national income. This is where everything began. But instead of applying the resulting model to this specific problem I used it to show that an exponential growth of national income from which a constant part was borrowed by the government solved the problem of the debt burden because eventually the debt was to grow at the same exponential rate as the income and thus retain a constant ratio to it. Later on I applied the model to the old problem of capital accumulation.

10. Richard A. Musgrave (b. 1910)

Birthplace: Königstein, Germany

Education:

1933:   first degree, University of Heidelberg, Germany
1937:   Ph.D. Harvard

Significant publications:

'The Voluntary Exchange Theory of Public Economy', *Quarterly Journal of Economics*, **53**, February 1939, 213–37.

'Proportional income taxation and risk taking', *Quarterly Journal of Economics*, **58**, May 1944, 388–422 (with E.D. Domar).

'On incidence', *Journal of Political Economy*, **61**, August 1953, 306–23.

Classics in the Theory of Public Finance, edited with A.T. Peacock, London: Macmillan, 1958.

The Theory of Public Finance – A Study in Public Economy, New York: McGraw-Hill, 1959.

Public Finance in Theory and Practice, New York: McGraw-Hill, 1973; 3rd edn 1980 (with P.B. Musgrave).

'ET, OT, and SBT', *Journal of Public Economics*, **6**, (1–2), July–August 1976, 3–16.

Significant honors and awards:

1962:   Vice-President of the American Economic Association
1978:   Distinguished Fellow of the American Economic Association
1978:   Honorary Vice-President of the International Institute of Public Finance

Experience:

1936–48:   Harvard
1948–58:   University of Michigan
1958–61:   Johns Hopkins
1962–5:   Princeton
1965–81:   Harvard
1981–   University of California at Santa Cruz

The interview took place at Richard Musgrave's office at the University of Santa Cruz on 17 June 1986.

Tell me about yourself.

I was born in 1910. I grew up in a small town called Königstein, which is by now a suburb of Frankfurt, Germany. I spent the first two years of my life in England; when I was two years old, and with the prospect of war, my family moved back to Germany. After my mother died, when I was 14, I went to a "landschulheim" boarding school. My primary interests were in literature, writing and politics. My political views were with the Social Democrats, which they still are. I am not ashamed to admit that I did not change my basic ideas very much. During those years I took a strong interest in public affairs, but it was more, I think, from the political than from a specifically economic side. My major intellectual interest was in literature.

You would have been eight or nine at the close of World War I. How did your family fare during the war?

We got along, getting farm products from the countryside and growing potatoes. The first major political event that shocked me was the murder of Walter Rathenau in 1922. And of course I remember the inflation – my sister and I having stacks of money to play with. From one mark to ten billion marks. So I had a very good education on inflation; it was so drastic that any later inflations seemed hardly worthy of the name.

I graduated from school in 1930, and from there went to Munich to study economics. I chose economics because of a political interest in social affairs, rather than an initial scientific interest in economics. As I said, during the school years I was interested in literature and philosophy, but I had a strong political interest. My father, foreseeing what would happen in Germany, also attempted to steer me in a direction which would be marketable abroad and would allow me to get out. So I went to Munich to study economics.

In my first year there, the introductory course was given by Adolph Weber, no relation to Max. The best lecturer, named Kisch, gave an introduction to the Civil Code. There was also an impressive theorist named Zwiedineck Südenhorst, who came from the Austrian School. But it was too early for me to appreciate him.

I also took Public Finance. The lecturer was Weddigen, not exciting, but the subject interested me because it seemed the most obvious link to public affairs. The economics we learned was a Gustav Cassel type of enlightened, but not doctrinaire, market economy approach. What we studied was mostly micro – but with little technical analysis.

In short, my first year at university was a good beginning, but no major intellectual experience. More impressive was the rising Nazi movement, especially since I lived just across from their headquarters on the Schellingstrasse. There were frequent political riots at the university.

How did your teachers explain the trouble in Germany after the war?

The reparation problem was discussed and of course the inflation. But the main concern was with the political turmoil and whether the Weimar Republic would survive.

Did any of your classes provide a theory of the trouble and prescriptions for what could be done about it?

No, I don't think so. What I learned was similar to Cassel's book which provided a systematic discussion of economics in general without particular attention to what went on.

After my first year, I went to Heidelberg, where I stayed from 1931 to 1933. There I was a little further along, and my real interest in economics developed. Marschak was there. He taught a course in macro and held a seminar on Keynes's *Treatise*, especially the equation in the Appendix. I think the course was called "Money and Capital". Public Finance was taught by Arnold Bergsträsser, part of an intellectual group led by Stefan George, a poet. He reflected the romantic, "organic" view of the state which has been part of the German public finance tradition. I remember writing a paper on Thomas Aquinas, which I was quite involved in. Alfred Weber, of location theory fame, brother of Max Weber, was also there. By then he had shifted into sociology and had become an important figure in that field. His teaching was obscure, but he was especially brave in dealing with the Nazi situation – one of the few people who were. Theory was taught by Brinkmann, a rather good micro theorist, who caved in when the Nazis took over. Otto Pfleiderer, assistant to Weber, also taught in the fiscal field. So it was at Heidelberg that I had my first significant contact with real economics and especially public finance.

So people talked about macroeconomic issues at that time?

Yes, Marschak did. He had been at Kiel, and had been associated with Gerhard Colm. He also taught a seminar on national income accounts, which were developed in Germany before Kuznets and others developed them in the United States. So that gave an overview of the economy.

Was the savings/investment issue discussed?

Yes, but in the context of the *Treatise*, not *The General Theory*. The German heretics, whom Keynes later praised, were not in the picture. Focus was on an ex post view of the circular flow and equilibrium in the national income accounts.

How would your teachers explain the unemployment?

It was viewed as a speculative breakdown in markets, lack of confidence, and the aftermath of reparations, inflation and the crash. There was no systematic pre-Keynesian or alternative-to-Keynesian view of it.

Were you relatively satisfied with the explanation the faculty gave of unemployment, of the Depression?

As mentioned before, I do not recall this to have been the major concern. The rise of the Nazi movement, its terror and the collapse of the Weimar Republic were of overwhelming importance. The dynamics of the political situation seemed so in the foreground. Book burning, beating, the riots, and all that. The collapse, from the Reichstag fire on, came during that spring term of 1933 and I left soon thereafter.

What did you do then?

I came to the United States as an exchange student and was sent to Rochester to continue with economics. There I was under the direction of Professor Clausing, who gave me a thorough tour through Marshall's *Principles*. There was also a Professor Gilbert, a public finance economist, econometrically oriented, applied, and very interesting. So this was a good year to get into an English/American perspective on economics, which, of course, was very different from what I had been given before, which had been in the broader social science tradition such as Max Weber. However, I do not regret that earlier phase. It has always remained in the back of my mind. Even though I turned away from it, it always remained.

Was there any macroeconomics taught at Rochester?

Not that I recall.

How did you then get to Harvard?

In 1934, after the Rochester year, I decided to stay in the United States. With two Jewish grandparents, this was not a difficult choice to make, even though there were still hopes that Hitler might collapse. I went to Cambridge and got a fellowship there. That was in the fall of 1934, giving me the good fortune to be there during the really fabulous second half of the thirties.

What courses did you go to at Harvard in 1934?

Well, the basic theory course then was Ec. 11, which was the first graduate course. That fall it was taught for the last time by Professor Taussig, who subsequently retired. The subject never went beyond Ricardo, but Taussig was a marvelous Socratic teacher. He would give a problem, raise questions and leave it to us to find the answers. Joseph Schumpeter, who had recently arrived at Harvard, took over the course in the spring term. He covered Walrasian economics. So you see we had two great teachers in that first year. The introductory course they taught was a totally different approach than is now the case. It was not a boning up on tools, but the teaching of a broad vision of economics. Both micro and macro were seen in an interconnected way. Schumpeter considered the broad movements of the aggregate economy. But his treatment was of an evolutionary system; it was not the neoclassical equilibrium model that came to dominate macro in the 1960s and 1970s. It was dynamic evolution. So, in his way, Schumpeter covered macro.

Who else was a student there at the time?

Most important, there was Paul Samuelson, who was a towering figure from the beginning, intellectually. Off and on, he would point out some errors in Schumpeter's math, and Schumpeter would like it. There was also Lloyd Metzler, another brilliant person, and many others. It was quite a group to be with.

But there was a fair amount of unemployment in 1935 in the United States, at that point. Was that discussed in the classes?

Well, not very much at the beginning. The hot topic in 1934–5 was monopolistic and imperfect competition. The macro revolution would follow next, when Hansen came to Harvard.

Can you tell us something about the Hansen seminar?

I think when they hired Hansen he really was known for the textbook, Garver and Hansen, a quite conventional text, and his little business cycle book, which was on the history of thought. He had done work in social security, but his major macro interest, and his interest in fiscal policy, was hardly anticipated by those who hired him; it developed after he got there. Hansen created his own demand when at Harvard, and that, of course, was in line with the rising excitement about the Keynesian message.

Prior to Hansen's arrival, there had been some pre-Keynesian macro theorizing at Harvard, by Lauchlin Currie and others, but it was the advent of *The General Theory* that galvanized interest in macroeconomics. In the afternoon, around four, we would go to a coffee shop to talk about *The General Theory* and what it meant. Paul Sweezy was one of the informal teachers. And then, of course, Hansen's Fiscal Policy Seminar. That seminar was a very, very active enterprise, with close linkage to Washington and public policy, with people coming in back and forth. Hansen's contribution, perhaps, was less in pushing theoretical analysis further than in explaining the Keynesian model and in his tremendous energy and good will to do something about unemployment. His was a very activist, concerned approach, and there was also the intellectual stimulus that he provided. He was so deeply bent in his stagnationist view that the problems of inflation were not to be taken seriously.

The balanced budget multiplier episode which Salant worked on created a good deal of excitement, as did Samuelson's multiplier–accelerator model. It was a splendid seminar, and one of the reasons was John Williams's contribution as a keen but not entirely unsympathetic critic. He was with the New York Fed, and skeptical about it all, but contributed a critical input, which was important.

I don't think Keynes ever visited the seminar, and perhaps he did not think much of it. He and Hansen were altogether different types, Keynes the refined intellectual and Hansen the down to earth observer and activist. Schumpeter and Keynes, of course, were great rivals, but that is a different story.

There was also a group of young economists who had their own Keynesian policy study group. An important figure in that group was Richard Gilbert, the primary author of a little book by "seven Harvard economists". But that might have been too doctrinaire for Hansen. His attitude was that permitting heavy unemployment was stupid, and that we should decently take care of the aged, but beyond that, let's have a market economy. There was no ideological or intellectual doubt about a market economy, combined with public policy guidance where needed.

What was your thesis about?

I was very much involved in the Fiscal Policy Seminar and its many problems, but my major interest and thesis topic was with the microeconomics of the public sector. When I came from Germany, I had the comparative advantage of knowing the European literature. Few English-speaking persons knew the writings of Wicksell and Lindahl, their discussion about the nature of public goods and how to provide them. I thought this was the central problem of public finance and I wanted to work on it. Also I had a strong interest in distributive problems, interests somewhat outside the macro field.

How did you happen to go to the Fed?

After I got my Ph.D. in 1939, I stayed on as an instructor for three years and then I looked for a job. The Fed made an attractive offer and I took it. I thought that it would be useful to work there for a while and to be part of the war effort. I didn't plan to stay because I knew in the back of my mind that I wanted to build a public finance model that would put together the many parts of the field. My first task at the Board was in the banking section, and to look at fluctuations in currency outstanding. I transferred to the fiscal section where I had the opportunity to work with Evsey Domar. A major concern was with debt structure and what would be the prudent way of financing the war. Another was to work with Treasury people on war taxation.

Later on I worked as a personal assistant to the Chairman of the Board, Marriner Eccles, and his quarrels with the New York Bank. I then left the Board in 1949 to return to teaching.

At that time, what would you say were the main intellectual influences on the thinking of the Fed?

The immediate problem was how to handle the war – financing it, budgets and economic relations with allies. There was also a good deal of thinking about post-war policies, resulting eventually in a return to stagnation when the war was over. The stagnationist view was suspended during the war, but the feeling was that, once the huge war expenditures were gone, stagnation would return.

But would you say that The General Theory *was really well known by everyone?*

Oh, yes, it was known. But how well is a different matter. By the end of the thirties it had become the economist's bible.

Now how about other groups out there? There must have been other – you know, you had a small coterie of Harvard people at the Fed; were there other groups? Angell, or, you know …?

Goldenweiser, who had been a director of research for many years, was rather eclectic. He was a good economist, a good banking economist, benevolently favorable to academic activity, but not an academic thinker on his own, and of course there was a great deal of day-to-day work to be done. Nevertheless, the Fed had frequent seminars, attended by many of Washington's economists, who were stationed there as part of the war effort.

Let's go back now to the Keynes visit to the Fed seminar – the one where Lerner was there.

Keynes was talking about problems of war finance and international financial arrangements in the post-war period. In the discussion, Abba Lerner argued that the problem would be over saving and unemployment, and Evsey Domar digressed on similar "Keynesian" positions. As I recall, Keynes harshly rejected the risk of post-war stagnation, holding that because of Social Security there would be a large reduction in private saving and so that would be no problem. And then he practically said no sensible person would still be a Keynesian in such a period. I remember feeling sorry for Abba's being left in the cold.

It's interesting. Alvin Hansen has a totally different memory of an encounter of Keynes and Lerner; Hansen remembers Abba saying at one point, "Why don't you forget all this stuff like deficit finance and everything, and just print money?" After he looked around and saw that no reporters were there, Keynes said, "It's the art of statesmanship to tell lies, but they must be plausible lies."

It's amazing how different recollections are. Mine is of Keynes being rather un-Keynesian at that meeting.

I left the Fed in 1949 because I wanted to go back to teaching and I wanted to write my public finance book. I went to Michigan, and I stayed there during the 1950s. We at Michigan had wonderful departmental, intellectual and personal relationships. Michigan at the time was a largely Keynesian department, with Warren Smith, Gardner Ackley, Kenneth Boulding and Larry Klein.

11. Tibor Scitovsky (b. 1910)

Birthplace: Budapest, Hungary

Education:

1932: first degree in law, University of Budapest
1938: M.A. London School of Economics

Significant publications:

Welfare and Competition, London: Richard D. Irwin, Allen & Unwin, 1951; 2nd edn 1971.

Economic Theory and Western European Integration, London: Allen & Unwin, 1958.

Papers on Welfare and Growth, London: Allen & Unwin, 1964: collection of papers including: 'A Note on Welfare Propositions in Economics', *Review of Economic Studies*, November 1941; 'A Note on Profit Maximization and Its Implications', *Review of Economic Studies,* February 1943; 'Two Concepts of External Economies', *Journal of Political Economy*, April 1954; 'What Price Economic Progress?', *Yale Review*, Autumn 1959.

Money and the Balance of Payments, Chicago: Rand McNally, 1969.

The Joyless Economy, Oxford: Oxford University Press, 1976.

Significant honors and awards:

1973: Distinguished Fellow of the American Economic Association

Experience:

1938–46:	United States Department of Commerce
1946–58:	Stanford
1958–66:	University of California at Berkeley
1968–70:	Yale
1970–76:	Stanford
1976–8:	London School of Economics
1978– :	University of California at Santa Cruz

The interview was conducted in October 1985 in Middlebury, Vermont, after Tibor Scitovsky had given a lecture at Middlebury College.

How did you happen to go into economics?

I really can't tell you, because I don't know myself. That, I suspect, must often be the case. I studied law in Budapest, because that, in the Hungary of those days, was the subject people able to go to a university chose if they lacked an overweening interest or passion for something specific. After a year, however, I realized that I could obtain the doctorate without attending lectures; and since my father wanted me to learn more English and become more independent, I went to Trinity College, Cambridge, to study international law. But I soon exhausted the university's meagre offering in that subject so, for the last two of my five terms, I switched to economics, which was one of the main subjects there.

I attended Dennis Robertson's lectures on economic theory and Maurice Dobb's on economic history and wrote a fortnightly essay for Joan Robinson, my supervisor. That was too little to teach me economics but enough to give me a taste for it; and Joan's sharp criticism and bluntness, which devastated me at first, taught me how to think for myself, for which I remained forever grateful. She was a charming and beautiful young woman at the time who chain-smoked cigarettes, wore a long scarf and was visibly still in love with her husband, however alienated they became later on.

Was it recognized that she was brilliant?

I honestly don't know, having had little personal contact with fellow students and even less with faculty. Her book on imperfect competition was rumored to be forthcoming but I had no inkling at the time of its originality, nor did I realize how unique it was in those days for a woman to write a book on economic theory. I do remember, however, that she was supposed to be a better economist than her husband, whose first appearance in print was to be the mention of an argument of his in Joan's forthcoming book.

Did you get any sense as an undergraduate of the friendship between Robertson and Keynes?

No, I hardly even knew Keynes's name. Two terms of two introductory lectures taught me very little about economics and even less about economists, partly because I did not study very seriously. I was so overwhelmed by the novelty and excitement of the Cambridge atmosphere. My fellow students' enthusiasm for English and German literature and avid hunger for learning just about every aspect and field of intellectual life were contagious. I was too busy learning about life and all the things kept from me during my excessively lonely and sheltered youth to leave enough time and energy for taking the study of economics very seriously.

How was the Depression there?

The time being the winter of 1930–31, I was not yet aware of it in Cambridge. But as I arrived home, my father's first question was, "Now that you've learned some economics: what does one do when there is a run on banks?" My immediate response, "One gets the government to declare a bank holiday", clearly impressed father, because within a few days, the Hungarian government declared a bank holiday, prompted by him, who was the prime minister's close friend from high-school days and president at the time of Hungary's largest bank, which had close ties to the Viennese Credit Anstalt, whose bankruptcy marked the beginning of the Great Depression.

At home I did my compulsory military service and completed my law doctorate, after which my father, who was completely trilingual, sent me to Paris to improve my French. I wanted to learn also more economics at the same time by enrolling in the 'Science Po', as the Ecole Libre des Sciences Politiques was nicknamed; but finding their teaching closer to economic journalism than to economic theory, I gave that up and concentrated instead on learning French full time at the Alliance Française.

In 1934 I became a teller in one of the Budapest branches of my father's bank as a preparation for a banking career; but by that time there were many signs of Hungary's getting engulfed in Hitler's national socialism, which I found so repulsive and frightening that I decided to quit and carve out a career for myself in the West. In 1935, therefore, with my parents' reluctant blessings, I left Hungary and went to the LSE (London School of Economics) to learn enough economics to be able to live by it.

Tell me about LSE.

The LSE, with its conservative economics faculty and its leftist and Marxist students and other faculties, was an excellent place to learn economics in, because it made one very aware of the gulf between the depressed economy and the faculty's elegant economic theories. The economics faculty consisted of Lionel Robbins, Friedrich von Hayek, T.E. Gregory, Frank Paish, Barrett Whale, Frederic Benham, Ronald Coase, Nicholas Kaldor and a few others. Hayek was the only member of the faculty to have an explanation for the depression; but his two books on the business cycle seemed too convoluted and confusing to carry conviction. Many of us sensed the faculty's inability to deal with economic reality and felt that something, perhaps an altogether new and different approach, was missing from their theoretical models of the economy.

Having read Marx's *Das Kapital*, I thought that the elements of conflict and exploitation ought somehow to be introduced into our model of the competitive market economy and worked terribly hard to find some way of doing that, reading way beyond what was required, learning mathematics, national income statistics, even suspecting the faculty of deliberately hiding from us such important and relevant books as Schumpeter's *Theory of Economic Development*, which was missing from the library and, like Kuznets's work and the very concept of national income and product, was never even mentioned in any of the lectures. My fellow students included such distinguished people as G.L.S. Shackle, Arthur Lewis, David Rockefeller and George Jaszi; but apart from the last-mentioned, I had virtually no contact with them.

And then, slowly, I became aware of the fact that some revolutionary new kind of economics was in the making in Cambridge. A young student came from there and presented a paper in the London–Cambridge–Oxford Joint Economic Seminar, of which I did not understand a word and felt that there was something seriously wrong either with him or with me. I soon began to suspect that it was I who was lacking something. The name of that student was Champernowne, who later was appointed instructor and became quite a friend. What he was talking about in that seminar paper had to do with what he had learnt in Keynes's lectures; and it was unintelligible to his London audience, because he wrongly assumed that we were familiar with Keynes's new ideas. It took me long to find all that out; and I knew nothing of Keynes's revolutionary new ideas until the appearance of his *General Theory*.

When that appeared, I persuaded the manager of the LSE bookshop to sell me a copy the evening before its official release and I remember dropping everything to concentrate on it day and night, because reading it was a tremendous experience, not only intellectual but emotional as well. For the book seemed to answer all the problems I had with reconciling the gloomy economic reality with the elegant theories we were being taught.

From then on, life at the London School became very exciting. The big weekly seminar of Lionel Robbins, the Department's chairman, became a battleground between the thoroughly and bitterly anti-Keynesian senior faculty, mainly Robbins, Hayek and the Director of the School, Sir William, later Lord Beveridge, and the equally strongly Keynesian young faculty member, Nicholas Kaldor, two young visiting scholars, Oskar Lange and Michal Kalecki, and us, the more vocal graduate students. A year later Abba Lerner, returning from a leave of absence, joined us Keynesians.

Those fights were pretty violent and we students faced the difficult but challenging problem of how to pass our examinations. For we knew that the senior faculty clung to its rights of setting and grading examination papers. We obviously wanted to get good grades; but how were we going to get them knowing the economic beliefs of the people who set and graded the papers, with which we did not agree at all. We did not want to be dishonest and write answers which we knew were wrong but would please the examiners. So we were forced to integrate and see the connection between Keynesian and pre-Keynesian economics. That was good training and hard work, because you really had to do some pretty hard thinking how to operate in that highly charged environment.

Do you remember any ways that people had of integrating the two?

To some extent. My way of doing it was published in August 1940 as my first paper ("A Study of Interest and Capital"), which argued that the rate of interest cannot equate the flow of saving with the flow of investment because it equates the accumulated stock of assets with people's desire to hold them and the same price cannot equate supply and demand in two different markets. That later became known as the stock-flow analysis and still is in my opinion the key to the Keynesian revolution.

I was disappointed by Hicks's IS/LM diagram, which he presented in his "Keynes and the Classics" as the key to the Keynesian revolution, because I felt that his diagram, though useful in some respects, missed the boat, just as did Lange who published much the same argument at the same time. I showed my paper to Lange who admitted that my paper and not his had the important key to Keynes's innovation; and thirty years later I was glad to see Hicks's admission that "as a diagnosis of the 'revolution' [the IS/LM diagram] is very unsatisfactory".

Tell me how you came to the U.S.

I learned a lot at the LSE but wanted to get a job as soon as I got my master's degree. After two short-term jobs, however, I received a Leon fellowship to come to the U.S., just at the outbreak of the war in Europe. While in London, I became known as a reasonably good and vocal member of Robbins's seminar; but having come to the United States, where no one knew me from Adam, I realized that, if I wanted to make a mark and earn my keep as an economist, I must publish. However, I was not bursting with ideas to write articles about, so outside pressure to write was quite painful but ultimately good for me. Moreover, I was stuck in the United States, unable to go back to England, because of the war, so I had to publish or perish.

In the States I spent some time at Columbia, because I was anxious to listen to Hotelling, whose writings I liked. But Hotelling left on leave shortly after I arrived and his lectures were taken over by his research assistant, Abraham Wald, who turned out to be one of the brightest and most stimulating lecturers I had ever known. I also made friends with James Angell, who was an exceptionally nice person. From there I went to the University of Chicago, where I was glad to see Oskar Lange on the faculty, with whom I became friendly at the LSE, and also got to know professors Jacob Viner and Frank Knight, and made friends with many of the students, starting my lifelong friendship with Melvin Reder. From there I proceeded to Harvard, where I found the Hungarian fellow-students from the LSE, George Jaszi and George Lanyi, who with Dick Musgrave, the tax expert, Bill Salant, Hugo Munsterberg, the Seurat specialist, and Andrew Jaszi, George's brother and a Goethe scholar, formed a congenial, lively group. Among the faculty I only got to know Schumpeter, Leontief and Paul Sweezy.

Did you talk Keynesian economics with them? With anybody? Did they know Keynesian economics?

At Columbia, no one said or asked anything about Keynes. Hotelling and Wald were in a very different field and Angell was very much a pre-Keynesian economist. In Chicago, Lange and Reder were very much interested, but no one else. At Harvard, Schumpeter was the only person who asked about my interest in economics and he obviously was not interested in Keynes's theories. With the others, I discussed plenty of economics but very little about Keynes's *General Theory*.

What about Alvin Hansen?

As you know, Harvard is a peculiar place where everybody is isolated from everybody else. I never met Hansen and did not know enough about him to try to look him up. Curiously enough, my only contact with him was years later, when I was discharged from the army and went to the Department of Commerce where I became a member of a small group supposed to assist the newly appointed Secretary of Commerce, Henry Wallace. The day I arrived, I was given an indignant letter Wallace received from Hansen in which he protested an argument that appeared in the Survey of Current Business, and to which I was to write the answer for Wallace's signature. It was a minor point, too unimportant for me to remember after all these years; but I recall that it was easy to answer, because it showed Hansen's misunderstanding of something in Keynes's *General Theory*.

Had the problem of stocks and flows been discussed in the literature?

I do not think it was. Kaldor had an article on the subject somewhat similar to mine but a little harder to understand, because he brought expectations into the picture, which was appropriate but obscured the main point. Somehow, both our articles were ignored, though to my mind they were crucial to understanding the theoretical underpinning of Keynesian economics. Decades later, Leijonhufvud created a great stir with his supposedly new interpretation of Keynes. He also gave a lecture on it at Stanford, which many of my students attended but came to me disappointed to report that he had said nothing that they did not already know from my lectures. That made me realize that he too stumbled upon the stock-flow argument but many years after Kaldor's and my article appeared, which he apparently had not read.

At the time, however, I was more concerned with establishing myself as an economist than with preaching Keynes's gospel; and I was so disappointed by the utter lack of attention my paper received that I abandoned Keynesian economics and wrote papers on whatever subject I felt I could make a contribution to. That accomplished what I wanted it to accomplish and I returned to Keynesian economics only six years later, after my military service and short stay in the Commerce Department.

How about Keynesian policy? Were you interested during this time period in policy: what the government should do? Or had the war pretty much ended questions?

The war, on the contrary, led to President Roosevelt's Victory Program, which was based on a very Keynesian approach and led to our winning the war. I knew about Keynes's coming to Washington in the 1930s but not making much of an impression on the President; I was all the more glad therefore to learn of Robert Nathan's move from the Commerce Department's National Income Division to the Office of Production Management, there to make full use of what he learnt from Keynes and Kuznets. While in Washington, I knew only from hearsay about our war production plans being based on Nathan's estimates of our potential full-employment GDP, until my military duties led me to read in a German periodical, of all places, an admiring account of it by Rolf Wagenfuhr, a German economist.

I ended my military service as a member of the U.S. Strategic Bombing Survey, where my first assignment was to acquaint myself with, and lecture the staff about, the organization of Germany's war production and its main figures. That gave me entry to a London library that subscribed to just about every important German newspaper and periodical; where, in a German economic periodical, I came across Wagenfuhr's paper describing the planning of *our* war production, which became my best source concerning the Germans' approach to the same problem.

Wagenfuhr was evidently surprised that instead of following established procedure and relying on the estimates of the armed forces' high command of their needs for fighting the war, the Roosevelt Administration estimated what the US GDP would become when we reached full employment, and subtracting from it civilian consumption and the minimum maintenance of manufacturing capacity, obtained a huge residual, which it then told the military high command was available for war production. That, to judge by the style of the article, was obviously very different from the Germans' way of going about it; but on learning that Wagenfuhr was later recruited into Speer's Armaments and War Production Ministry, I conjectured that the Germans would at that stage follow our example. My first assumption proved correct but my conjecture was quite wrong. Wagenfuhr was given an office but no responsibilities in the Speer Ministry and spent his time writing a history of Germany's war effort, which never reached its full potential, as we soon found out in the Strategic Bombing Survey.

But to return to peacetime Keynesianism, I had plenty of Washington friends and colleagues in the National Income division of the Commerce Department, who I suppose accepted the argument in Keynes's *General Theory*; but the subject lay dormant during the post-war prosperity. Only after my short Washington stay, when I went to Stanford to teach, was my enthusiasm for Keynes aroused, feeling that, when crossing the Mississippi, I would move into pre-Keynesian country, where I would be one of the first to spread the gospel of Keynes.

Who was at Stanford?

The chairman was Bernard Haley, a terribly nice and decent person, tolerant, liberal, able to stand up for his high principles and anxious to build up a varied and good department. The ablest senior person was Ed Shaw, not a Keynesian but as broad-minded as Haley, because he hired Lorie Tarshis, whom he encountered in Keynes's Cambridge seminar, just as Haley hired me, having heard me hold forth at the London School. The rest of the faculty was quite innocent of Keynes.

Lorie Tarshis and I arrived at the same time and, glad at meeting a fellow-Keynesian, we immediately became good friends. We were doing all the macroeconomics. Lorie used his own introductory textbook on Keynes, which he had just published and which I liked much more than Samuelson's. It was not very good on micro but superior to Samuelson's on the macroeconomics of Keynes. I also used his text in the introductory macro course but was mainly teaching more advanced courses, where I used articles and Keynes's *General Theory*.

Which articles?

Hicks's "Keynes and the Classics", Kahn's paper on the multiplier, several of Lerner's papers, Joan Robinson's *Introduction to*, and *Essays in, the Theory of Employment*, Modigliani's life-cycle hypothesis, my own "Study of Interest and Capital" are some of those I remember. One thing we discussed was the mistake a lot of economists, Keynes included, made in predicting a major depression after the war. As you know, we had a long period of prosperity instead; and it was very instructive to the students to find out where and why all those economists had gone wrong.

How did you know they were wrong?

By that time it was obvious and not very difficult to know. Most people based their predictions on time-series data – such as the correlation between GNP and the intersection between the investment/savings curve – and completely ignored the large wartime accumulation of both personal and business savings in liquid funds. As a soldier drafted into the U.S. Army, I knew that the large holdings of Victory bonds by members of the armed forces were largely forced savings; and business firms' depreciation allowances and undistributed profits also went largely into Treasury Bonds, considering that the wartime rationing of raw materials and shortage of machine tools rendered real investment in equipment and equipment maintenance very difficult. At the end of the war, all those liquid funds could be and were used, by demobilized soldiers for long vacations and by householders and businesses for replacing and modernizing worn-out appliances and equipment. What seemed so obvious to Keynes's followers with the benefit of hindsight failed to occur before the event even to Keynes himself.

Were there numerous fights between Keynesians and non-Keynesians in the late 1940s and 1950s?

There were no fights within the department or the university; but an avalanche of indignant letters kept coming to the president of the university from rich alumni, not only because we were teaching Keynesian economics but also, and perhaps mainly, because Lorie Tarshis, the author of the highly popular and then only Keynesian introductory text, was on the faculty. Those letters painted Keynes, and so by implication also Tarshis, as a communist, perhaps because that was the worst they could say of a person, short of using four-letter words; and they were outraged. They threatened to stop all donations to the university and mobilized everybody, including even Herbert Hoover, to write to its president and urge the immediate firing of Lorie. It is much to the president's and Bernard Haley's credit that they stood firm in that storm, defending academic freedom and doing absolutely nothing.

I was amazed, since Keynes to me seemed to be the saviour of laissez-faire capitalism and so the very opposite of a communist. It was pretty obvious that most of the letter writers never even saw Lorie's text, only heard about it or, at best, read the long vituperative review of it in the *Review of Books of the National Economic Council*, a very conservative organization. Although I was just as filthy a Keynesian as was Lorie, I escaped that storm simply because he had written the book which was a best seller, while my articles on Keynes were read by no one and my first book, *Welfare and Competition*, did not deal with that subject at all.

12. Leon Hirsch Keyserling (1908–87)

Birthplace: Charleston, South Carolina

Education:
1931:   LLD, Harvard

Significant publications:
Toward Full Employment and Full Production, Washington, D.C.: Conference on Economic Progress, 1954.
Progress or Poverty, Washington, D.C.: Conference on Economic Progress, 1964.
The Toll of Rising Interest Rates, Washington, D.C.: Conference on Economic Progress, 1964.
Agriculture and Public Interest, Washington, D.C.: Conference on Economic Progress, 1965.
Wages, Prices, and Profits, Washington, D.C.: Conference on Economic Progress, 1971.
Goals for Full Employment and How to Achieve Them Under the 'Full Employment and Balanced Growth Act of 1978', Washington, D.C.: Conference on Economic Progress, 1978.
'Liberal' and 'Conservative' National Economic Policies and Their Consequences, 1919–1979, Washington, D.C.: Conference on Economic Progress, 1979.

Experience:
1933:   Lawyer for the Agricultural Adjustment Administration
1933–7:   Secretary and legislative assistant to Senator Robert Wagner of New York
1942–6:   General counsel to the United States Housing Administration

1946–9:   Chairman Council of Economic Advisors

The interview was conducted in June 1984 in Leon Keyserling's Washington home.

Tell me about how you got into economics.

I entered Columbia in 1924. My first getting into economics was accidental. When I went into the gymnasium to sign up, I signed up for Greek, and I happened to get to the table of an instructor in government, who said, "Why do you want to take that dead language? Why don't you take history, or government, or economics?" Well, if he had mentioned history last, I would have said "history", but he mentioned economics last, and so I said, "Put me down for economics."

I walked into the first-year course in economics with my freshman cap, and the instructor said, "Don't you read the syllabus? Don't you see that Economics I is open only to sophomores?" So I started walking out and he called me back and said, "Well, you go up to the head of the department on the sixth floor and if he says you can take economics, you can take it." So I went up and the man didn't look at me, or shake hands, or ask my name. I told him what I wanted to do. He said, "How old are you?" I said, "I'm sixteen." He said, "Any man who's sixteen years old can do anything in the world he wants to." He signed my card, and his name was Rexford Guy Tugwell.

This introductory course was the typical standardized classical course, using a book by Richard T. Ely, who was very well known then. In my second year, one year ahead of my class, I took a seminar with him; we got along famously, and five years after that, after I graduated from law school, I went back to Columbia to study economics. He gave me a job and that got me to come to Washington, in 1933, almost on the first train, when the New Deal went into effect. So that's how I got into economics. Once I got into it, I was more interested in it than in any of my other studies.

What do you remember learning in economics?

I learned how people lived, because the course that Mr Tugwell taught – one of the courses he taught – this was the most influential course I had because it was entirely institutional and pragmatic; it was based upon a textbook that he had written called *American Economic Life and the Means of Its Improvement*. In it we studied what was called the three levels of living: riches, comfort and poverty, what they meant, how people lived and what factors contributed to which of these three groups they were in. We ended up, as the title of the book suggested, on the means of improvement – how could American economic life be improved. Tugwell's course opened my eyes to what economic problems were all about and how important a part of them was the question of the distribution of income. In fact, that question is the conditioning factor on *most* economics problems. Unfortunately, it is a subject that is now very largely neglected because, fundamental though it is, it is, or smacks of being, controversial and therefore it's avoided in most of the study of discourse.

Did you have any courses on the business cycle?

Yes, I took a course with Wesley C. Mitchell, who was the outstanding so-called expert in those days on the business cycle; but surely the thing was in its infancy, because the business cycle was attributed to many factors and was taught not so much as a problem of analyzing its significance as it was of being descriptive of the different possible causes. And how elementary it was, and how early it was in the thinking: one of the causes was given to be sun spots.

Was there any premonition that you might run into trouble and the big depression might be coming? Or was it very much that things would continue to be good?

There was almost no talk about the big depression that was coming. As we all know, very few, if any, of the economic leading lights foresaw it. I remember in 1928, majoring in economics, I took a course with a man unknown, and one of the big central features of the course was to have all of the boys – there were no girls then at the school – have all of the boys invest a little money in the stock market and watch it and see what it was doing. This was not so much with the idea that the stock market was an indicator of something, but rather as the idea that the stock market was good, and important in itself, and that making money in the stock market was a part of the normal process of being alert and sensitive about American business.

If you liked economics so much, what made you decide to go to law school?

Tugwell used to ask that question, and maybe his phrasing of the question answered it. He said, "I always wonder why all of my best students go to law school." Law school seemed to offer a challenge to ability, and opportunity to become famous, and in those days economics didn't seem to offer so much. But I had really set myself on law school from the time I entered college, but when I finished law school, I came back to Columbia to study graduate economics and contacted Tugwell. He immediately offered me a job, while I was studying, as a young instructor in economics. I also did some work for the General Education Board of the Rockefeller Foundation.

The Depression started when you were in law school, right?

That's right. I will never forget standing in Harvard Square on that Black Monday, or whatever it was called, when you saw the papers lying on the pavement with the huge notices of the stock market crash. But, strangely, you didn't hear much discussion of it. Neither the students nor the professors seemed to be alert that anything was really happening between 1928 and 1931. When I got back to Columbia in 1931, there was a large awareness of it; and I helped Tugwell rewrite his book on American economic life and the means of its improvement, and I wrote in a lot of chapters about the Depression, and even about what might be done about it.

While at Columbia I didn't study for a master's; I studied for a Ph.D. In fact, I completed *all* the requirements for the Ph.D., including the orals and the examinations. I didn't go on with writing a thesis because, in March of 1933, I went to Washington, and became so engrossed in what I was doing there that I never had time to get back to writing a thesis.

In that period, '31 to '33, did you hear of Keynes at all?

Not really, because, while he had done some writing, the great work, *The General Theory*, didn't come out until much later – '36 or '37. I was very much impressed with the writings of Hawtrey, who slightly preceded Keynes and who really said most of what Keynes said, but in a simple way; it was only when Keynes put it into rather complicated formulae that he got accepted by the economists. Hawtrey's explanation was simple and right; it had to do with the distribution of income and the imbalances of the system.

I'm not saying that the intellectual value of Keynes's work was overstated, because I think he was very great; and I think the recent effort to criticize him and undermine him is entirely unwarranted and leads to very bad policies. But the things that we think of in connection with Keynes's contribution to economic policy happened long, long before hardly anybody had heard of Keynes.

If you try to state simply the main idea that the public thinks Keynes had, and one of the ideas that he did have, it's that he placed a good deal of emphasis upon the distribution of income. He said that, other than that distribution, saving could not be absorbed fully by investments, and that if investment didn't equal saving you would have more and more unemployment. Therefore, the government should tap some of these excess savings and do public works. That was the essence of part of his teaching. He had many other arguments, about interest rates and the propensity to consume, but the distribution of income was central to the part of Keynes's argument that one associates with policy: spend money through the government to compensate for the inadequate spending in the private sector caused by the fact that some of the saving became frozen and didn't flow into investments because there wasn't enough consumer demand to support a higher level of investment. Now the curious thing is – that you hardly ever hear – is that all of this was fully developed before Keynes.

Were you studying this in graduate school?

No, no. I'm talking about what was being *done*, rather than what was being *studied*. From the very beginning of the rising unemployment in 1930, in '30 and '31 and '32, a number of years before the general public really heard of Keynes, public officials – senators like Robert F. Wagner of New York and Edward Costigan of Colorado and Bob La Follette, the younger, of Wisconsin – were introducing bill after bill on public works to take up the unemployment, which was raw Keynesianism but didn't come from Keynes. The idea that the government should spend money to employ people goes back a long, long way.

But how about in what you were learning at Columbia?

Unfortunately, even between 1931 and 1933 the economists really weren't taking very much interest in what to do about the Depression. The teachers of economics, even in the face of the '29–'31 aspects of the Depression, were not very much interested in it. Aside from Wesley Mitchell's course on the business cycle that I had taken while I was still in college, the Depression simply wasn't discussed. And even though Mitchell's course was about the business cycle, he wasn't analyzing what was going on. He was giving a theoretical course on what the business cycle was and when it had happened and some of the theories about it. It wasn't really a pragmatic or empirical study of what was happening. So it was only, as I was saying, senators like Wagner and Costigan and La Follette who were repeatedly introducing bills on public works spending, although they didn't get accepted until 1933, long, long before there was any popular appraisal of Keynes. For example, Wagner had a bill called the Employment Stabilization Act, which became law in the 1930s and which certainly didn't trace back to Keynes, or, for that matter, to any well-known economist.

But – there you were in college, or in graduate school. Did you know about these bills then?

Oh, yes, I knew about them.

Did you ask your teachers: were these good? Did they make sense?

I don't think there was much room for that kind of discussion, because they were standardized courses that didn't run along those lines. I took a course in banking with a man named Willis, who had something to do with writing the Federal Reserve Act; I also took a course with a man by the name of Sinkovich, and I didn't know any more about what the course was about when I got through than when I began. I took a course in the traditional aspects of labor, of labor relations, with Leo Wolman – and so forth, but they were compartmentalized courses which were still running along upon the momentum of what they'd always been. They weren't really talking about the Depression and what to do about it.

Well, how about students? Did they spend a lot of time talking about it?

Not much, no. As a matter of fact, if one looks at the second volume of Arthur Schlesinger's *The Age of Roosevelt*, one can see some passages where he points out that, when Roosevelt was faced with a problem of what to do, none of the leading lights of the economics profession had anything to offer. And what he got came mostly from people here in Washington who were self-appointed students and from people interested in the subject; it didn't come from the academic profession.

So you came to Washington, then, in 1933?

I came to Washington with Rexford Guy Tugwell and that was that. My first job was in the Department of Agriculture where he was slated to be Under-Secretary. It happened that, since he was interested in the National Industrial Recovery Act, as was Jerome Frank, who was the solicitor of the Department – or *going* to be the solicitor of the Department of Agriculture – I got involved in the drafting of the NIRA, and that way came in contact with my predecessor in Senator Wagner's office. But when I got drawn into that drafting, I had my first meeting in Senator Wagner's office, and I was there with the group of hard-angled New Dealers, Henry Wallace and Tugwell and various others, and they talked for a couple of hours. I didn't say anything. Then Wagner said, "I'm tired; I've had a long day. We've got to stop now." I said, "Well, I just want to say this: I don't want us to leave here with the impression that everybody is in agreement. I don't agree with anything that's been said." Wagner said, "What do *you* think?" I said, "Well, I think if you want to get the ball rolling, you've got to get some purchasing power into the hands of the people. You've got to do something about wages; you've got to do something about public works." And he said, "I agree with you," and the meeting broke up.

The next morning he called me up and offered me a job because my predecessor was leaving to go to New York and practice law. That's how I got the job with Wagner, which I took two weeks after I entered the Department of Agriculture. So my stay in the Department of Agriculture was very, very fleeting. I soon began to work for Senator Wagner as his legislative assistant. That was the point through which all of the important New Deal legislation passed, either because it originated in his office or because he was asked to introduce practically all of it.

Where did the ideas for the New Deal legislation come from?

Well, if I ever get to write a book, it will argue that not many of them came from F.D.R or the White House. If you run down the list: the TVA got started with George Norris in Muscle Shoals way back in the Coolidge Administration. The New Deal and Roosevelt's leadership and popularity and glamour afforded an atmosphere in which these things could be done, but they didn't originate in the White House. The NIRA originated as a plan for suspending the antitrust laws so that business could cooperate, so to speak, in the stabilization of competition. And that originally came from what was known as the Slope Plan, originating with

Gerard Slope, the dynamic chairman of the General Electric Company. In Wagner's office we wrote the $3 300 000 000 public works program, which Roosevelt was very lukewarm about, and the way we got the $3 300 000 000 was that was the sum of the projects that he had in his files from when he was working on the Wagner–La Follette–Costigan bills. So we wrote that into the NIRA. We wrote in wage and hour provisions, which were the predecessors of the Fair Labor Standards Act of 1938; and we wrote in the famous Section 7A on collective bargaining, which was the predecessor to the Wagner Labor Relations Act of '35. So we wrote those in right in his office. So much for the NIRA.

The Agricultural Adjustment Act also didn't come from the White House. It was the subject of farm thinking going back to the fact that the farm depression started in 1922. The farm problem was the great political issue of the 1920s. That Agricultural Adjustment Act came from the people surrounding Henry Wallace, who had been editor of the largest farm paper in America; and his father had been a Secretary of Agriculture under Coolidge. So much for those twin cylinders of the early New Deal.

Then we came on to the National Labor Relations Act, which was vitally important in that it established, really established, unionism. That was done entirely in Wagner's office, and Roosevelt did everything he could to put stumbling blocks in the way of it. That particular story is told in Schlesinger's second or third volume.

The Housing Acts, all of the big Housing Acts – the FHA, which established mortgage insurance; the United States Housing Authority, which established slum clearance and low-rent housing; the Housing Act which wasn't enacted until 1949, which is the most comprehensive of all, which was called the Wagner–Ellender–Taft bill – they all originated in Wagner's office. They didn't come from the White House at all. We didn't get any help from the White House on them.

The Social Security Act was sent up by Roosevelt, but what had happened there was that Wagner and others had been agitating for unemployment insurance for many years. Wagner introduced the first resolution to study it, and then in 1934 you had the

Wagner–Lewis bill on unemployment insurance which pressed Roosevelt to set up his committee for the study of social security, which was headed by Professor Witte of Wisconsin. And that culminated in a draft of the Social Security Act, which Wagner introduced, and which *did* come from the White House.

So that' s about the history of the labor New Deal legislation.

How about Keynes's book that came out in late 1936. Was it read, was it discussed, at all?

Well, it's hard to imagine, I think, getting down to the realism of the situation, it's hard to imagine Senator Wagner or Senator Costigan or Senator La Follette, or any of them, deeply immersed in the reading of John Maynard Keynes.

How about Leon Keyserling, the A.B.D. (all but dissertation)?

Well, of course I read Keynes. But I can't say that it influenced anything, because we were *doing* these things. I'm not deprecating Keynes; the reason that he is regarded as having started everything is that you have to consider the college professors. The college professors had nothing to contribute to any of this legislation. They didn't even appear as witnesses when the hearings were held, with rare exceptions. They were remote. It was only when Keynes came out with something that spoke their language and that was sufficiently difficult, that they thought that, because Keynes had revolutionized Say's Law, and because Keynes had revolutionized the classical economics, that he had revolutionized the American national economic policy – which just isn't so. Without any deprecation, every one of those laws would have been enacted in just the form it was, if there had never been a Lord Keynes – because that isn't how they evolved.

When did Keynes first come over to the U.S.? Do you remember?

No, I don't remember exactly when, but he came over fairly early in the New Deal. And the report is that he had a meeting with Roosevelt; he came away feeling that Roosevelt didn't understand anything he was saying. Of course, Keynes came over later, more prominently, in connection with Bretton Woods, but that was much later.

When did you leave Senator Wagner's office?

Technically I stayed there until late 1937, which was four years; but actually, during the next nine years, until he retired because of illness, I was always called upon from other jobs whenever he had important work to do.

It was in that connection, just by way of example, that I drafted all three of the platforms on which Roosevelt ran for re-election, because Wagner was chairman of the Platform Committee and you didn't have big nationwide platforms like you have now. Wagner would say to me, "We've got to have a platform", and I'd draft a platform and Wagner would take it – I'd go with him – to Chicago or Philadelphia, or wherever the convention was held. The Platform Committee considered it, changed a few words, and it became the platform. I remember that in 1940, which is the second of the two platforms on which Roosevelt ran for re-election (because when he ran in '32, it wasn't his platform, he was a candidate), after the platform had been drafted as I described, Senator Wagner sent it over to Roosevelt to read and Ben Cohen and Tommy Corcoran brought it up to the Shoreham, where Senator Wagner lived, with Roosevelt's comments. And I read it aloud out there. Roosevelt had made only one comment on the whole thing. Where it said, "We will not send our men to fight in foreign wars", Roosevelt had written in, in his own handwriting, "except in case of attack". That was the only change he made in the platform.

Now, when he went to Boston to make his famous speech later on in the campaign, and when he made his statement that "to tell you again and again and again, we will not send our men to fight in foreign wars", he did not add "except in case of attack". He just said, "We will not send our men to fight in foreign wars", but that was permissible politics; there was nothing indictable about that.

In 1937 I went over to the United States Housing Authority, and I worked on the U.S. Housing Act: that was the first great nationwide slum clearance and low-rent housing program. It was a standardized program. There were local housing authorities, and we granted them funds for projects and supervised their design and other standards and reviewed the rents they charged. And that went on until 1941. I was still there. Originally I was Deputy Administrator and General Counsel. By the time I'm talking about now, I was Acting Administrator. We shifted over to a war housing program or a defense housing program and supervised the building of defense housing, to house literally millions of war workers.

Was the New Deal legislation pulling the economy out of the recession, independent of the war?

Well, I don't think there's any statement that has wider currency and is more unfounded in fact than the statement that the New Deal did nothing to reduce unemployment until the war came along, or at least until we became the arsenal of democracy, in 1939 and 1940. This is simply not so. When the New Deal came in with 13 000 000 unemployed, 25 per cent of the workforce, there was no knowledge of what to do about it. There was no established experience. There was no consciousness by the people that anything could be done about it. And yet with all those difficulties, from 1933 to 1937, as a percentage of the unemployed, as a percentage of the workforce, we reduced unemployment more than at *any* time since, despite much easier problems since that accomplishment.

In 1937 we had a sharp depression within a depression, caused not by the New Deal but by the fact that the opponents of the New Deal in Congress – some of the conservatives in the administration, like the Secretary of the Treasury – convinced Roosevelt, who was really fundamentally conservative in his economic thinking, to cut back sharply on government spending. At that time, government spending was no more than $6 billion a year, and cutting back sharply on it caused a sharp recession in '37. But even if you look at the period from '33 to '39, including the years '37 to '39, the reduction in unemployment percentage-wise was greater than at any time since. There were still 8 000 000 unemployed, but as a confrontation with a public problem, it was better than we've done at any time since, when we've had unemployment – very high unemployment – and done very little about it. We had 8 per cent unemployment very recently, coming down from 10, to be sure, but that's only a one-fifth reduction. We did very much better in the New Deal.

Did you see the war economic experience as validating the ideas of the New Deal: that government spending could drive the economy?

Well, it didn't validate it, but the idea really validated was the idea that a big war creates a full economy. We accomplished during the war prodigies of production and real economic growth, and reduction of unemployment. We got down to a level of unemployment that nobody had dreamed of, and we did this by a very wide range of planning programs. There was complete planning of the economy. There were goals and they were reconciled. There were decisions as to how much consumption and investment should be had, and all government programs conspired to use tax policy and monetary policy in a way to bring those adjustments about. So, those were the things that explain what happened during the war. Whether they would have happened to the same degree *if* those programs had not been manned so largely by people who were the outgrowth of the New Deal is a speculative question that I can't answer. I suppose that some of them were done a little more vigorously and with a little more regard for what needed to be done, realistic economics and otherwise.

Well, there were some examples. Even at the start of World War II, the big factors in the steel industry and other aspects of the business community said that we shouldn't expand the production of steel – that we should fight the war with the steel that was being produced, cut back on civilian consumption accordingly, and that also there should be no cuts into how much would be used in the war, because they said, "Otherwise, you'll come out of the war with so much steel capacity that we'll have another Great Depression." Well, they were beaten and overruled, and that was very largely a New Deal influence. Robert Nathan, who was one of the real economists of America, was chairman of the planning commission of the War Production Board, and he was an instrumental factor in overruling that, and we greatly expanded the production of steel. It's a great thing that we did so, because pretty soon the war effort alone was using more steel than the total amount that we'd been producing at the beginning of the war, so had we not expanded there wouldn't have been any steel for the post-war domestic market.

How about price controls during that time?

Price controls were extremely effective, because we meant it. After a flurry of price increases in the first year or so, prices were amazingly stable. Price control was strong and it invalidated what we've heard recently as to why you can't have price control. One argument was that, if you have price control, the prices start shooting up when you take them off. Well, this is like the argument that, if you have some degree of murder control by laws against murder, if you took them all off, there'd be more murder, and therefore you use that as an argument that the control laws are what caused the murders and you should never have them. Really, if it were true that the prices shot up when you took the controls off, the argument should not have been against controls; the argument should be that you should have kept them on longer. Or kept them on permanently. The second argument was that they caused black markets. Well, that's like saying that every law creates some violations. But the black markets were a mere bagatelle compared to the fact that we got the goods where they needed to be, at home and overseas, and did it very well. The black markets were sensational but didn't matter very much.

Tell me about the Pabst contest.

Well, in 1944, the Pabst Brewing Company decided to have an essay contest: "Post-war Full Employment". There were 37 000 entries, including a great many economists. One amusing story: the preliminary judges were the economics faculty of Columbia

University; and the final judges were four men, including Wesley Mitchell and Beardsley Rummel, president of Macy's, who was famous in connection with the pay-as-you-go taxes, and A.F. Whitney, the president of the Brotherhood of Railroad Crewmen Trainmen, and Clarence Dykstra, the president of the University of Minnesota. I believe those were the final judges. The first prize was won by Herbert Stein, who became chairman of the Council about thirty years after I was; I won the second prize, with an essay entitled "The American Economic Goal".

In my view my essay "The American Economic Goal" was far more influential because the Employment Act of 1946 was based on it. I organized the four senators who were the main sponsors and was very active in connection with its passage. The idea of having the President declare the goal of maximum employment, production, and purchasing power, define it – and use polices to get it – was really a reiteration of my essay.

What was the fear among economists that would happen after the war, and what was your *fear?*

Economists were predicting that shortly after the war there would be eight million unemployed. This was merely a projection of the past because there had been high unemployment in the genuine depression of 1920–22. I wrote an article in the *New York Times Magazine* to the effect that there would *not* be eight million unemployed because of the things we were doing during the war to cushion the shock, such as veterans' benefits, schooling, loans – all kinds of things – housing; and I gave many other reasons; and, in fact, the transition was made quite smoothly, under Truman.

So, you were still at the Housing Administration, or ...

During the war, in 1942, I initially was with the U.S. Housing Authority, of which I had been Acting Administrator, building defense housing. There were sixteen warring housing agencies in Washington, and as we moved toward the war in 1941 and on into '42, the idea was created that something needed to be done about those sixteen warring housing agencies but no discussion of *what.* So the President invited his most trusted counsel, Judge Samuel Rosenman, to look into it. Rosenman came to Washington and had interviews with the two top men in each of the sixteen housing agencies, and then he had the President appoint me, off the record, to work out a plan. And I worked out the consolidation of the sixteen agencies under one National Housing Agency, working with Roosevelt. That was promulgated in February 1942 by an Executive Order.

I went over to be General Counsel of the National Housing Agency, which, when peace came, became the Housing and Home Finance Agency, and that in turn became the Department of Housing and Urban Development. So that really all started from the Executive Order that put the sixteen agencies into one.

How about the Employment Act of '46? What can you tell me about that?

My interest in the Act was that it reflected the ideas in my Pabst essay. I got Senators Wagner and O'Mahoney and Representative Wright Patman and Senator James E. Murray interested in it – and after a hard-fought battle for a year and a half or two, it became law in '46. Now in the meantime Truman had become President and he didn't take much interest in it at first, but then I was invited to come over and address the President's War Mobilization Committee, composed of members of labor and industry and public servants. The chairman was William H. Davis, who was a public service representative. He had also been Economic Stabilizer later on in the Korean War. I came over and addressed them and Fred Vinson, who was then Secretary of the Treasury (Truman later put him on the Supreme Court). Vinson and the committee became convinced of its importance; Truman became actively interested in it, and it became law in 1946.

They took out some words there, about full employment. Can you tell me anything about that?

Oh, they changed it to "maximum employment", and there was a lot of talk about it being watered down. It was absolutely mean-

ingless – the difference. Neither "maximum employment" nor
"full employment" means "no unemployment". You have got to
have frictional unemployment. You have got to define "full employment" or "maximum employment", whichever term you use
and, just from the viewpoint of English, I don't know much
difference between "full" and "maximum".

*What about inflation? Was there worry at the time that inflation
was going to take over?*

There was nothing in the Act about inflation. Inflation is a by-
product of high unemployment, not of full employment, contrary
to a lot of theory but not supported by the evidence.

*Your wife, the former Mary Dublin, is an economist, who had
been to England. When did you meet her?*

I met Mary in 1934.

*Did she come back from England telling you about Keynes, or
Keynesian ideas, at all?*

No, because she had been at the London School of Economics
from '31 to '32. She came back talking a whole lot about Harold
Laski and Friedrich Hayek, who was teaching there, but I don't
recall her talking appreciably about Keynes. She told one story
about going to a lecture of Keynes's, so there was an interest in
him. Keynes eventually married a foreign dancer. She had been
sitting next to Mary at the talk and expressed a tremendous
admiration of what Keynes was saying. And then she said to
Mary, "He is so beautiful. I do not understand a word of what he
says, but he is so beautiful." And so they got married.

When did you become chairman of the Council?

I really became chairman in 1949 when Nourse resigned – I was
acting chairman. Literally, I became chairman early in 1950, but
I was really chairman from '49 until the end of the Truman
administration in '53.

And at that point, what were the guiding principles? Was there Keynesian economics there; did it come from any economists, or was it still very much generated quite separately from the economics profession?

It was generated within the Council.

How about Keynesian economists who came to Washington? Weren't there some – you know, part of the Harvard seminar? Any tie-in there?

During the period that I was on the Council, for better or for worse, we knew very little about the economics profession, *except* for some very good professional economists who were on our staff. The best of those were a man by the name of Gerhard Colm, who had been in the Budget Bureau, and another, named Walter Salant, who functioned for many years at Brookings thereafter; and we had Paul Homan, who was editor of the *American Economic Review.* So our staff was chuck-full of economists, in addition to the first chairman, Nourse, who had been president of the American Economic Association and the head of the economics institute at Brookings. So we were filled with economists, but we didn't get much from the outside.

I remember we had consulting meetings with some groups, and once we had a group of very well-known economists come down; I won't mention their names – some of them are still famous. We didn't get much from them, and we didn't repeat it. But we got a great deal from our conferences with business, labor and farm groups. We were going to have a business advisory council, and it was suggested to me – I was chairman then – that we take the business advisory councilmen to the Department of Commerce. I said, "You got a hundred odd people there. You can't do anything with a hundred people – except go to Greenbriar and play softball." I said, "You let me pick ten of them" – I said this to the White House – and I picked ten of them, and of the ten I picked, three of them became Cabinet members under Eisenhower: George Humphrey, the Secretary of the Treasury (who was the head of Pittsburgh Consolidated Coal); Charlie Wilson of General Motors, who became Secretary of the Treasury; and Marion Folsom of Eastman Kodak, who became Secretary of Health, Education and Welfare – these were three of my ten.

How about Alvin Hansen?

Alvin Hansen was one of the great ones. And when I've said that the economists – the academic economists – did not make much of a creative contribution to national economic policy. I should have stated that Alvin Hansen was an exception. He was always policy-minded, in his writings and in his speaking. I was very close to him. Alvin Hansen had dinner here, not long before he died, when he was living in Washington. Alvin Hansen said to me many times, "The one thing I most fear is that the economists will take a higher and higher definition for what constitutes full employment. Instead of saying that full employment is 3 per cent, they'll say 5 per cent is full employment, 7 per cent is full employment ..." – he said that to me many times. He said that's what worried him most.

Did he play much of a role in getting economic ideas across?

Yes. He was particularly interested in policy. That's how I came into close contact with him. And he was an advisor to the committee that drew the social security program, testified on it. Another economist who showed some interest in public policy was Sumner Slichter. I had Sumner Slichter come down and testify on the National Labor Relations bill.

What were your main concerns about the economy during this time?

Our main concern was about an expanding economy, economic growth and achieving very low unemployment. We felt that this would in itself moderate the problem of inflation, which it did, because we had price control for a while, but the main thing was the management of the industrial buildup, selectively – the things that were needed – so that we had an average rate of 3 per cent inflation. We got it down to 0.8 per cent in the last year.

Was there any concern about what might happen with labor markets – that if they were maintained really tight you'd start getting wage inflation – or not?

I've never subscribed to the doctrine of wage inflation. I've made studies of it for the last twenty-five years, and, during periods of high economic growth and relative full employment, the wage rate increases have always lagged behind the productivity gains. It is only when you get into a recession that the wage increases exceed the productivity gains, because the productivity gains collapse and the wage movement does not collapse. This is fortunate because, otherwise, you'd never get out of the recession.

When was that relationship between productivity and wage increases first seen?

Oh, we had the formula during the Truman years, particularly during the Korean War, to have wage increases equate the productivity gains. We pretty well maintained that. We had a wage stabilization program under a man named Feinsinger during the Korean War.

Judging everything that's happened, is there anything that you'd say economists could have done, or should have done, during this time period to get their ideas out? From your description, they sound pretty much irrelevant to the whole process.

There's something about the general run of economics teaching, study and writing. Pick up a copy of the *American Economic Review* and see what anybody – if they can understand it – could gain as to what could be done about economic policy; you'd get very little. It's strangely remote.

Index

.